Practical
Pre-School

Building a Portfolio for

Early Years Care and Education S/NVQ Level 3

ownsend

OOK REE

C15 and M7

Illustrated by Cathy Hughes

About the author

Mary Townsend started her career as a nursery nurse working in day nurseries. While her family were young she worked as a childminder and ran a playgroup for five years. She then trained as an infant teacher and worked in infant schools for 14 years. She went on to lecture in a college of further education and during that time set up an assessment centre and became an NVQ co-ordinator and internal and external verifier.

More recently as an independent consultant, she has carried out projects for the Early Years National Training Organisation and the Qualifications and Curriculum Authority. Her current work includes inspection of training in Early Years Care and Education NVQs for the Adult Learning Inspectorate and policy development in the Early Years and Childcare Unit for the Department for Education and Skills.

She is deeply committed to raising standards in the early years sector and firmly believes that a well delivered and assessed National Vocational Qualification can make a significant contribution to achieving high quality care and education for our children.

While we have made every effort to contact people whose articles are featured in this book, we apologise if any authors have not been notified.

Published by Step Forward Publishing Limited
Coach House, Cross Road, Milverton, Leamington Spa, CV32 5PB   Tel: 01926 420046
© Step Forward Publishing Limited 2001
Building a Portfolio for Early Years Care and Education S/NVQ Level 3, Book 3   ISBN: 1-902438-56-6

Building a Portfolio *Book 3* • • •

Chapter 4: M7 Plan, implement and evaluate learning activities and experiences

contents

All articles have been published previously in *Practical Pre-School*,
except for 'An overview of the National Curriculum' pages 67-68.

Chapter 1

Introduction

This book covers Units P2, C15 and M7 of your NVQ Level 3 in Early Years Care and Education. As we recommend that these units are best left until later, you're probably coming towards the end of your NVQ, or at least the end of the core units. That means that you will soon have a nationally recognised qualification which will enable you to get a job anywhere in the United Kingdom, or even further afield. Early years provision is growing rapidly in the UK, and many more qualified early years practitioners are needed.

NVQs are based on the National Occupational Standards which have been agreed by experts working in a range of settings across the early years field. They cover all the competences expected of an early years practitioner. There are three levels - Level 2 for people working under supervision, as an assistant or voluntary worker; Level 3 for people working under their own initiative as supervisors; and Level 4, for people in a managerial role, with responsibility for complex and non-routine tasks, or responsibility for quality control in a number of establishments.

> *'I didn't really think about why I did things before, but now I think much more about how it is going to help the children.'*
>
> NVQ candidate

This qualification will help you to gain a better understanding of children's needs - it will help you to reflect on why you do certain things with and for children. And the great thing about NVQ is that you don't have to give up work to do it, because it's based on the work you do every day. You can also work towards an NVQ as a volunteer, or combine a part-time job with voluntary work in order to gain wider experience. You may not even have to go to college at all - that will depend on how much experience you have, and whether you have done any previous training. We will talk about this in more detail later.

NVQs are not like other qualifications. Instead of doing a course at college, you gather your own evidence that you can do all of the things you need to do to keep children safe and happy, and help them to develop. A lot of your evidence will come from what you are doing with the children every day. You will put all your evidence into a folder, or portfolio.

For Level 3 there are 11 mandatory units which you have to do, and you choose three optional units to suit your own job role and interests. What you choose will depend on which kind of setting you work in, or which area of work you are most interested in. You should by now have been given a copy of your candidate handbook with full details of the units. Don't be put off by your first look through it. It looks complicated, but once you have worked through one unit, the others will seem much more clear. You don't have to start at the beginning and work through the units in a particular order. You can choose which unit you feel most confident about, and start with that.

By now, you may have had an induction at your NVQ assessment centre. The staff will have explained what NVQs are all about, and explained how the centre operates. Each centre operates differently, although they all use the same Early Years Standards. The centre will allocate an assessor to you, who will work with you throughout your NVQ. You will get to know your assessor really well, and work closely with her or him. She will help you to plan what sort of evidence you will need to provide. She will also visit you in your setting and observe you working with the children.

The aim of this book is to help you to gather your evidence from the things you do every day with the children, rather than having to work through set tasks and assignments which are often not appropriate to your situation. That means it will be individual and meaningful to you, which is what NVQ is all about. We will look at the different ways you can gather the evidence and give you some useful formats to use, as well as resources to help you with your planning. Throughout this book, we will be referring to your candidate handbook. This is the book which contains the Early Years National Occupational Standards, which you will have been given when you registered. You will always need that with you.

You need to bear in mind that your centre may require you to work in a particular way, and in that case you may not have the freedom to gather the evidence in the way we recommend, but you will still find the book very useful.

How do NVQs work?

NVQ Level 3 is made up of 11 mandatory units and three optional units. Each unit describes a particular area of early years work. Each unit is broken down into elements, which identify all the things you need to be able to do, to show you are competent in that area of work.

Let's take an example - Unit M7. The title of the unit is 'Plan, implement and evaluate learning activities and experiences'.

Find it in your candidate handbook. Read the list of elements at the beginning of the unit. Don't worry about all the other reading at the beginning of the unit yet. We will go back to that. These are the elements:

M7.1 Plan a curriculum to facilitate children's learning and development

M7.2 Development individual learning programmes for children

M7.3 Implement planned learning activities and experiences

M7.4 Evaluate planned learning activities and experiences

Much of the planning you carry out – short-, medium- and long-term - will provide most of the evidence you will need for this unit. If you're not sure what some of the elements mean, look at the 'Notes on this element' on the appropriate pages in the handbook.

'I understand a lot more now. I can put it into practice straight away because I'm working with the children every day.'

NVQ candidate

You will notice that each element has two main parts - performance criteria and range. The **performance criteria** (we will refer to these as PCs) are all the things you need to show you can do for that element - for example, in M7.1 PC3 states 'Overall curriculum plans are developed which include a variety of learning activities and experiences to meet the identified needs of the children in the setting'.

Break that statement down. 'Overall curriculum plans are

developed …' Think about what planning you carry out in your setting, and what you have done already to provide evidence for other units. You probably already have a lot of evidence, at least of short-term planning, but you need to have evidence of medium- and long-term planning, too.

The PC also states '…which include a variety of learning activities and experiences …' - it's not just about planned activities but about how you ensure that children get a range of other experiences, too, like using the local environment and community, taking advantage of unexpected things that happen during the day, giving children lots of opportunity to play freely and discover things for themselves.

Lastly, '… to meet the identified needs of the children in the setting'. This means that you need to have carried out child observations, monitored the children's learning and development and talked to parents and colleagues, before you can plan effectively. So there's a lot to think about in just one performance criterion.

Useful tip

Some performance criteria can seem very complicated. If you break them down into bits, as we have shown you, it will help to make them clearer. It will also stop you missing vital bits.

Now look at the **range**. This means all the different situations you may have to plan for – short-, medium- and long-term plans, for individuals and groups, in spontaneous as well as planned situations. The range will be different for each element, but by the time you have completed all the units, you will have covered every aspect of child care and development you are likely to come across.

This does not mean that you will necessarily have done all of these things. Sometimes, you will not be able to show that you have actually carried out all of the range, but you will need to show evidence that you could do it should the need arise.

Your assessor will normally want to observe as many of the performance criteria and range as possible, but for M7 and C15 in this book there is less observation needed. Only M7.3 requires observation, because that element is about implementing your plans. In P2 there is more assessor observation. Your assessor will also plan with you how you will provide the rest of the evidence you need. We will look at the different sorts of evidence you can use later in the chapter. If you need any help with ideas for activities to provide for the element or unit you are working on, you will find some useful resources in each chapter.

There are two other important sections in each unit which you need to be aware of. At the front of your candidate handbook you will find a section called the 'Statement of underlying principles'. They include:

- the welfare of the child

- keeping children safe

- working in partnership with parents/families

- children's learning and development

- equality of opportunity

- anti-discrimination

- celebrating diversity

- confidentiality

- working with other professionals

- the reflective practitioner

These are the principles which every early years worker must always adhere to if they are to commit themselves to giving children the best possible care and education in their early years. They have taken into account the United Nations Convention on the Rights of the Child and the Children Act 1989. You may have had them explained to you in your induction, but if not, you need to go back to the front of your candidate handbook to find a full explanation of what each one means. If you can, talk them through with your assessor. It would also be useful to discuss them with your colleagues in your work setting.

When you're gathering your evidence for each unit, you must always be aware of the underlying principles. To help you to do this, there is a grid at the beginning of each unit which shows which underlying principles, or values, you need to show evidence of in each element. (Throughout the book, we will refer to them as values, for short.)

Go back to the beginning of Unit M7 and look for the grid entitled 'Values statement' under the heading 'Principles of good practice'. Under each element it shows you which PCs refer to some aspect of the principles, or values. Try using the grid now to find the relevant element and PC, and think about how you might show that you are aware of the values. If you have any difficulty with this, go through it with your assessor.

Here's an example:
Go to the column headed **Element 1**. Look down the grid until you come to number 5. This means **performance criteria 5** in Element 1.
Look across to the left to see which value it covers. You will find **anti-discrimination**.

Now go to Element 1 in your handbook (headed M7.1) and look at PC5. It says 'Overall curriculum plans include varying strategies which will help the children develop positive attitudes to equal opportunities and anti-discrimination issues'.

Element 1 is all about planning an appropriate curriculum, which means that you must, through the activities and experiences you plan, ensure that all children, regardless of gender, ethnic background and disability, have access to an appropriate range of experiences. It also means that you need to show children by your own attitudes and values in the implementation of the curriculum the importance of respect for all members of our society.

Remember!
Celebrating diversity is not just about celebrating festivals like Diwali or Chinese New Year. It's about integrating it into everything you do so that it becomes a natural part of life, not something strange and different.

Finally, we need to look at the description of **knowledge, understanding and skills.** You will find this at the end of each unit, after the last element. This is where you need to provide evidence that you have the knowledge and understanding to show that you know why you do the things you do with the children in your care. This section looks a bit daunting, but don't panic! You will be able to cover a lot of it through the evidence you will be collecting for each element.

This section is divided under four main headings:

- Development

- Curriculum practice

- Equipment, materials, environment

- Relationships

However, you will find when you start working with them that there is quite a lot of overlap from one section to another, and we will show you how you can cut down on the work by taking several points together. We will do this within the chapter for each unit, so don't worry about it at this stage.

Many assessment centres will provide teaching sessions either in the daytime or evening, or learning packs which you can use at home, and will usually recommend some text books. Your local Early Years Development and Childcare Partnership (EYDCP) will probably also have courses you can attend. Your setting should receive information about these. If not, ring your local education authority and ask what is available. It is especially important that you attend training on first aid and child protection carried out by experts in these fields.

Although it is not a requirement for NVQ to take a recognised course in these areas, all early years practitioners should have a thorough knowledge of both.

You are not required to attend a course to gain your underpinning knowledge for NVQ, unless attendance at college is a requirement in order to gain funding. If you are an experienced practitioner, you may feel that you already have the knowledge you need, or feel confident to fill any gaps through your own reading and research. If you are less experienced, you will gain a great deal from attending these sessions, and from sharing your ideas with other candidates.

note:
This book does not aim to provide you with all of the underpinning knowledge you will need for your NVQ. It is a resource book and guide, to help you to gather your evidence for each unit.

Gathering evidence

NVQ is different to other qualifications in that, instead of taking an examination, you show that you are competent by collecting evidence of what you do in your day-to-day work with the children. The role of your assessor is to judge whether your evidence is sufficient to prove that you are competent.

Your candidate handbook has an explanation of the different sorts of evidence you can use. You will find this in the section at the beginning entitled 'The assessment process'. You may have already had the methods explained to you at your induction, but we will explain them again here.

There are two main types of evidence:

- ◆ Performance evidence - what you can do

- ◆ Knowledge evidence - what you know

At the beginning of each unit there is a description of the different ways you can collect your evidence. It's not the same for every unit, but it will always be from the following approved methods of evidence collection listed in your candidate handbook:

- ◆ Direct observation by a qualified assessor

- ◆ Questioning

- ◆ Witness testimony

- ◆ Work plans

- ◆ Inspection of the setting by a qualified assessor

- ◆ Reflective accounts

- ◆ Log books, diaries and notes

- ◆ Work products

- ◆ Case studies, assignments or projects

- ◆ Child observations

- ◆ Simulation, role play or skills rehearsals

- ◆ Skills transferable from other performance

- ◆ Past achievements

- ◆ Formal written or oral tests/extended questioning

To make it easier for you to collect the evidence, we will look at some useful formats you can use. Your assessment centre may have their own formats, so you need to check first. Evidence does **not** have to be written. If you feel worried about doing a lot of writing there are other methods you can use. For instance, you can record your evidence onto a tape recorder, or use a word processor. We have already said that your assessor will ask you oral questions. You may be able to make an arrangement with her to do extra questioning. This will depend on the amount of time she is allowed for assessment because, of course, it will be more time-consuming for her. If you feel that you may be eligible for extra support, talk to your assessor. Many centres are able to access funds to help candidates with additional needs. Some assessment centres have access to a range of specialised equipment available for people with disabilities.

Direct observation
The most important type of evidence is direct observation by a qualified assessor. You will see in the section on performance evidence in your candidate handbook that there are some PCs (performance criteria) which must be observed. Your assessor will also have to observe at least one aspect of each range category. For the rest of the range, PCs and knowledge, you will provide other types of evidence from the list above. Your assessor will write down what she observes on an ***observation record*** which is provided by the assessment centre. She will give you this to keep in your portfolio. An example of what it may look like is given overleaf.

Date	OBSERVATION RECORD	PCs range	Knowledge evidence
21.7.00	Sarah supervised snack time with the children - fruit and drinks. She let the children pour their own drinks, and they passed the cut-up fruit - a choice of apple, orange and banana - around the table. Sarah talked with the children and was aware of their needs, giving help where necessary. When they had finished she asked them to wash their hands in preparation for the cooking activity they were about to do, and cleaned the table with antibacterial spray.	C2.1.1,5,8 R2,3,4 C2.2.11 R2,6	C2KE2,7,11
	She helped the children to put on aprons. It was a large group but other adults were helping. Sarah showed the children the scales, and how to weigh out the ingredients for the pizza base. The children helped with the weighing, and Sarah melted the butter in the microwave. She talked about how it had changed from solid to liquid as she showed the children the difference. She put the ingredients into several bowls and the children took turns in mixing the dough.	C10.3.1,5,6 R2,3,6 M7.3.2, 3 4,5 R2,3, 6,7,8,9	C10KE8,11,16,17,21,31 M7KE2,8,10,22, 23
	Sarah then gave the children cheese to grate, or vegetables to cut up, and she and the other adults supervised them closely. There was a lot of conversation about colour, shape and so on. Once the vegetables and cheese were ready, every child had a piece of dough, which they rolled out. They really enjoyed this. Sarah placed the vegetables and cheese within easy reach of the children, and they chose what they wanted to put on their pizza. There was a brief squabble between two children, which Sarah dealt with calmly. She gave praise and encouragement throughout the activity.	C3.4.1,2,3,4, 6,7 R2,4,6 C11.2.2,4,5, 6,7 R7,9,11 C6.2.1,2,3 R1,4 C6.3.3,5, 6,7,8 R2,4,6	C3KE11,13,16 (This observation may not cover the whole of the knowledge evidence for these sections)

Signed Anne Other ....(assessor)   Sarah Bright ....(candidate)

Questioning

Your assessor will often ask you questions about what she has observed, to check your understanding. She will write down answers to any oral questions she asks you. She will give you these to keep in your portfolio. The question sheet may be a similar format to the one below:

Date	ORAL QUESTION RECORD	PCs range	Knowledge evidence
20.10.00	1. Unplanned activities for creativity/imagination? When the children are outside playing in the sand, they think of imaginative ways to use it, eg digging a hole to Australia. On climbing frame they imagined it was a train & they were going on a journey.	C10.4.2 R2,3 M7.1.7,R6	
	2. Importance of process/end product? The important thing was that the children were being creative, artistic and using their imagination. They were not being directed, they were free to choose what they wanted to do. It's the doing that counts.	C10.4.10 R2,5	C10KE27
	3. Factors affecting memory and concentration? If they're feeling ill or tired they lose concentration. If they're going through emotional difficulties, eg parents splitting up. If they're very young.		C10KE6 M7KE5
	4. How is children's expression constrained by stereotypical roles? Some children make the assumption that the boy will be the doctor, the girl the nurse. Attitudes such as boys play football, girls skip. We need to encourage equality.	C10.4.11 M7.1.5	C10KE25 M7KE3

Signed........Anne Other........................(assessor) ......Sarah Bright.................................(candidate)

Witness testimony

For things which your assessor is not able to observe easily, or to cover areas of the range, you can ask other people you work with to write a witness testimony. If you are a childminder you can ask parents and other professionals who visit you to write a witness testimony. You may need to explain the National Occupational Standards to them, so that what they write is relevant. You will need to have a list of people who have supplied witness testimonies in your portfolio, with a note of their job role or status. An example is given below.

Date	WITNESS TESTIMONY	PCs range	Knowledge evidence
6.11.00	The nursery has an open door policy so parents feel welcome to come to the nursery at any time. Sarah is very relaxed with the parents and encourages them to talk to her about their child's development, and any worries and concerns they may have.	C11.1.1 P2.1.1,4,5 R1,2,3 P2.3.2	C11KE8 P2KE4,6
	She also shows the parents the activities the children have been doing that day when they come to collect them, and encourages the children to talk about what they have done. Often parents just like to chat, and Sarah is always willing to listen. She upholds the nursery's policy on confidentiality at all times.	P2.3.5, 6,7,8 R1,4 C5.3.10, R3,6	C11KE12 P2KE10 C11KE31 P2KE8
	Sarah was concerned about a Chinese boy who was not speaking much at nursery. She talked to his mum, who said his English is good and he chatted away at home, and she was surprised he didn't at the nursery. Since then Sarah has encouraged him to join in with group activities and he is gradually starting to talk more.	P2.1.8,10 C11.1.5 R2,4 C11.5.6 P2.1.9 C5.1.8,10 R3	

Signed.......... V Goode ....witness   Sarah Bright ....(candidate)

Status of witness.............. Nursery Manager ....

Work plans

If you are involved in planning the routine and curriculum in your setting, you can use your plans as evidence. If you do this, you will need to write a brief explanation of how you were involved in the planning. It would be useful extra evidence to say how the plans were put into practice, and to evaluate their effectiveness - what the children gained from them, whether you would change them next time and so on.

If you are not involved in the planning, you will need to produce some evidence that you are able to plan. The activity plan on pages 28-29 will help you to do this. If you answer the questions thoroughly, this activity plan will cover much of the knowledge evidence you will need (an example of a completed activity plan is also provided, on pages 14-15, to give you an idea of what is expected.)

Inspection of the setting

For some units, such as E3 which covers health and safety and planning the environment, your assessor will need to inspect your setting. She will ask you questions about how far you are responsible for these areas of work, and whether you understand the reasons for things being the way they are. She

will usually record this on the direct observation and oral question records.

Reflective accounts

These are a really useful way of writing (or talking) about things you have done which your assessor was not able to observe. There is no special format, you can write on ordinary A4 paper. (Alternatively, you can put your reflective account onto audio tape.) An example of a reflective account is given below.

Perhaps something unexpected happened in the nursery, or you dealt with an accident, or a query from a parent. It could cover areas of the range. It's useful to try and identify which elements or units it will be relevant for, then you can make sure you cover the relevant details. When you write your account, try to reflect on why you dealt with it the way you did and what you learned from it. Don't forget to refer to the knowledge evidence section, and cover any relevant points. A significant feature of the NVQ is that it aims to make early years workers into reflective practitioners who are constantly reviewing the way they do things, so that they can improve

---

Reflective account of a visit to the library

Every week we take a group of children to the library in the afternoon to look at new books and choose some books for the nursery. We sometimes use the computer in the children's library as well.

C11.4.1,6 M7.1.3, 6 R5, 7

On the way there the children talk to me and to each other about different things we see. One week they saw a fire engine with its lights flashing. The children were excited to see it and this prompted a discussion about when they had seen fire engines before. Often interesting topics and memories about past events are discussed on the walk to the library. The children also develop their listening skills and safety awareness when they listen to instructions, such as how to cross the road safely.

C11.3.1,3,4,6 R1,2,3,4 C11KE14

At the library the children choose books and look at them, sometimes share books together and sometimes listen as a story is read aloud. They handle books and get used to holding them the right way round and turning the pages one at a time. They look at the pictures on the page and some children talk about what is happening in each picture. I talk to the children about what is happening in each picture. I talk to the children about how to look after books and show them where the title and author of the book is. When I read a large story book with simple words I follow the words with my finger to show the children that words carry meaning and how print differs to pictures.

C11.3.2 C11KE6,7,25,27 C5.2.7 C5.5R8 M7.1.5

About a month ago we attended a session at the library which celebrated black culture. A librarian told stories to the children which included 'Lima's Red Hot Chilli'. The children then tasted some Caribbean food including mango, honey cake and a fruit drink. The children enjoyed the morning's activities, and celebrating a different culture with young children helps to overcome discriminatory and stereotypical ideas they may have formed. It is important to show respect and value different cultures, religions, languages and dialects to increase the self-esteem of children from different cultures. In the same way books can also counteract stereotypes based on gender or disability by showing positive images of, for example, women as engineers or doctors.

Signed......Anne...Other...............(assessor)   .   Sarah..Bright..................(candidate)

---

their practice. None of us ever stop learning, no matter how experienced we are.

Log books, diaries and notes
These can be used to record your day-to-day work with the children. You may if you wish keep a daily diary, but they can become repetitive. It's useful to have a sample of your routine, but once you have written that for perhaps a week, be more discerning about what you write.

You may find it helpful to carry a notebook around with you to record things which happen during the day. You can then write anything relevant in more detail in quiet times during the day, or when you get home. Aim to pick out significant events rather than list all the routine things you do day after day. To record these events you can use the free description format of a reflective account, or you may find the format shown on page 16 helpful because it's a bit more structured.

Work products
You can use things like:
- policies and procedures of your setting - you must write a short note to show either how you have been involved in preparing them or how you use them in your daily work.

- curriculum plans - write a note to say how you were involved in planning and carrying out the activities. Evaluate how successful they were and what the children gained from them.

- examples of activities you have done with the children - only if you feel they are needed to support the evidence. Don't include a lot of children's work.

- menus, charts, details of outings and special events - explain how you were involved in preparing these.

- letters to parents, children's records, child observations and anything else you feel is a relevant piece of evidence - you must get permission from your supervisor or employer, and always remove names and check that the child or adult will not be recognised from anything in the piece of evidence, in order to maintain confidentiality.

- photographs of yourself working with the children, with a caption saying what the activity is, and how you are involved.

Remember!
Whatever evidence you use from your workplace, do check with your employer that you can use it first.

ACTIVITY PLAN

NAME: Sarah Bright   **DATE:** 15.6.00   **ACTIVITY:** A sound game   **AGE OF CHILDREN:** 3 - 4yrs

Before the activity:
Describe the activity you are planning. Describe how it fulfils the values statements for the element or unit you are working on.
I will play high notes and low notes on the piano. The children will listen to the notes and place a teddy on a ladder - at the top if they hear a high note, at the bottom for a low note. They will take turns to play high or low notes, while the others say if it's high or low.

Why have you chosen this activity? What do you think the children will gain from it? *(Think about areas of development.)*
The game will improve children's listening skills and help develop auditory discrimination. It will help children describe different sounds, so extending their vocabulary.

Which children will be involved? Why? *(Will it be free choice? Have you targeted children who need particular help with, for instance, colour recognition?)*
A group of 6 to 8 children will play the game. The group should not be too large as the children might become restless waiting for their turn.

ACTIVITY PLAN continued

What equipment/resources/preparation do you need?

A piano, a ladder, a teddy.

What will you do during the activity? *(Language you will use, help you will give, etc.)*

I will talk about hearing, using our ears to hear all sorts of different noises and sounds. Then I will show the piano to the children and discuss the different notes, using high, low, in the middle, notes. I will try to extend the game to include loud and quiet, fast and slow. I will supervise the children and encourage them to take turns. I will encourage and praise them.

After the activity:

Did the activity go well? Why? If not, why not?

The activity went quite well, as the children enjoyed moving the teddy up and down the ladder.

Would you change it next time? If so, how and why?

I would make the game slightly longer, by using other instruments, such as a xylophone, so that the children have more 'hands on' experience.

How would you adapt the activity for older/younger children? For children with additional needs or disabilities?

For older children I would get them to play loud and quiet, fast and slow. For children with a hearing impairment I would use gongs and instruments that vibrate a lot, and get them to feel the vibration of the instruments, and do more on rhythm than high and low.

What did the children gain from the activity? Was it what you thought they would?

The children had to concentrate by listening carefully to the different sounds. It helped them to develop their auditory discrimination.

What did you learn from it?

Once children understand an idea or a game, it gives them the confidence to develop other ideas, and try other things a bit more complicated.

Evidence covered:

C10.1.1, 2, 8, R2 C10.2.2, 3, 4, R4 C11.2.1, 6, 7 C11.4.2, 7, R1, 3 C11.5.3, R1, 3, 4 M7.1.3, R1, 5, 7
M7.3.2, 3, 4, 5, R2, 3, 6, 7, 8 M7.4.1, 2, 3, 7, 8, R2, 3, 4, 5

Signed ....Sarah Bright............. (candidate) If anyone observed you ask them to sign that this is a true record, and to comment if possible.

Signed ....A. N. Other.......... Role: ....Assessor...................

Comment: The children enjoyed this activity and gained a lot from it, but I agree, adding some more instruments would extend the experience for them.

CANDIDATE DIARY

NAME: Sarah Bright   **DATE:** 22.9.00   **INCIDENT:** Council's recycling lorry came to nursery to empty the newspaper container

What happened? Who was involved? *(Don't use names - number of staff/children/parents)*

The children heard the lorry at the gates of the nursery so we decided to take the children outside to watch the newspapers being collected. The children enjoyed watching the lorry pick up the container and empty the papers.

How did you react? What did you do?

I used this unplanned opportunity to talk with the children about recycling things such as paper, cans, glass bottles and so on. We talked about what happens to the papers after they have been collected, and where the lorry was going to next. Also as we watched the lorry I used language such as up, down, full, empty.

Why did you do it this way?

It was a good chance for the children to see at first hand what happens to the things we recycle at nursery, and introduce them in a very simple way to the concept of looking after the environment. It was also a good opportunity to extend their language skills.

Did it work? If not, why not?

Yes, the children were really interested.

What have you learned from it? What would you do differently next time?

(Think about the values statements)

That it's important to be flexible, and take opportunities to give children new experiences when they arise. I wouldn't do anything different next time.

Which PCs/range/knowledge does this relate to?

C11.2.4,6,7 R7,9,13,14
C11.4.1,2,3,5,6,7 R1
C10.2.2 R1,2,7,9
C10.3.2 R2,3
M7.3.7, R1,6,7,8
M7.4.4, R1

If anyone observed you ask them to sign that this is an accurate record
and to make a comment.

Witness.......... V. Goode ....

Status ....Nursery Manager...

Witness comment (if applicable)

This was a spontaneous event which proved valuable and rewarding.

Case studies, assignments or projects

This covers a range of other evidence, such as:

- assignments and projects set by your centre:
  - your centre may ask you at the beginning of the NVQ programme to carry out a project to cover all aspects of child development, because several of the units ask you to show your knowledge of this, and it's easier to cover it all together.

  - your centre may ask you to do an assignment for Unit C15, Child Protection, because there is very little which can be directly observed.

- written work to cover areas of the underpinning knowledge and range which you have not covered with other, work-based evidence, perhaps because it is outside your experience or you needed to do some reading or research.

- a case study of a particular child, carried out over a period of time.

Child observations

There is a whole unit dedicated to child observation, but don't wait till you get to C16 to start carrying out observations of children. You need to get into the habit of observing children, because it is an important skill. Observations help you learn a lot about child development, and individual children's needs, and they help you to plan appropriate activities for your children. They are also useful evidence for most of the units. You need to gain permission from the parents before you include observations in your portfolio. Some employers ask for parents' permission for this when their child joins the setting, so check what the position is in your setting. If you are not confident about child observation, read the chapter on C16 in Book 1. A helpful format for you to use when you record your observations is provided on page 18.

Simulation, role play, skills rehearsal

If you are not able to demonstrate a particular competence in your workplace - for instance, if you don't have the opportunity to bath babies or make feeds - you could be observed doing these things in a classroom situation. Or if you wanted to demonstrate your ability to handle a difficult situation with a parent which it would be inappropriate to observe, you could be observed in a role play. These are only used in exceptional circumstances.

Skills transferable from other performance

This can be used when it would be inappropriate to carry out direct observation, such as in the case of a child's disclosure of abuse. Some of the skills you would need in this situation may be observed in other work situations, such as how you support a distressed child, how you communicate or how you handle difficult situations.

Past achievements

You may have a great deal of past experience as well as other relevant qualifications when you embark on your NVQ. You will be able to draw on this as evidence for your portfolio. Your centre will normally be able to advise you on this, and may take you through a process called accreditation of prior learning (APL) or accreditation of prior achievement (APA). In order to include any evidence from the past, you will need to prove that it is your own work, and that the information is not out of date - for instance, the work needs to show an awareness of equal opportunities and anti-discriminatory practice; information related to child safety and protection must take account of the Children Act; and curriculum practice must take account of the Early Learning Goals or the National Curriculum. Evidence from the past cannot take the place of direct observation, but it can be used to cover parts of the range and knowledge evidence.

Formal written or oral tests/extended questioning

It is not usual to use tests as evidence for NVQ, because it is a qualification based on assessment of your competence in the workplace. However, there is a possibility that it may be used in the future for some aspects of assessment.

> **Remember!**
> It is absolutely vital that you keep all of your evidence together in your portfolio, with your assessment plans, and keep it in a safe place.

How do I reference and record the evidence?

Your centre will usually show you how they want the portfolio organised. It's usually best to divide the evidence unit by unit, but not essential. If you're working with several units at once, it might be better not to separate it into units, because you need to number it as you go along, so that you can record it onto the unit assessment records. Have a look at your candidate handbook with the standards in it. The format for recording your evidence varies slightly from one awarding body to another, but you will often find that for every PC, range and knowledge evidence statement you have to say what sort of evidence you have used, and what page number it's on, so that your assessor and internal verifier can check it. You need to number every piece of evidence as you do it. This is not easy to get to grips with at first, so ask your assessor to explain how she wants you to do it.

CHILD OBSERVATION

Title of observation:

Settling in

Type of observation: *(eg target child, free description, developmental check-list)*

Time sample

Aim of observation: *(Which aspect of child development/behaviour are you aiming to observe?)*

To observe how a child copes with settling in to nursery

First name of child: *(or fictitious name)*   Sandeep   **Age:** *(yrs & mths)*   2yrs 9mths

Description of setting: *(where observation is taking place, number of staff, children, equipment available, etc)*

Nursery playroom, 3 staff, 15 children. Morning session - registration time, play and structured activities, drinks time.

The observation: Write this on a separate piece of paper, or other format you have chosen. Write what you actually observed in detail, using present tense.

Evaluation: Comment on what you learned from the observation - link this to your aims. Evaluate what the child's needs are, and make recommendations for future planning.

Signatures: Sign your observation and ask someone who witnessed the observation to sign it if possible.

Signed S. Bright (candidate)   **Signed** Anne Other (witness)

Observation

9.00 Sandeep is cuddling her mum and looking anxious. She is watching the other children playing but doesn't join in.

9.30 Sandeep's mum says goodbye and a member of staff sits with Sandeep. She cries for about a minute and then goes to sit with the rest of the children for register time, with the members of staff.

10.00 Sandeep is sitting at the painting table with an apron on. She is absorbed in sponge painting. She finishes her picture and gets up from the table. She watches another child washing his hands. She looks anxious again.

10.30 Snack time. Sandeep sits at the table with the other children but doesn't speak. She is offered a piece of toast but shakes her head. She drinks her orange juice.

11.00 Sandeep is playing with the play people on the carpet. She looks at another child also playing there but doesn't speak.

11.30 Sandeep's mum returns to collect her. She is sitting with the other children listening to the story but as soon as she sees her mum she runs to her smiling.

Evaluation

Sandeep was obviously quite anxious about her mum leaving her but she only cried for a very short time. She spent a lot of time watching other children but didn't speak to anyone, child or adult. She did enjoy painting and later in the morning started playing alongside another child. She will need a lot of reassurance over the next few days. Staff need to gently encourage her to join in with things, but not be too insistent. She will join in when she's ready

Evidence covered:

C16.1.1, 2, 3, 4, 7, 8, 9, R1, 3, 6, 7, 12   C16.2.1, 2, 3, 5, R2, 4, 5   C5.1.2, 4, 5, 7, 8, R2, 5
M7.1.1, 2, R4   P2.1.1, R1, 3   P2.2.3, 6, R3, 4, 7

Personal skills review

In Book 1, we suggested that Unit C10, 'Implement planned activities to promote children's sensory and intellectual development', might be a good unit to start with, but that depends on your experience, the age of the children you work with and which areas you feel most confident about.

The personal skills review provided will help you to identify the areas of your work you are confident about, and areas where you need to take some action to improve your competence. Read through the summary of units and elements and use sections 1- 4 in the skills review first of all to help you to decide which unit to start with. You can photocopy and use the blank review sheet on page 21 (Personal skills profile). You will need your candidate handbook to help you.

When you have chosen a unit, do another personal skills review, this time based on the unit. You may find it easier to do this element by element at first.

◆ Go through the PCs and range for the element you are working on and fill in the appropriate boxes 1 - 5 on the review sheet.

◆ Go to the knowledge evidence section at the end of the unit and pick out the statements which are relevant to the element you are working on. Note which you need some help with in section 6 on the review sheet.

◆ Decide which activities you can arrange for your assessor to observe (box 7), and what other types of evidence you can use.

Note: As you become more confident, use this format to look at the whole unit rather than just one element.

The personal skills review will help you to be prepared for when you and your assessor plan your assessment. If you have done other units already and you feel confident to go straight into planning, you can leave this section out.

Action you may need to take

If you have identified areas you may have difficulty with you will need to discuss with your assessor what you are going to do to put these right. For instance:

Section 2 You may simply need to practise an activity until you feel more confident. Ask your assessor or colleagues for guidance if necessary. If you need ideas for activities you will find the resources in this book helpful.

Section 3 You may need to ask your employer to give you the opportunity to move to a different age group, or to allow you to do things not normally within your role. If there are serious gaps, you may need to spend some time in another setting - for instance, if you work in a creche where you never have the same children for more than an hour, or you only have children under two years old, you do need to consider getting wider experience.

Section 4 If you want to use something from the past as evidence, your assessor will have to make sure that it is sufficient, takes account of current legislation, local regulations and best practice, and that it is authentic and reliable - that is, that it's your own work. Past experience cannot take the place of direct observation.

Section 6 When you fill in this section, remember to check the knowledge evidence. We have identified the relevant knowledge evidence for each element in each of the chapters. You may need to attend some training, ask for support, or do some reading and research to improve your understanding. Your centre may offer training sessions, or learning materials and supported study.

Assessment planning

At this stage you may want to arrange a meeting with your assessor so that you can start planning your assessment. If this is your first unit, we would recommend that you plan together, but once you are confident, you can plan on your own if you wish. You will find a chapter on each of the mandatory units, either in this book or in the other two books in the series, to help you with your planning. Your centre will have an assessment plan format, but an example of what it might look like is given on page 32 (completed version, page 22).

◆ There are two ways of planning your assessment:
You can take each element separately and plan an activity which your assessor will observe and other evidence you need for that element, **or:**

◆ Plan a whole session which will cover a range of activities and provide evidence for more than one element or unit - we sometimes call this **holistic assessment.** We recommend this method because it is a more effective use of your own and the assessor's time. We will explain this more fully in the section on cross referencing below.

Start by choosing an activity for your assessor to observe which will cover as many of the PCs and the range as possible. Remember to check which PCs must be observed, and remember too that at least one aspect of each area of the range must be observed. It's a good idea to plan the activity using the activity plan format we suggested earlier in the chapter, so that you can make sure that you are well prepared, and also to show your assessor that you have a good knowledge and understanding of the element or unit.

Decide how you will provide the other evidence you need. You will find suggestions about the most appropriate types of evidence at the beginning of the unit. Don't forget to include any work plans from your normal work practice, with a note to say how you were involved in preparing and carrying them out.

Cross referencing

The NVQ process encourages working across elements and units - we call this **holistic assessment.** This means that you can use one piece of evidence in several units. Because every page of evidence is numbered, you simply cross reference to the relevant page, regardless of which unit it is in. For instance, your assessor may have observed you playing a colour matching game with a group of children, which you planned for Element 3 in C10 (we usually write this as C10.3). She will probably have noted how you encouraged children to relate to each other and take turns (C5.2) and how you encouraged and praised children (C5.3). You were probably encouraging concentration (C10.1) and developing language skills (C11.2,5). If your assessor planned to spend some extra time observing tidying up and getting ready for dinner, she would also see evidence for C5.3 - encouraging self-reliance; for E3.1 - maintaining a safe environment; and for C2.2 - contributing to children's personal hygiene. In the same way you can cross reference for areas of the range. You can also do this for any of your written evidence. Some candidates are unable to cope with this at first, and you may need to grow into it. As you become more familiar with your handbook, you will find it easier to cross reference.

You will probably find it easier to concentrate on one unit at a time, but be aware of when evidence can be cross referenced

PERSONAL SKILLS PROFILE

1. Things I feel confident I can do

2. Things I don't feel confident about doing

3. Things I don't have the opportunity to do

4. Things I have done in the past

5. Areas of the range my assessor can observe

6. Things I don't understand (check knowledge evidence)

7. Possible activities my assessor could observe

8. Other types of evidence I could provide

ASSESSMENT PLAN

Description of evidence/activity	To cover PCs/ range	To cover knowledge evidence	Date due
Cooking activity to be observed Write an activity plan for the cooking activity Reflective account of other activities carried out to develop maths, relational and physical concepts Cross reference to evidence from previous course on concepts	C10.2 R4,5 C10.3.1,3,4 5,6,7, R2 C10.3, R1-6	C10KE10,11,19,20 21,22,23 M7KE2,3,5,10, 17,20,23	
Assignment to cover all areas of development		C3,C5,C10,C11 KE1 and others	

Signed.........Sarah Bright..................................(candidate)   ....A. N. Other......................................(assessor)

Date.........23. 6.00..   Date..............23. 6.00......................................

CROSS REFERENCING SHEET

Unit	
Description of evidence	**Unit/page reference**

to other units. To help you to do this, we have given you a simple format (see page 23). Put a copy at the beginning of each unit, and as you find evidence which you think will fit, list it on the sheet, with the page reference. At this stage, you don't need to worry about exactly which PCs, range or knowledge evidence it fits, as long as you know where to find it. When you start working on that unit, you can go back to the evidence and cross reference it into the appropriate place.

Knowledge evidence

Try to incorporate as much knowledge evidence as you can into your activity plan, candidate diary, reflective account, child observation or other work-based evidence. If there are still gaps in your evidence, you can write paragraphs on each relevant point. You should aim to make this short, clear and to the point, and wherever possible, use examples from your own work practice. Don't copy chunks from books, nor include photocopied pages.

Alternatively, if you feel confident that you can give an oral account of your knowledge and understanding, arrange this with your assessor, or include an audio-tape of your answers as evidence.

You may find it easier to pick out the relevant bits of knowledge evidence for each element, to ensure that you have covered all of the evidence but not repeated anything unnecessarily. You will notice in your candidate handbook that alongside each statement in the knowledge evidence there is a reference to the element it is linked to. To help you to identify it, we have included the reference numbers of the relevant statements in each of the elements in the chapters.

The resources in this book will help you with your underpinning knowledge. There are some good practical ideas, and some thought-provoking articles which will help you to reflect on your own practice and improve it. We have placed each article in the unit it is most relevant for but you will notice that many of the articles are relevant for more than one unit.

You will probably need to do further reading from study materials and recommended text books, or make arrangements to attend training sessions. Your centre will be able to advise you on this. A list of books you may find useful is given here.

Suggested reading list

Children with Special Educational Needs by M Alcott (Hodder & Stoughton) 0 340 70152 8.

Babies and Young Children by Beaver, Brewster *et al* (Stanley Thornes) Book 1 (2nd edition) 0 7487 3974 2; Book 2 0 7847 3975 0.

Child Care and Education by T Bruce and C Meggitt (Hodder & Stoughton) 0 340 64328 5.

A Practical Guide to Caring for Children with Special Needs by Dare and O'Donovan (Stanley Thornes) 0 7487 2871 6.

DfEE publications:
    Early Learning Goals
    Curriculum Guidance for the Foundation Stage

National Curriculum documents:
    National Literacy Strategy
    National Numeracy Strategy

Observations and Assessments by Harding and Meldon-Smith (Hodder & Stoughton) 0 340 78138 X.

A Practical Guide to Child Observation (2nd edition) by Hobart and Frankel (Stanley Thornes) 0 7487 4500 9.

Good Practice in Child Protection by Hobart and Frankel (Stanley Thornes) 0 7487 3094.

Child Protection and Early Years Work by J Lindon (Hodder & Stoughton) 0 340 70558 2.

Equal Opportunities in Practice by J Lindon (Hodder & Stoughton) 0 340 70559 0.

A Practical Guide to Equal Opportunities by H Malik (Stanley Thornes) 0 7487 3652 2.

Working with Parents by M Whalley (Hodder & Stoughton) 0 340 73076 5.

Planning for Learning series (Step Forward Publishing – for details ring for a catalogue 01926 420046).

Date	OBSERVATION RECORD	PCs range	Knowledge evidence

Signed..(assessor)   ....(candidate)

Date	ORAL QUESTION RECORD	PCs range	Knowledge evidence

Signed..(assessor) ....(candidate)

Date	WITNESS TESTIMONY	PCs range	Knowledge evidence

Signed..witness ....(candidate)

Status of witness..

ACTIVITY PLAN

NAME: **DATE:**   **ACTIVITY:**   **AGE OF CHILDREN:**

Before the activity:
Describe the activity you are planning. Describe how it fulfils the values statements for the element or unit you are working on.

Why have you chosen this activity? What do you think the children will gain from it?*(Think about areas of development.)*

Which children will be involved? Why? *(Will it be free choice? Have you targeted children who need particular help with, for instance, colour recognition?)*

What equipment/resources/preparation do you need?

What will you do during the activity? *(Language you will use, help you will give, etc)*

After the activity:

Did the activity go well? Why? If not, why not?

Would you change it next time? If so, how and why?

How would you adapt the activity for older/younger children? For children with additional needs or disabilities?

What did the children gain from the activity? Was it what you thought they would?

What did you learn from it?

Signed .... (candidate) If anyone observed you ask them to sign that this is a true record, and to comment if possible.

Signed .... Role: ....

Comment:

CANDIDATE DIARY

NAME: **DATE:**   **INCIDENT:**

What happened? Who was involved?   *(Don't use names - number of staff/children/parents)*

How did you react? What did you do?

Why did you do it this way?

Did it work? If not, why not?

What have you learned from it? What would you do differently next time?
(Think about the values statements)

Which PC's/range/knowledge does this relate to?

If anyone observed you ask them to sign that this is an accurate record and to make a comment.

Witness..   **Status** ....

Witness comment (if applicable)

CHILD OBSERVATION

Candidate's name   **Date**

Title of observation:

Type of observation: *(eg target child, free description, developmental check-list)*

Aim of observation: *(Which aspect of child development/behaviour are you aiming to observe?)*

First name of child: *(or fictitious name)*   **Age:** *(yrs & mths)*

Description of setting: *(where observation is taking place, number of staff, children, equipment available, etc)*

The observation: Write this on a separate piece of paper, or other format you have chosen. Write what you actually observed in detail, using present tense.

Evaluation: Comment on what you learned from the observation - link this to your aims. Evaluate what the child's needs are, and make recommendations for future planning.

Signatures: Sign your observation and ask someone who witnessed the observation to sign it if possible.

Signed...(candidate)   **Signed**.......................................(witness)

ASSESSMENT PLAN

Description of evidence/activity	To cover PCs/ range	To cover knowledge evidence	Date due

Signed...(assessor)   ....(candidate)

Date...   Date...

Chapter 2

Unit P2: Establish and maintain relationships with parents

About this unit

This unit, which is about establishing and maintaining relationships with parents, is an essential aspect of your work with young children. Parents play a central role in their children's welfare and development, and it's vital that you recognise and take account of that in everything you do with the children in your care. The way you welcome and respond to parents at the start will determine whether you have a good relationship with them in the future.

Read through the elements and familiarise yourself with the requirements. In some settings, you may find it difficult to meet all the requirements for this unit, if you don't have the opportunity to work closely with parents. For instance, in some schools only the class teacher has direct contact. If this is a problem for you, you will need to discuss it with your assessor, who may need to negotiate with the class teacher about allowing you some contact with parents so that you can fulfil the requirements of the unit. Good opportunities for this would be school open days for the new intake, when parents spend some time in the school with their children. If there are parent helpers in the classroom, or if parents are involved in school outings, you may be able to work with them on these occasions. Maybe you take a voluntary group, such as cubs or brownies, where you meet with parents.

If you work in a day nursery or other setting where children are admitted throughout the year, look out for opportunities to work with new parents when their children start. Many of you will meet and talk with parents every day as they bring and collect their children. If your setting keeps a daily diary for parents to refer to, make sure you fill it in carefully, and discuss it with parents at the end of each day. If not, try to do this informally.

The first two elements are about settling-in arrangements and welcoming new parents, so these are best done at the start of a new intake of children. You may already have some evidence for this unit in C5, which also deals with settling children in to new settings. The emphasis in C5 is on the children, whereas in P2 it is on the parents, but there is likely to be some overlap. Check your cross referencing sheet for evidence you already have, and don't repeat work unnecessarily.

A useful tip!

Fill in the unit assessment records with each piece of evidence as you collect it, starting with your assessor's observation. That will prevent you doing too much.

Values

All work you do with parents should be carried out in the context of the requirements of the Children Act 1989, so make sure you know what they are. The Children Act is an important piece of legislation for early years workers, which sets out clearly the responsibilities of parents and other people who care for children, and focuses on children's rights and needs more than any other past legislation. It also encourages closer co-operation between those who work in the early years sector, and children and their families.

For all elements, you need to be aware of the need to work in partnership with parents, and also that the welfare of the child is paramount. The two go hand in glove. You have to show that you are a reflective practitioner, able to evaluate your own attitude and practice in relation to parents and the central role they play. Make sure you know where the boundaries of your responsibilities are, and when you should refer parents on to other more senior colleagues in the setting, or to other professionals outside the setting. You must also be aware of good practice in relation to equal opportunities and anti-discrimination - of how to communicate with parents from all cultures and backgrounds as equals and to take account of differences in family values and beliefs. You need to recognise the difficulties that may be faced by children and parents whose culture and language is different from the predominant culture and language of the setting.

Below are some suggestions about how you can build a good partnership with parents. It may be difficult to achieve all of them in some settings - for instance, working parents will not often get the opportunity to help at their child's nursery. You will probably be able to think of points to add to the list.

◆ Ensure that parents understand what **you** are trying to achieve, and that you understand what **they** are trying to achieve.

◆ Ask parents for their views and **really listen** to what they have to say.

◆ Try to reach **all** parents in some way, even if they cannot be directly involved.

◆ Encourage parents to help in the setting if they are able to.

◆ Give parents the opportunity to use their skills to benefit the children - for example, by getting them to talk to the children about their job or special interest

◆ Make provision for parents who have difficulty in communication or other particular needs

◆ Give parents the opportunity to develop new skills.

◆ If possible, have a place where parents can meet and talk.

Getting started
In this unit you will need to show how you:

◆ develop relationships with parents new to your setting

◆ plan settling-in arrangements with parents

◆ exchange information with parents about their children

◆ share the care and management of children with their parents

You may need to go through the personal skills check-list to see if there are any areas you will find it difficult to provide evidence for. You will find this on page 21 in the introduction. If you think direct observation will be a problem because you don't get to work with parents in your setting, you will need to discuss this with your assessor. If you feel you need to do further training or research, find out what courses are available at your centre or your local early years partnership.

Element P2.1 Develop relationships with parents new to the setting

Element P2.2 Plan settling-in arrangements with parents

Key issues
As these two elements are so closely linked we will look at them together. Your setting needs clear procedures for settling in new children, and these procedures need to be shared with parents. Most settings have a brochure with all the necessary information, which they give to prospective parents. Some

make home visits to introduce themselves and give parents all the information they need. Practices on settling in differ widely from one setting to another, but it's good practice to encourage parents to stay with their children for at least part of the first few sessions, to ease the transition from home to the care setting. This is particularly important for younger children, once they have reached the age where they are anxious about strangers, which may be from about eight months old, until they reach the age when they are ready to socialise in larger groups, at about three years old. Of course, this will depend on the individual child and their previous experience. Some children cope with change more easily than others. Where parents are working, it's not always possible for them to stay for long periods, but you should insist on at least an introductory visit and encourage them to stay as long as they are able when the child first starts, especially if the child is finding it difficult to settle in.

Parents will often be apprehensive about leaving their child in an early years setting for the first time, so you will need to be able to put them at their ease and reassure them. They will have more confidence in a setting which has carefully thought out settling-in procedures. It's important for the child, who will probably also be apprehensive, to see that you and their parents have a good relationship. Find out what parents would prefer to be called, make sure that you get their name right, and make them feel welcome when they come in. Show that you respect and value the information they give you about their child - they know their child better than anyone! If they are from a minority ethnic background, they may find communication difficult - but don't assume that this is the case because many are fluent English speakers, and have been born and brought up in Britain.

Useful information!
Your local community education association or intercultural support service may offer interpreters if you have any language barriers with parents, and also offer advice about particular requirements and expectations of families from different minority ethnic groups.

You need to treat everything parents tell you in strict confidence, and only pass on information to those in your setting who need to know. There may be times when parents do not keep to the requirements of the setting - perhaps being consistently late picking their child up, or allowing behaviour which you cannot accept in the setting. Or they may come to you for advice on family problems. Be aware of the limits of your responsibility, and refer parents on to a senior colleague if necessary. If you are a childminder in sole charge of the children, refer any serious concerns to your local health visitor or social services department.

There are many benefits to building good relationships with parents:

Benefits to children:
◆ continuity between home and setting

◆ children settle in more easily

◆ children are more confident

◆ children benefit from skills of visiting parents

◆ opportunity for interaction in home language for children whose first language is not English

◆ extra help in the classroom

Benefits to parents:
◆ more aware of what is going on in setting

◆ more aware of child's progress

◆ more confident and relaxed about the setting

◆ feel valued

◆ able to use their own skills and interests

◆ have opportunity to learn new skills

◆ able to socialise with other parents

Benefits to setting:
◆ better relationship with parents

◆ better understanding of the children and their families

◆ parents bring special skills and interests

◆ extra help in the classroom or with outings, clubs, social events

◆ financial support and fundraising

◆ help in planning and policy making

You will probably be able to think of some more.

Which type of evidence?

Remember that these elements are closely linked to C5.1, 'Enable children to adjust to the setting', so refer to your cross referencing sheet and check whether you can cross reference any of the evidence. You can also use **work products** such as parent brochures, as long as you include a short summary of how you have used it or been involved in preparing the materials. You will see from the evidence requirements for P2.1 that your assessor needs to **observe** six of the ten PCs and one aspect of the one range category, and for P2.2 all but one of the PCs and one aspect in each of the two range categories. Of course, she can observe more if she has the opportunity.

You can provide the other evidence through a **candidate diary** or **reflective account** of, for instance, times when you have had difficulty in communicating with a parent, supported a parent who was anxious, or been asked for information which was beyond the scope of your responsibility. Use these accounts to cover the range if possible, or if you haven't had direct experience, write a brief account of how you would deal with these situations if you needed to. The range for the whole unit has a lot of overlap so it would be a good idea to write about all of the range together. Ask your supervisor or a colleague to write a **witness testimony** that you only pass on information obtained from parents when it is for the benefit of the child and that you treat all information confidentially.

> **Don't forget!**
> Check your knowledge evidence and cover as much as you can in your reflective accounts and other evidence.

The **knowledge evidence** statements related to these elements are 1, 2, 4, 5, 6, 7, 8, 9, 10, 11, 12, 13, 14, 15, 16, 17, 18. There are a lot of points, but there is some overlap, so try to link them together. You will see from point 9 that you need to be clear on current good practice and legislation, particularly the Children Act 1989. You also need to know about your own setting's policies and practices in relation to new parents.

If you don't feel confident that you have sufficient knowledge and understanding of the issues, check whether there are any courses at your centre or local partnership you may be able to attend. Discuss your setting's policies and procedures with your supervisor. Make sure you are fully aware of any good practice in your setting which promotes partnership with parents, and contribute your own ideas if you get the opportunity. The articles later in the chapter will give you useful information, and you can supplement those by further reading from the book list.

Element P2.3 Exchange information with parents about their children

Key issues

Exchange of information is an important aspect of developing relationships with parents. When new children start, your setting will collect some important information from the parents about the children's medical history and any medical conditions they have, dietary and religious practices, family circumstances, perhaps what skills and abilities the children already have, any concerns, and so on. It's crucial that you take account of this information when you are caring for the children, so that there is continuity of care and respect for the families' values.

Once parents and their children have settled in, it's important to maintain and build on the relationship by ensuring that there is ongoing sharing of information between the parents and the setting. Share information about what the children have achieved, things they have enjoyed and so on. If you or the parents have any concerns, you can pick up on these before they become a big issue. Some settings keep a diary which staff and parents contribute to, so that there is two-way communication. Parents will really value this exchange of information because it gives them a picture of their child's day, and reassures them that you are observing and monitoring their child.

Think of ways of sharing information about children's activities, such as a photograph display of children carrying out activities with captions describing how they benefit the children, good work sent home for parents to see, workshops where parents try out some of the children's activities, open days or evenings. Many settings have regular newsletters, or a noticeboard. There are some useful ideas in the article called 'Sharing information' later in the chapter.

> **Remember!**
> Parents are busy and will be less likely to read lengthy letters. Keep correspondence brief, easy to read and eye catching. Check whether there are parents who need information translated into home language.

Which type of evidence?

Read through the evidence requirements for the element. Check whether you already have some of the evidence from C5, P2.1 or P2.2. If you have, record it on your assessment records. Your assessor will need to **observe** all but the first two PCs, and one aspect of each range category, unless she has done so already. She may wish to **inspect the setting** to see what arrangements are made for the safe storage of children's records, or ask you **questions** about how you use the records to inform your practice. You can use examples of

children's records with the names and addresses removed, or write a fictitious one to illustrate the format your setting uses. You may be able show a **work plan** or write a **reflective account** of how you have used some of the information in your planning of routines or activities. You may have already covered the range, but if not, add this information to your reflective account if you can.

The **knowledge evidence** statements for this element are 5, 10, 15, 16. Try to include these in your other evidence.

> **Remember!**
> You don't have to provide all of these types of evidence for every element. Cross reference as much as you can. Don't write more than you need to.

Element P2.4 Share the care and management of children with their parents

Key issues

This element is about how you share the care and education of children with their parents. It's important that you show parents that you value them as the most important carers and educators of their child. This element is linked closely to the other elements, and you may have already covered much of the evidence.

As an early years worker you should aim to provide continuity between the home and care setting as far as you can. Remember that you may have children from a wide range of social and cultural backgrounds, so find out as much as possible from the parents about their needs and expectations. You need to take account of parents' views as far as possible. This is perhaps easier to achieve where you have parents who share the setting's philosophy, but more difficult when they have very different values.

There will inevitably be times you need to reach a compromise, or when you cannot comply with the parents' wishes - for instance, if parents suggest that you smack their child if they behave badly, or express discriminatory views about activities you provide to make children more aware of different cultures. In these situations, you need to be able to justify your reasons for why you cannot comply with their wishes. Always behave politely and professionally if disputes or disagreements arise.

Parents may also look to you for advice and support if they are having difficulties. Try to make time to listen without other things distracting you. You need to be able to reassure them and boost their confidence in their role as parents. Don't go beyond the limitations of your work role, and know who to refer parents on to if you need to.

A good start to sharing a child's care and education with their parents is to ask parents to complete a profile of things their child has achieved, enjoys doing, is anxious about, and so on, before their child starts at the setting. This can be followed by a consultation where you exchange ideas and views on the child's care and agree on joint strategies for helping their learning or managing their behaviour. This will need to be followed up by a regular exchange of information and ideas. This approach is easier if you operate the key worker system, where each member of staff is responsible for a small group of children, and the parents know who to go to.

It will be particularly important to work closely with parents where you are caring for a child with a disability or special need. You may need to work with other professionals, too. There is an article on Portage - a scheme for teaching pre-school children with special needs new and useful skills in their own home - later in the chapter, which will give you an insight into ways of working with parents of children with special needs.

Remember!
It's absolutely crucial that you maintain strict confidentiality about any information passed to you about children and their families in the course of your work.

Which type of evidence?
There are only two PCs in this element which your assessor has to **observe,** and one aspect of the range category. The others are not easy to observe, or it may not be appropriate to observe them because of the issue of confidentiality. You may have covered some of this element already, so check first. You may be able to write a **candidate diary** or **reflective account** of incidents, for instance where you had a discussion with a parent which resulted in joint action being taken, or where you responded to an anxiety they expressed, or how you dealt with an issue where they didn't agree with the policy of the setting. A parent may be willing to write a **witness testimony** about how you supported them.

The **knowledge evidence** statements for this element are 3, 6, 18, 19. It's very likely that you have already covered these in the other elements, so do check. You will find the following articles helpful in giving you ideas about the best ways to build a partnership with parents.

Do you make time to talk to prospective parents and show them round? Do you insist on appointments or can visitors call in any time? What is the best approach and why? Sue Rose offers some guidance on what works well

Managing visits from parents

For many parents their first visit to your setting will be their first brush with the educational 'establishment'. It is vital to get it right if good foundations are to be laid for learning together. No matter who we are or what qualifications we have, this visit will often prove intimidating. Imagining our parenting skills judged and possibly found wanting makes some of us nervous and others loudly aggressive. It's our job to ease this tension.

Parents from minority ethnic backgrounds may find it particularly daunting, especially if English is not their first language. Make sure your environment and displays are welcoming to all groups of the community, and arrange for an interpreter if necessary.

I find it helps to praise the child's carer in whichever way seems appropriate:

❑ 'You've obviously spent a lot of time singing together.'

❑ 'My goodness, he can already count to seven.'

It's helpful to have advance warning of visitors but even then conditions may not be perfect. It is useful to bear priorities in mind:

❑ the children already in your care

❑ the parents

❑ the staff

❑ anybody else!

It is best if one member of staff can be the welcomer. This will not always be the same person, especially on unplanned visits, but it should always be someone with enough

knowledge of your aims and objectives to give both the right flavour and correct information. Questions answered inconsistently provide huge scope for misunderstanding in the future.

The guided tour

It is usually a good idea to begin a visit with the 'guided tour', highlighting the strengths of your establishment as you go:

'We have a big sunny kitchen. The children have their milk here just like home', or 'We have a high ratio of adults to children so that we can encourage speaking and listening skills.'

If you know that there are drawbacks in your facilities, point out how you manage to use them to your advantage. (A block of safely

piled chairs can make an effective display area.) Mentioning safety aspects also tells parents that you are alert to the most pressing of all parental needs. It doesn't matter how wonderful your maths opportunities are if children land in hospital when the home corner collapses on them!

Visits present an ideal time to establish good practice:

'We always help the children to name their pictures in the top left-hand corner. This helps to establish the left to right eye movement necessary for reading.'

'Capital letters are only used for the first letter of a name.'

Astute visitors will pick up on this kind of thing, eager themselves to get it right. Visits are also an ideal time for the parents to talk to you about their child - their skills and difficulties, their likes and dislikes and so on. Remember, they know their child better than anyone. The more you know about the child, the better you will help them to settle in.

Time to join in

Having completed the look around, urge parents to let their children join in any activity of interest, offering them a short time later to bring up any issues arising from this watching/joining in period.

Other staff/adults should take this opportunity to make friendly comments to both carer and child as they go about their activities. This immediately shows a shared commitment to the caring and the teamwork which is so important in creating the right atmosphere. Often a visitor will find it easier to ask questions of a staff member or parent helpers, if you have them. The importance to parents of their own peer group is often overlooked in the push to make our settings educationally excellent. Parents need to be in touch with each other. Once visitors are happily chatting to other adults in the group, the welcomer can resume whatever they were engaged in before the break. At most only ten minutes will have been lost.

Opportunities for the whole group

Visits should, wherever possible, be long enough to enable children to overcome their initial shyness. Once they have watched everyone else for a while they begin to relax and sometimes offer some conversation, occasionally to grown-ups, but more often to other children. Such visits present a wonderful chance for more established children in the group to practise emergent social skills:

❑ helping them to feel welcome

❑ being kind to little ones

❑ showing them where things are

❑ sharing

Older children often like to offer visiting adults a cup of tea and will usually rush to show visitors project books or photographs of significant events, if you have them. Sometimes they are delighted that they already know a child who is visiting and be proud to tell you that they live next door to Grandma.

The newcomer will need to touch base with their special person, but will hopefully find something familiar with which to play. This building on experience gives immense confidence and the eventual readiness to move into more challenging areas.

Providing information

An hour is long enough for a visit and for some children only half an hour is sensible. If your setting operates a circle time or group singing, it is not usually a good idea for the very young visitor to be part of that. Group sitting is an alien concept for small children. Better by far to stop while you're winning, leaving them with a happy memory. The welcomer needs to size up the situation, drawing the visit to a close quite firmly by offering some written information for the parents to take away. This information could be in the form of a brief letter something like the one below.

Parents need to be told when places may become available, how many sessions to start with and what they should expect to happen next. There may need to be clarification about funded places as many parents find this issue totally confusing. An enrolment form can be offered with a provisional starting date.

You could invite them to make a return visit at a convenient time. The best time for visits is normally well after the to-ing and fro-ing of children's arrival and parents' departure. The time when children are actively engaged in play experiences is often the most appropriate and easily managed for both group and visitors.

Practice sessions

The practice session visit is a really good idea. A group of new children and their families may be invited at a time when no other children are present. This may be difficult in some settings and involve some extra work, but is well worth the effort in terms of settling in. Staff/helpers have the chance to get to know the newcomers without the pressure of a normal workload. Families, including dads if you can make it a Saturday, can ask questions as you circulate and everyone can have a bash at the clay or a bang at the woodwork bench. There is plenty of time and space to note a parent's interaction with their child and get a feel for how confident the child is.

With outline strategies in place every visit, however inconvenient, can be seen as a pleasant surprise. Spontaneous events like this give an opportunity to extend and enrich children's lives. Seize it with both hands and your setting will always be in demand!

Sue Rose

Name of group

Details of contact

Welcome

Dear Mums and Dads,

This is a small leaflet telling you about our group before your child comes. There has been a playgroup here for 30 years. We have qualified staff with long years of experience in education for under-fives. We provide a caring and stimulating atmosphere in which children are encouraged to develop skills and confidence.

Times of opening:

We are open (x) sessions a week with holidays similar to the local school. Sessions are from .... (Details of days and times)

Fees:

The fees are £   per session until your child becomes eligible for Local Education Authority funding, which allows up to five sessions per week free. (For more details please talk to the playleader.) (Methods and timing of payment)

Staffing:

We have a high ratio of one adult to (x) children enabling us to give individual care to your child. It is important that children talk to a variety of adults and have lots of help when they are coping with new experiences for the first time without you.

Ways in which you may become involved:

If you are good at something please share it!

The crucial handover period when children arrive at pre-school or nursery is not always given the thought and planning it deserves. Sarah Stocks sets out some strategies

Arrival time: making families welcome

Imagine arriving at a party that you didn't really want to go to, being dropped off by someone you would rather stay with, entering a loud and busy room and being left to find your way around or pluck up courage to join in established conversations. If your host is ignoring you into the bargain you would be forgiven for turning tail and leaving straightaway!

No matter how often you have done it and no matter how confident you and your child are, arriving at nursery or pre-school represents a break away from the parent or daytime carer and the more challenging atmosphere of an early years environment. Unfortunately, this crucial handover period is not always given the thought and planning it deserves. Getting this aspect of your day wrong will jeopardize your ability to win the trust and attention of both the child in your care and his or her parent.

Situations to avoid

Before we look at some suggestions for arrivals time, let's first look at the problems that might occur if the child and his or her family are not welcomed and integrated into the group. If a parent has to leave her child standing forlornly in the middle of a room, unspoken to by an adult and excluded from ongoing activities by other children then you may assume that:

❏ The child will be upset, gaining little positive value from her time in the group.

❏ The parent will leave feeling that they have abandoned their child. These bad feelings will affect the way they deal with the handover period the next time and you will have clingy children and parents who do not feel able to leave - a vicious circle!

❏ Your relationship with the parent will suffer.

❏ The stressful atmosphere in the room will affect all the children's responses to you and the activities you have planned for them.

Be ready

Be ready to greet the children as they arrive. The first activities should be set up, your hands should be free and all staff should be available. The activities on offer should be chosen to allow inclusion of arriving children easily. Keep the atmosphere as calm as possible.

Say hello!

Smile and say hello to every parent and child. Yes! Every child, every morning! Ensure that parents know the routine, where to put coats, who to hand the child over to, and so on. Larger groups may find it useful to have a leaflet to hand out to new parents - 'How to drop your child off' - they will appreciate it. Don't stand in a huddle - spread yourselves out around the room, it makes you more accessible.

Make eye contact

Touch the child. Take his or her hand and lead them to an activity, get low enough to establish eye contact and make sure they are happy before you move away. Let the parent see that you are caring for their child, he is happy and safe and that you are going to settle him in properly. A backward smile or nod and a reassuring word as you lead the child away will reassure the parent that all is well. Encourage parent and child to say goodbye to each other. A parent who 'sneaks' away when the child is not looking is storing up problems for the next time!

Settling-in policy

Have a coherent, enforced settling in policy which allows the new child and parent time to be at the group together. A rough guide would be a whole session to begin with, then half a session, then the first hour and then to be dropped off like all the other children. A child should not move to the next stage until he is happy with the stage he is on. Allow for individuals and their differing needs.

Message system

Have a system for parents to leave messages - a book to write in is ideal. It is too easy to forget one of the six important messages you were given in a five-minute period at the busiest time of the day! Do not let the written message system replace your availability, however, some things need to be said. Remember, too, that not all parents find writing as easy as you - be sensitive to parents who may not be able to write.

Firm handling

Be prepared to be firm with parents who want to spend too long chatting. A polite 'May we continue this later Mary? I can see that Sophie needs a hand!' will usually do the trick. More persistent parents may need firmer handling; it may be that they have problems of their own that they need help with. You may be able to help but arrivals time is not the right time to do it. Make a note to speak to her at a more convenient time.

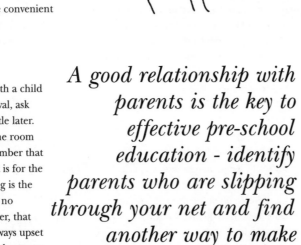

Children who cry

If you are having difficulties with a child who is often disruptive on arrival, ask the parent to bring her in a little later. This will reduce the stress in the room as other children arrive. Remember that it is as hard for the parent as it is for the child! Leaving your child crying is the hardest thing to do and serves no purpose. It is fair to say, however, that individual children who are always upset may well have problems other than ones caused by your arrivals policy! Knowing your children and being confident that you are providing a welcoming environment will help you decide if a persistent crier has other problems.

Late arrivals

Children who arrive late still need to settle in and you should make time to greet them properly. It is rarely the child's fault that he or she is late! If you have a persistently late arriver a quiet word to the parent may suffice. Explain that it makes it hard for you to concentrate on your job if you have to keep stopping.

A good relationship with parents is the key to effective pre-school education - identify parents who are slipping through your net and find another way to make contact with them.

Carers

If the child is being dropped off by a carer other than the parent you should afford them all the same respect, attention and support you would to the child's parent. They are acting on the parent's behalf and will welcome your support and inclusion. The child has the same rights as one dropped off by a home-based mother and will benefit from this understanding approach.

Regular contact

A key worker system should ensure that all parents are spoken to regularly, otherwise the group leader might keep an eye on those who do not seem to be speaking to anyone. Some parents are intimidated by people they see as 'officials' and will not approach you. A good relationship with parents is the key to effective pre-school education - identify parents who are slipping through your net and find another way to make contact with them. If the family does not speak English then consider using an interpreter, certainly for the first few sessions and thereafter at parents' evenings or social events.

Finally, a good honest look around you is always a valuable exercise. Don't be afraid to stand back and watch. If the atmosphere is relaxed, happy and productive then you must be doing something right! Remember new problems are inevitable, treat each one as an opportunity to improve and give yourself praise where praise is due!

Sara Stocks

Collection time may be all that parents ever see of your group. The impression they get of you in these short minutes really matters. Sara Stocks sets out some plans of action for making home time stress-free

Collection time: **keeping calm**

The end of the session has come, a session during which you have played with, stimulated and encouraged the children in your care. They are sitting beautifully waiting for their mummies and daddies who will come in, thank you for all your hard work and leave, on time, with all their belongings. Then a warm after-glow of satisfaction will weave its way around the hall as you and your staff leave, on time and ready for another day ......

OK! OK! Like all good fairy stories it strikes a chord, and like all good yarns it has elements of truth but this scenario just does not seem to happen often enough does it? How can we make the end of the day as good as the rest of it? After all, it is as much a shop window as the arrival time and is all the parents may see of your group. The impression they get of you in these short minutes really matters.

Options for collection

How you organise the collection time depends largely on the type of group that you run. Groups who have staggered collection times often decide that the best option is to organise free play activities that the children can leave relatively easily. Parents should then be able to come in quietly, collect their child and leave without too much disruption. For most children this works well but there is always the child who, at the first sight of her parent, immediately begins to throw herself around the room, disrupting every game within reach, refusing to put on her coat and generally causing mayhem! Try to arrange an earlier collection time for this child until she settles down.

Spot the signs

The end of the session is a good time to see parents and children together. Being aware of relationships within the families who attend your group is important. If you

witness dramatic changes of behaviour at collection time it could possibly signal a problem. As usual, the key is observation and communication with the parents. The child who plays quietly and apparently happily all morning but who bursts into tears when seeing his parent is not as settled as you thought he was!

Ready, steady ...go!

Groups who have a set collection time have fewer opportunities for the type of disruptive behaviour mentioned above - but it may not stop the most determined children of course! If you have everything ready the parents can quickly pick up the child and go if it looks like there is going to be a problem. Have a named tray/box/bag for pictures, accessible coat racks and a clear system for collection of belongings. A set policy on toys from home will save you endless hours of looking for Batman's tiny plastic belt....

Collection time, if all else is going smoothly, is a good moment to speak to parents. However, those you need to speak to are often the ones who do not hang around so do plan for these conversations. Make sure another member of your team is available for other parents while you catch the parent you are waiting to speak to.

If you need a parent to sign an accident book you could have a sticker system. As the injured child's details are entered into the book he or she will be given a 'getting better' sticker. This sticker then alerts the parents to the fact that they need to sign the book before they go.

Issues of security

Security is extremely important. You must know the adults who are going to be collecting the child, and if there is anyone

prohibited by court orders from seeing the child. It is very rare for children to be taken from organised groups but it is not a matter for complacency. It is avoided through efficient and effective communication with the carers of the child and constant staff vigilance. If a person that you know is not supposed to have contact with the child turns up you may have to lock the door and call the police. Do not be afraid to do so, you may regret it bitterly if you don't! Ask a helper to soothe the child and play down the importance of your actions to the other children.

A more common risk of damage to children is being injured by traffic when they leave the building. Make your access as safe as possible and remind parents regularly of road safety issues.

Leaving work on time is a luxury that most childcare workers have learned to live without! But there are ways of helping to ensure that late departures are rare.

Being punctual

Although many people may take it for granted, leaving work on time is a luxury that most childcare workers have learned to live without! But there are ways of helping to ensure that late departures are rare. The usual reason is late collection of children. Most parents have been late for a child at one time or another and the sad sight of the child's face, left at playgroup or nursery by herself, is reprimand enough even if the delay was unavoidable.

A system used successfully (by a manager with a flair for rhyme!) was to put up notices such as the one overleaf. Tackling a problem with good humour is more likely to get you the results you require than going in with all guns blazing at the first sign of trouble.

Persistent offenders

There are, however, parents who are consistently late. If you have a persistent offender who does not respond to polite requests, then you could take the route most often taken by groups who charge per hour - charge them for the time at an inflated price. The extra money could go towards paying overtime for the staff. If you do not have this option, or if it is failing to make any difference, then you will have to speak to the parent again. Be very clear, polite but absolutely adamant that the child must be collected on time. Give clear reasons, explain how it makes the child feel, how the staff are being put out and suggest that if everybody was consistently late then the group would not be able to function. The last point on this subject is important too - be punctual yourselves. Open on time and be ready to go on time and the vast majority of your parents will be punctual too.

during a day spent caring for children is very important. Don't underestimate this function of your group. If there is a place where parents can chat while they are waiting, then so much the better. You may decide it is best for the parents to wait outside and for all of them to come in at the same time. Although this is an efficient way to organise your collection time there is no doubt

Make someone's day

Do not forget that parents love to hear what has happened that day. A funny anecdote or a word of praise is very valuable indeed. You really can make someone's day!

Encourage a chat

Collection time from pre-school or nursery is a social event in itself for many parents and a valuable one too. Making friends in the community and talking to other adults

that the child who scans each face for his mum only to find she is late again may wish there was another way! Be sensitive!

Finally, be as welcoming and as available on departure as you were on arrival, know your families, have efficient systems that will support you and your staff in most eventualities and then - take a well-earned break, you deserve it!

Sara Stocks

A plea from the heart for all parents and collectors

We love to have your child here
We love to help them play
We love to guide them
Teach, provide them
With a fun and worthwhile day.

We gladly give our time up
We enjoy all that we do
But when it's home time
Coats and go time
What we need is YOU!

Please be on time as often
As it's possible to be
The children need you
Love to see you
And so, most days, do we!

Sharing information with parents is crucial and needs to work both ways. Sara Stocks looks at the two most obvious ways of exchanging day-to-day information - noticeboards and newsletters

Sharing information

You may well use your noticeboard for posting information, but have you thought what else it could be telling people? Your newsletters may well be a convenient way to tell parents what you want them to know but are they getting the real message? You have the opportunity to gain support, earn praise, reassure, develop relationships, support others, stay legal and much more - all from your noticeboard and newsletters!

Making the most of your noticeboard

If your noticeboard is an old green felt board, with fading hand-written notices that have been there for several months, then take it down now! That impression of being out of touch, shabby amd uninteresting is not one any group would want. Check your image - it may be time for a make-over. Here are a few more pointers to bear in mind:

❑ Don't make each notice the same shape and colour. The eye is drawn to unusual shapes and will drift over regularity. There is nothing wrong with circular, hexagonal or even star-shaped notices! Use different styles of print, ink colours and paper types. Use backing card for some notices, outline others.

❑ Date all your notices, visibly. If a notice has been up for more than four weeks either take it down if it is no longer relevant or change it and put it back up in a different place.

❑ A picture paints a thousand words . . . use photos whenever you can. If a caption in a trade magazine or a cartoon in a paper amuses you or has particular relevance - put it up.

❑ Remember that some parents may not be able to read English, and you may need to translate, or check with them that they have got the message.

❑ Have a marked spot for urgent news/information or use a large red cardboard arrow to direct attention to the relevant notice.

❑ Allow parents a section of the board to use for themselves. They can advertise second-hand goods, look for babysitting help, offer help, advertise social events and generally 'own' a part of your public image.

❑ Put your board where people wait! This may sound obvious but it is not always possible to have a permanent board - many pre-schools tidy up the noticeboard along with the toys! Have a free standing easel or other support to hold the board up and put it as near to the parents as you can. It is well-known that most noticeboards are only read by people who have nothing better to do at the time!

❑ Make sure that your 'legal notes' such as insurance certificates, inspection reports and notification of up and coming inspections/results are clear and visible - you are required to display them.

❑ Noticeboards are often in corridors or foyers. Encourage people to stop and read them but try not to make an obstruction of the crowds who will stop and admire your dynamic new image . . .

❑ Every group now has policies covering every aspect of their provision. It is a good idea to display them but the sheer volume of words prohibits a full display. To encourage parents to read the policies, why not display one a week and make it clear that all policies are available for inspection?

❑ When you are thinking about changing your board be aware of notices around you - in supermarkets, surgeries, shops,

schools. Learn from others' mistakes - which boards appeal and why?

What makes a good newsletter?

Do your newsletters strike fear into the heart of every recipient? Does every parent raise an eyebrow and say, 'Oh no, either they've got head lice or the fees are going up again'? Look back over your past six letters, count the occurrences of complaints, bad news, information, humour, good news or requests for help and see how your letters balance out.

Dear Parents....
At pre-school this term we did the usual things. We had the usual break snacks and outings and most children seemed ok. We need more of you to come and help out. The fees are going up again. We have no new equipment to tell you about and we will see you all back at the beginning of next term. The dates and times are on the last letter we sent you ....
Yours sincerely
The pre-school staff

No marks for guessing how many parents still had the last letter! Newsletters should contain news. Parents want to know what you have bought, what inspectors/fieldworkers/visitors have said about the group, funny things that the children have said - wise to leave these comments anonymous! - planned activities, trips and visits, up and coming themes, staff news, new members, leavers, and so on. If you find you are struggling for news it could be a sign that your group is not as active as it could be, so take note.

Find out if there are any parents who have difficulty with reading letters - perhaps because English is their second language or they have a visual impairment. Ask them whether they would like a translation, an enlarged copy, or help with reading the letter.

Keep a record of every letter you send for reference - you often need to refer back to them. If you have important information (such as the dreaded fees increase) and you want to ensure each parent has had a copy you could ask them to sign for receipt of the dated letter.

To make sure that your readers stay with you to the end it can be handy to include some sort of request on each letter - 'Please can all children come with a hard boiled egg next Tuesday'. Parents also like to feel that they are helping and, for the most part will respond to specific requests with enthusiasm.

Graphics can be awkward for some groups to produce but those lucky enough to have a computer expert producing the letter can get some spectacular results. Even without this technology you can still have great fun:

❑ Use coloured paper (the children could even colour it with wash for you before you start).

❑ Get an arty staff member (or parent) to doodle a little design on the top or design a proper logo.

❑ Personalise your letters by using parents' names.

❑ Get the children to stick stickers on the blank spaces and deliver them personally.

❑ Drop a dot of lavender oil on the corner and see who notices.

❑ Number them and use them in a prize draw for a small treat.

❑ Include tear-off slips to get firm offers of extra help for particular days, sessions, skills, trips, reordering sweatshirts and so on.

❑ Got a group decision to make? Have a vote - include ballot papers.

❑ Roll them up and tie with ribbon - it makes it much more special.

❑ Ask the children to draw the intended recipient on the top of the letter.

❑ Put the children's names in big clear letters on the top and encourage them to find their own at home time.

Letter writing can be a chore but don't underestimate the value of newsletters and noticeboards. They will support and reflect the excellent work you do in the creation of real and useful links between home and nursery or pre-school.

Your parents' evenings, open days, social events and committees will all rely on this fundamental communication. Make sure this is one channel that stays open and used - it is always time well spent!

Sara Stocks

❄ Notice boards ❄

There is no reason why notices should always be square or rectangular, you can have any shape notice you like! Cut them out with pinking shears now and again.

4th May 1954
Date each notice visibly, if you still have notices up after four weeks, take them down or change them.

Outline messages or use a backing sheet

Use a big red arrow to point out urgent messages, or have a designated spot - the hot spot?

Pictures paint a thousand words...

...Use photos, cartoons and items of interest you find in trade magazines to liven up the board.

The Parents' Corner - a space to post items for sale, announcements, requests for baby sitting, offers of help, etc etc.

What can you do to give parents an insight into what nursery education is all about and encourage them to volunteer their help? Pam Taylor offers some starting points

Getting parents involved

Parents have an important role to play in acting as co-educators and as a support to the daily running of a session within a pre-school or nursery. Parents want the best pre-school education for their child, regular communication with staff and an insight into how a nursery ticks. Providers need to develop effective partnerships with parents/carers. This covers the information given to parents about the provision, children's attainment and progress and the opportunities provided for parents to be involved in children's learning.

Yet, despite this, providers often find it difficult to get parents involved as helpers. It can be different for those pre-schools run by a committee for a community because parents are often expected to help out on a rota basis to keep costs down. Private nurseries are in a difficult situation. Their parents are paying for a service and may be reluctant to give up free time or unable to because they work or have other children to care for.

Providing an insight

Parents with their first child in nursery often have no insight into what happens during a session - how it is structured and the different activities a child will participate in. After all, the usual comment from a child when asked what he did in nursery today is 'nothing'. Although most parents are sensible enough to realise that

this is not so, unless they are educated to the range of structured activities and reasons behind the children doing them, they might think the children just play, run around and occasionally do an art/craft activity. Once parents have an understanding of what goes on they might decide they'd like to help out generally or feel that they have a specific skill to offer. So how do you go about enlightening them and getting them to volunteer? Firstly, how friendly are your staff? Do they take the time to chat to parents, make time for them or do they just pass the time of day at the beginning and end of a session? Parents have to feel comfortable, feel they could chat to staff

> *Parents have to feel comfortable, feel they could chat to staff about things generally and get along with them if they are going to help out during a session.*

about things generally and get along with them if they are going to help out during a session.

Do you offer parents a leaflet answering all those questions that they might be embarrassed to ask such as:

❏ What exactly is a parent helper expected to do?

❏ How much time and how often would I be expected to come?

❏ How many children would I be expected to work with?

❏ Are there any jobs that need doing that don't involve working with the children?

❏ How will my child react to me being in the nursery?

❏ Is there anything that I should be aware of concerning nursery if I do come in and help?

Offer support

Once parents/carers have made the move and volunteered, do make sure they are supported by a member of staff throughout the session. Find out what they'd like to do with the children, don't just assume everyone is happy in the art/craft area. Find out if they have any specific skills that could be used that would fit in with planning or just be a bonus as an activity that the children would enjoy. Give parents a taste of several activities so that next time they help out they can tell you what they would like to do. After all, no parent is going to return unless they enjoyed it and felt appreciated.

Those helpers that have enjoyed being part of the nursery session might gain enough confidence to want to gain a qualification that will allow them to work with children in the future.

Give information
Staff should take the right opportunity to chat to a capable helper, bringing up the subject of training for a qualification. Often

really good working with young children'. Provide information - 'The next course starts ....., do you want me to make enquiries for you?'

Successful parental involvement needs total long-term staff commitment and planning. Parents have a lot to offer and are a valuable resource.

parents think that they are not good enough to gain qualifications. They also think that all courses are held during the day when they have family commitments. Let them know that courses are run for people like themselves, often in the evenings, ideal for parents with young families. Give them information on courses being run locally, explain briefly what the course might entail. Once they have had time to think about it, follow it up by posing the right questions. 'Have you thought any more about our chat last week?' Boost their confidence: 'You'd be

Successful parental involvement needs total long-term staff commitment and planning. Parents have a lot to offer and are a valuable resource. Remember, the best recommendation for any nursery comes by word of mouth via parents. Any parent helper has a lot of knowledge about what goes on during a session and can only be a natural advertisement for the good work that goes on in your nursery.

Pam Taylor

Parents' evenings are a chance for parents to really understand what has been going on at nursery or pre-school and gain an insight into the workings of their child's day. Sara Stocks offers some hints on how to go about organising them

Holding parents' evenings

The old days of parents facing their child's teacher across a desk and being told whether they were 'good' or 'bad' are long gone. Parents' evenings are now an essential part of the overall care of the child, an opportunity for two important parties to discuss and share experiences with each other. Your inspector will want to know how well you liaise with your parents and will look for evidence that you have made the most of the opportunities that a valuable relationship with them offers.

Achieving this dialogue is not as easy as it sounds. It is all too easy to hide behind the formality of an interview, losing the real value of the occasion which is the contact between the two of you. A parents' evening is, of course, a chance to share the reaching of milestones and measurable targets (or not, as the case may be) and for you to give out information. You mustn't forget that dialogue is a two-way process, so take the opportunity to ask the parents their opinion, too.

The feel good factor

Parents who come to see you will be a little nervous. They are on your territory and they are hoping to hear good things about their child. They will remember the evening long after you do, so make it count. Normal good manners rules apply - don't keep parents waiting too long, greet each parent as they arrive and ensure that enough staff are around to make them feel welcome. If you know you need interpreters make sure they are available.

Even though you may have to tackle difficult issues with some of the parents there is no

reason why each parent who visits you should not leave feeling that they have had your undivided attention and that you understand and really care for their child.

The starting block

As the professional you will be expected to kick proceedings off. You must make sure you are somewhere private and that you have all the information the parent will want to know. This may include:

❑ Copies of child observations you have made
❑ Examples of work the child has done
❑ Your planning records to show what the child has done over the term
❑ The accident book records should they be required
❑ Your register, in case you want to discuss attendance issues
❑ Photos or other records that you think the parent might like to see

Your parents will expect you to know their child well. It is reassuring to be given little anecdotes, examples of things the child has

said, comments he or she made that were amusing or witty. It shows an understanding of the individual child and confirms that you really do listen to the children in your care.

Work from notes where necessary but don't be too formal, chatting is fine! Getting to know the parents better is one of the benefits of organising a parents' evening - make the most of it.

The bearer of bad news

It is a well-known fact that all parents know that they have the most perfect child ever - the cleverest, kindest, funniest! Some parents find it upsetting to be told otherwise! If you do have to tell a parent something that they may not want to know be absolutely sure of your ground before you do so. If you do have concerns about a child, make sure they are clear. Being told something vague is far more worrying than a clear comment - 'We are concerned that Emily does not find socialising very easy' is far better than 'There is something wrong with Emily'. Be positive! Even if you are really concerned about a child, make sure that you tell the family how you are hoping to tackle the problem and consult them about any plans you are making.

Of course, most children are fine! However, that has never stopped nearly all parents worrying. Be prepared to soothe and reassure in large measure. There is nothing wrong in confirming the perfection of each child in your care and praising the parents for how wonderfully they are doing, but do be honest about where children need extra support.

Cashing in!

There is an aspect of parents' evenings that is often missed - consider what a golden opportunity for you it is to have so many of them in the same place at the same time.

- ❑ Do you need to raise funds? Don't be shy! Set out your stall and ask away!
- ❑ Do you need extra help? Put up a prominent sign designed to prick any consciences.
- ❑ Do you need more equipment? Display a 'wants' list.

Blow your own trumpet!

Another function of a parents' evening is to blow your own trumpet! If you have done activities that you are particularly proud of or if your recent inspection report was glowing then make a point of showing off, you deserve it! Display photos and the results of good activities, have reports, letters of praise and comments from officials clearly available for parents to browse through. It makes you feel good and them feel more confident - after all, they are entrusting you with something very precious.

This confidence is something that you work hard to earn. Too many people lose a lot of ground by handling parents insensitively on these more formal occasions.

Social event?

It is tempting to make the most of having everyone together to make it a social event and there is no reason why this should not happen. A few words of warning though:

- ❑ Do not undervalue the importance of what you are trying to achieve on a parents' evening by dressing it up to be something else. A parents' evening is an important occasion on its own.
- ❑ Make sure that you do not achieve the opposite of your intentions. Parents who hate quiz evenings may be discouraged if they have to endure one to get to you to discuss their child.
- ❑ Allow busy parents who really want to see you but do not have time to stay and chat to do so without feeling guilty. The feel good factor of a parents' evening is important.

Good practice

One of the best ideas I have come across in the handling of a parents' evening is the setting up of subject area tables around the room where parents can have a go at different activities. The idea is that each table has a notice showing what a child might be learning whilst doing the activity which is already laid out on the table. The parents then do the activity so they can find out for themselves the value of hands-on learning. To have parents who really understand the value of your activities is a great asset and removes that 'they are just playing' attitude so hard for nurseries and

pre-schools to overcome. This type of information sharing makes a follow-up interview with a teacher or nursery nurse much more valuable.

Sharing the intentions behind your planning of activities with the parents makes for easier interviews on parents' evenings. If a parent has experienced one of the sessions for themselves they will understand how many parts there are to an activity and that even if their child cannot achieve certain sections of the activity they will have managed some. We all want our achievements noted and by really understanding how the activities work parents will be able to go back to each child and praise them for their individual progress, measured in real terms and not in end results.

Parents' evenings are only a part of the network you will have in place to involve parents in the early years experience of their child. You may have committees, social groups, fund-raising groups or even be totally managed by parents.

Parent power is a force to be harnessed, whether you choose to do it one way or another it is not optional! Involving your parents is a sure-fire way to make sure that you really know your children, and knowing the concerns of the parents enables you to support the entire family.

Sara Stocks

Starting up a parents' committee

Committees are notoriously complex creatures! They can either be a nightmare to operate, degenerating into a moan and groan group that the staff dread hearing from and only the most difficult parents ever want to join or they can be an absolute boon. Starting up a parents' committee is not therefore for the faint hearted or the novice. Handling groups of people in any circumstance is not easy and you must make sure that you know what you are letting yourself in for.

Make the aims and objectives of the group clear and provide written copies of such aims for all members and other parents.

Have a clear hierarchy and allocate responsibilities within the group so that everyone knows what their task is. Committees tend to function best with clear roles - chair, treasurer, secretary, and so on.

If you do not want the formality of a committee you may like to create a parents' group. Again, be clear what the aims of such a group are. The benefits of well-run committees and groups are many and may well include:

- ❑ Valuable fund-raising
- ❑ Staff support
- ❑ Administrative support
- ❑ New ideas
- ❑ Social opportunities
- ❑ Improved communication between staff and parents
- ❑ Occasional extra help and help with inspections, productions and parties.
- ❑ Some parents have wonderful hobbies and skills that you will want to use to the group's advantage. A parents' group is a good way to find out about it.

Many of you will have come across children with special needs in your work. You might also have heard that they have received Portage, and wondered what exactly what this meant and what was involved. Glen Cossins explains

What is **Portage?**

Portage is a scheme for teaching pre-school children with special needs new and useful skills in their own home, through making their parents more effective teachers of their children. It originated in the USA in the 1960s, in Portage, Wisconsin, and was introduced into the UK in 1976.

There are now around 150 registered Portage services throughout the country that meet the criteria as laid down by the National Portage Association. Services work with children with a range of special needs, including Down's Syndrome, cerebral palsy, and autism, as well as children with visual or hearing problems and language delay or disorder.

National Portage Association
For more information about the National Portage Association, visit the Portage website on www.portage.org.uk or contact:
Brenda Paul
NPA Administrator
127, Monks Dale
Yeovil
Somerset BA21 3JE
Tel: 01935 471641
Email: portageuk.freeserve.co.uk

Portage services vary considerably from region to region. They may be funded through education, health or social services, or be joint funded. A Portage team may include people from a variety of backgrounds, such as teaching, speech and language therapy, community nursing and health visiting.

Some services have volunteer home visitors; these are often past Portage parents. To become a Portage home visitor, you have to undertake a Portage Basic Workshop which lasts the equivalent of three days. It looks at the core principles of the Portage approach, as well as how to use the Portage materials to make assessments, to select teaching targets and long-term goals and to keep records.

How does Portage work?
Parents have a major role in choosing and carrying out the weekly tasks that encourage their child to develop skills in a variety of areas. During the first few weekly visits the home visitor and the parent will use the Portage check-list to identify what skills the child already has, those that are emerging and what the priorities are for the next few months. The check-list covers development up to the age of six in social, self-help, cognitive, motor and language skills, and a picture of the child's strengths and weaknesses is built up.

Together the parent and the home visitor decide on appropriate long-term goals, and activities to promote these goals are rehearsed each week for the parent to practise throughout the following week. These activities are written down on activity charts that carefully identify all the aspects that need to be considered, such as:

❑ a clear description of what the adult and child will do;

❑ what toys will be used;

❑ what help it might be necessary to give the child; and

❑ what rewards will be given.

The activity charts are used to record the progress during the week and over a period of time.

This might sound rather formal and clinical, but in practice it isn't. Parents want to know what they can do for their child, but often feel they do not know where to start. It is often necessary to break down an individual skill into smaller parts that are more achievable, and this can be difficult to do at first. However, it is important so that even small steps towards the goal are recognised and celebrated. It is also important to recognise and build on the things that the child can do and enjoys, as so often the messages about the child have been negative and based on what he or she can't do.

The regular weekly visits mean that there is constant feedback between the parent and home visitor. The relationship that is

> *It is also important to recognise and build on the things that the child can do and enjoys, as so often the messages about the child have been negative and based on what he or she can't do.*

developed through this contact means that some weeks the home visitor spends more time listening to the parents' feelings than talking about the activities, but this is a very important aspect of Portage support.

The parent and home visitor choose activities that are based on play, and which can be incorporated easily into the daily routines of the household. Other members of the family become involved, including brothers and sisters who often play an important part in the activities. Parents become more competent and confident about their teaching, more articulate about their child's skills and more aware of the different ways that children learn. As one parent says, 'The Portage method gave us the specific tools to help (our son) progress. No longer did I feel that we were working towards unobtainable goals, for I was helped merely to work towards the next, the closest milestone, and have confidence that having reached it, the following one would be attained as well. Looking back it seems as if there was a miracle, although I know there was a lot of hard work as well. Somehow the Portage activities never seemed a burden – we just included them into our daily routines and found that they served to enrich our family life.' (from *To A Different Drumbeat: A Practical Guide to Parenting Children with*

Special Needs by Clarke, Kofsky, Lauruol Hawthorn Press 1989 ISBN 1 869890 09 4)

The positive reports of registered Portage services that have been inspected under the nursery education scheme have identified the strong partnership with parents and the effective assessment and recording processes as particular strengths.

What contact might Portage have with other settings?

When the time comes for a child to become involved in a group outside his home, for example his local playgroup or day nursery, you may well have contact with his Portage visitor. Effective liaison is one of the fundamental aspects of the Portage approach.

The home visitor could be involved in a number of ways. She might visit the group with the child in the initial stages or call in to see how things are going as time passes. She may discuss his current long-term goals with you, and how to approach some of them in your setting. This may be helpful to you when drawing up an individual education plan. She will ask for your observations of the child's progress in particular areas so that a full picture can be gathered, especially when it is time to review the long-term goals.

Over the years the Portage model has been adopted in countries around the world and adapted into many different settings, other than the home. In response to the many pre-school children with special needs who are attending non-specialist provision, and in recognition of the implications of the Code of Practice for the Identification and Assessment of Special Educational Needs, the National Portage Association produced a training package called *Quality Play*. The aim of the course is to raise awareness that all children, including those with a special need or disability, have rights to effective participation in a wide range of play

experiences. It looks at ways to help practitioners working in group situations, such as playgroups and day nurseries, to develop strategies aimed at analysing and supporting the play of individual children of all abilities. The approach links closely to the five stages in the Code of Practice.

There are continuous developments in the Portage delivery. For example, some services are looking at ways of extending aspects of the Portage approach as a child moves on into mainstream school, involving close liaison between the home visitor, parents and school staff. They have developed the Portage goals to include new skills needed for successful transition into school and they also provide training and ongoing support for teachers during the first two terms that the child is in school.

The National Portage Association works to encourage the principles that lie at the heart of Portage. As well as the Basic Workshop, which is open to people who may not be home visitors but who are interested in knowing how the Portage principles can be adapted into their setting, it is continually developing and monitoring further training modules. Examples include autism, play, early motor and communication skills, as well as aspects such as working with children with profound and multiple learning difficulties and the multicultural dimension of Portage.

Glen Cossins is South West Regional Representative for the National Portage Association, a registered nursery inspector, early years trainer and consultant.

Chapter 3

Unit C15: Contribute to the protection of children from abuse

About this unit

We would strongly advise that all early years practitioners attend a course on child protection which is delivered by a person competent in dealing with child abuse and approved by the local social services department. This is a difficult and sensitive subject and needs to be handled carefully. All local authorities will provide training in child protection. You can get information from your Early Years Development and Childcare Partnership.

The legal definition of child abuse is set down by the Children Act, 1989. Here is a brief summary of the responsibility of the State:

The primary justification for the State to initiate proceedings seeking compulsory powers is actual or likely harm to the child, where harm includes both ill treatment (which includes sexual abuse and non-physical ill treatment such as emotional abuse) and the impairment of health and development, health meaning physical or mental health, intellectual, emotional, social or behavioural development.

Values

The most important values to be aware of in this unit are the welfare of the child, keeping children safe and working in partnership with parents and families. A key aspect of your work with children, and of ensuring their safety and wellbeing, is observation. By now, you will have carried out a number of observations of children, and have learned how much you can find out about a child through observing them. You need to be constantly observing children - not always in a formal way, but as you go about your daily work. If you observe children regularly you will become much more aware of when they are tired or unwell, happy or excited, upset or anxious, from the way their behaviour changes.

If you have any suspicions about an injury to a child, or the child's physical or emotional wellbeing, discuss it with a senior colleague. Your setting should have an agreed procedure for suspected child abuse. Make sure you know what it is. There may be a simple explanation for an injury, so the appropriate member of staff needs to seek an explanation from the child's parents first. If you are not happy with their explanation, you have a responsibility to pass on any concerns you have about a child's safety, either to your superior or, if you are in charge, to

social services. Parents have a right to be informed and consulted throughout any procedures necessary for child protection, but the social worker involved in the case will be responsible for sharing information with the parents. Confidentiality is absolutely essential - only tell the people who need to know. You will need to be able to give accurate details to social services of why you have concerns, or of any disclosure which was made to you, so it's important to write down the details and dates.

Getting started

In this unit you are going to show that you can:

◆ Identify signs and symptons of possible abuse

◆ Respond to a child's disclosure of abuse

◆ Inform other professionals

◆ Promote children's awareness of personal safety and abuse

Make sure you are clear about the correct procedures by reading your setting's policy and talking through them with a senior colleague. Your own assessor may not have sufficient expertise in child protection to carry out your assessment. Some centres use special assessors with this expertise to assess this unit.

Element C15.1 Identify signs and symptoms of possible abuse

Element C15.2 Respond to a child's disclosure of abuse

Element C15.3 Inform other professionals

Key issues

The first three elements, which we will deal with together, take you through the three stages of identifying abuse, responding appropriately to disclosure of abuse and informing the relevant people. Abuse may be physical, emotional, sexual or neglect. You need to be observant of any changes in a child's behaviour, such as becoming withdrawn or showing sexual behaviour inappropriate for their age, or signs that they may be suffering abuse such as physical injuries, bruising, inflammation, bleeding in the genital or anal area, weight loss or failure to grow, or signs of neglect. If you have any concerns that the signs are more serious than the normal day-to-day ups and downs, tiredness or illness of children and the normal accidents that happen, it's your duty to report it, and keep a record. You may be involved in a case conference at a later date, so you need to be clear about what you saw or heard.

> **Remember!**
> It's imperative that you participate in an approved training course on child protection. In the training you will learn how to recognise the signs, how to respond to disclosure and the procedure for reporting incidents.

Which type of evidence?

Some child protection training providers are aware of the requirements of NVQ, and may give you an *assignment* or a list of questions which link in with the knowledge statements. You may have some handouts which include exercises you have carried out or scenarios you have commented on during the training. You can include these as evidence, but you may need to support them by answering *oral or written questions* from your assessor to show that you have the necessary understanding. You will not usually be in a position to be able to supply direct evidence. Even if you were, it would probably not be appropriate to use that evidence in your portfolio. However, your assessor may have *observed* how you have comforted a distressed child in another situation, or how you handled a difficult situation calmly, which will indicate to a certain extent how well you would cope with a child abuse situation. If you do provide any evidence from your own experience, make sure that you don't break confidentiality - be certain that no-one could identify the child from your evidence.

Element C15.4 Promote children's awareness of personal safety and abuse

Key issues

This element is about how you promote children's awareness of safety. It's important that your setting has an agreed policy on how you achieve this, which has also been discussed with parents. Look at the notes on this element, to ensure that you are familiar with all of the requirements. You need to teach children how to make choices and to assert their own rights in an appropriate way, and encourage them to express their fears and feelings without fear of being ridiculed or rejected. This is linked in to children's social and emotional development in C5. Some children will come from a background where this is not the accepted way of behaving, and you need to take this into account when talking to children. It's important that parents understand your policy, and how you are helping children to protect themselves. You may need to make modifications to the policy in order to accommodate parents' wishes.

At a simple level during everyday activities you will be introducing children to different parts of the body, so that they are able to name them. You need to respond simply and honestly when they ask you questions about bodily functions.

You also need to make them aware, within their level of understanding, of the difference between good and bad secrets, and about 'stranger danger'. Stories are a good way of teaching children about personal safety. There are some good quality books on the market to introduce children to 'stranger danger', the difference between good and bad secrets, and so on. One example is *Come and Tell Me* by Helen Hollick (published for the Home Office by Dinosaur). These can be a good starting point for discussion appropriate to the children's age and developmental levels. Letterbox Library specialises in educational books, including books written to deal with specific issues related to children's welfare.

We do need to make children aware, but we don't want to make them frightened of all adults, so be careful in your approach. You need to be prepared for the possibility that such books may encourage a child who has been suffering from abuse to disclose it, or a child may become frightened and upset. You need to have discussed as a staff how this will be handled whilst ensuring that you are fulfilling your responsibility to the other children. It would be best to have two members of staff with the group when discussing these issues, in case there are any children who become upset and need individual attention.

Which type of evidence?

Your assessor will want to *observe* PCs 1, 3, 6 and 7, and one aspect of each range category, if possible. Check to see whether you have any evidence in C5 which will supplement this observation. You can ask your supervisor or colleagues to provide a *witness testimony* and you can write a *reflective account* of ways you have helped children to be more aware of how to protect themselves, make choices and express their fears and feelings. If you have appropriate books you have used with the children, write a *book list*.

The *knowledge evidence* statements for this element are 4, 5, 8, 9, 10, 12, 21. Try to cover these in your reflective account or written assignments. You will find the articles later in this chapter helpful, but we stress again the importance of proper training in this area.

You have a duty to help to protect all children within your care and are well placed to observe and report any causes for concern. But what does this mean in practice? Liz Wilcock and Sheila Collins offer guidance

Child protection: what you need to know

It is a sad fact that child abuse has been happening for many, many years with research showing that it can be found in all socio/economic groups and in all cultures. It is when a child abuse case hits the media headlines that most people become aware of the problems. No-one ever feels comfortable discussing child protection issues and everyone dealing with child abuse will have come to terms with their own feelings and emotions, which can range from concern, shame and fear to anger and revulsion.

One of the underlying principles of the Children Act 1989 is that the welfare of the child is paramount at all times. As childcare workers you have a duty to help to protect all children within your care and are well placed to observe and report any causes for concern. Often it is the fact that a childcare worker has been able to listen to and observe a child that has helped to ensure that a child at risk receives the protection he or she needs and that their family gains help and support.

Remember that you are not alone and that many people share responsibility for the welfare of children. All agencies, whether voluntary or statutory, and all childcarers have to co-operate with the police and social services in their legal responsibilities to protect children.

In every area there should be an area Child Protection Committee whose responsibility it is to establish and operate the local child protection procedures. All childcare facilities should have their own policies and procedures in place,

with which you must be familiar. These will have been based on the handbook/guidance issued by the local Child Protection Committee. Ask to see a copy of the handbook/guidance.

If your facility needs help in compiling a policy of its own contact your local social services under-eights advisers who will be able to refer you to appropriate guidance. If you are a childminder, discuss with your under-eights officer how you should act if you suspect any form of abuse.

In simple terms:

❑ Some types of abuse occur because of the deliberate actions of an adult.

❑ Other types of abuse occur because an adult fails to take action.

There are four main categories of abuse:

❑ Physical

❑ Sexual

❑ Emotional

❑ Neglect

Some children may experience more than one type of abuse at any one time. (More details are provided overleaf.)

In many areas the child protection co-ordinator will run courses on child protection which will give you an in-depth knowledge and understanding of what child abuse is and the local procedures and routes of referral to follow if you have any concerns. We strongly recommend that you ask at your local social services or contact the NSPCC about courses.

Remember that you are not alone and that many people share responsibility for the welfare of children. All agencies, whether voluntary or statutory, and all childcarers have to co-operate with the police and social services in their legal responsibilities to protect children.

The areas of abuse cannot easily be separated from one another. It is likely that if a child is being, for example, physically or sexually abused, the child will also be showing signs of emotional abuse and neglect.

What is child abuse?

Physical abuse

Non-accidental injury - deliberately inflicted. Examples - hitting, shaking, squeezing, burns, bruises, broken limbs, scalds, weals, bites, cuts, gripping. Giving a child inappropriate drugs or alcohol. Attempting to poison, suffocate or drown.
Physical abuse can cause long-term problems. Examples - scars, internal injuries, brain damage, even death.

Neglect

Persistent or severe failure to meet a child's basic needs. Examples - lack of adequate food, inappropriate diet, exposing a child to cold, leaving a child unattended, inappropriate clothing, failing to attend to personal hygiene. Failing to seek medical attention.
Neglect can lead to a child having health problems. The child may be failing to thrive.

Sexual abuse

Taking advantage of a child for the sexual gratification of an adult. Examples - inappropriate fondling, masturbation, oral sex, anal sex, full intercourse, use of foreign objects, exhibitionism, exposing a child to pornography, making pornographic materials, sex rings, ritualistic abuse.
Sexual abuse can have long lasting effects. This will include having difficulties in later life in forming trusting and stable personal

Emotional abuse

Persistent lack of affection and physical interaction with a child. Examples - continuously failing to show love and affection, persistent rejection, criticism, belittling, bullying, frightening, harassment, taunting, threatening, ridiculing, 'scapegoating', ignoring.
Emotional abuse can cause a child to become nervous, withdrawn, lacking in confidence and self-esteem.

Would you know what to do if you suspected that a child in your care showed signs of abuse? This article takes a general overview of how to handle a situation - and how to protect yourself. Remember that you must find out the procedure for your own area/facility

Dealing with child abuse: **what to do**

❑ If you are uneasy about anything you see or hear, discuss it with your colleagues/line manager/local authority adviser. Often your own instincts or reactions - 'gut feelings' - are right. Children in your care may not have reached the stage where they can vocalise, or may not have the ability to express themselves if they have a special need.

❑ If a child approaches you and discloses information, you must listen to and believe the child. Reassure the child that it was right to tell you and that you will try and help. **Never promise to keep the allegation/disclosure a secret.**

❑ It is important to get the child to talk to you but not to lead the child or suggest what might be happening. Listen but do not probe as this could prejudice later action. Do not state an opinion or make a judgement.

❑ Do not assume that because a child says that something used to happen that it is not still going on.

❑ Ensure that the child knows that you will need to tell someone else, that you will talk to your manager/local authority adviser or social services duty worker.

❑ Share your concerns/information with the designated person and together decide what action to take. Remember that the welfare of the child is paramount. Is the child likely to be at risk at this time?

❑ Keep a written record of events but make sure that all information recorded is factual not supposition or opinion. Try to write down exactly what the child has said including dates and times. Also record details of their appearance and behaviour and if you know the child well, any changes

that have occurred. Many areas/facilities have a proforma which should be used. Remember that this could be used as evidence if a child protection case conference is convened. If through your observations you have cause for concern, although the child has not told you anything or is not yet able to talk, record your concerns in the same way.

What next?

The designated person in your facility (or you if you are a childminder) should share the concerns with the duty social worker at your local social services. Ensure that this number is readily available. A decision will be made as to whether a referral should be made. The information supplied by you may be crucial in building up knowledge about the child or may be the last piece of evidence needed to take action.

If it is decided not to take action at this time, you may be asked to monitor the child and record any further concerns/disclosures. If it is decided that action should be taken by social services they will decide what has to follow - not you or your manager. You should always be informed that a response has been made but information about action taken will remain confidential with the child protection agencies.

Such action will include interviewing the child and contacting the parents. Possibly the child may have to have a medical examination. Other family members may have to be interviewed and enquiries made of other agencies such as schools, health visitors, doctors, youth club leaders. Arrangements may have to be made when a

child's safety is seriously at risk but usually a family will be supported as a whole unit.

A child protection conference may have to be arranged and any evidence you/your facility has gathered will be needed. You may not be asked to attend.

Protecting yourself

Consider a real situation that you may find yourself in:
You become aware that a little girl in your care has soiled herself. It is nearly time for all the children to be collected and it is busy. All other adults are involved with the children. You take the child to the toilet and clean her, talking to her all the time to reassure her. You notice that one of the cheeks of her bottom is rather red. You help her into fresh pants and trousers. She is happy now and you tap her on the bottom in a friendly manner saying 'Off you go!', and she goes to join the others. You are then asked to clear up in another room so you do not see her being collected by her mum.

The next day, you arrive for work and are

summoned to the manager's office. You are told that the child's father has been in to make a complaint about you smacking his daughter on the bottom and that he has reported this to social services.

What would your personal reaction to this be?

It is likely that you will be upset at the allegation and worried about the consequences.

What would you need to know?

You will need to establish your position with the manager. What will happen next? Am I to be sacked from my job? Will anyone listen to me? The manager is likely to tell you that someone from social services will be coming to speak to you about the incident. This will be your opportunity to explain the situation as it happened.

What will you tell social services?

The facts. Of course, you will be upset and may not be able to state the facts in a clear way. It may be useful to jot down the events as you recall them, as this will help when you speak to the person from social services. A colleague may be present with you for support.

How can you protect yourself from such a situation arising?

It is easy to say - 'Never be left unattended with a child'. In reality, there will be occasions when a member of staff is in that situation. There are ways in which you can protect yourself. Firstly, always tell another member of staff where you are going and for what reason. If possible, stay in sight of other people (you don't need to be in full view), and within earshot also. If you have changed a child's clothing, make sure that another member of staff is aware of the situation. Make sure that you inform the parent of the reason for the change of clothing. If you are not available to speak to the parent, ensure that other members of staff are aware of the need to inform the parent when the child is collected.

In this way, you will be able to tell the person from social services that:

1. You did change the child's clothing,

possibly seen but definitely heard by another member of staff.

2. Other staff were aware that this was what you were going to do.

3. The child was dealt with appropriately. The playful tap on the bottom was nothing more than that.

4. Other members of staff were able to inform the parents of the child's change of clothing in your absence.

> This article highlights general issues to do with child protection. Always refer to your own LEA guidance for details about specific procedures.

The way forward for you

Remember:

The more we hear about child abuse, especially sexual, people caring for children worry about touching/cuddling and playing with them. Young children need close and warm relationships with both parents and others who care for them on a regular basis. Cuddles and affections are all normal, good childcare practice. The important thing is not to force any attention on a child which they dislike and respond sensitively to any distress.

Remember:

That there may be other reasons why a child may not be his or her usual self. It is important to remember that a child is not being abused every time he or she cries or gets upset. You need to get the full picture.

Remember:

To find out what appropriate procedures you should take in your facility. A good general rule is to

Assess the situation

Discuss with your line manager/adviser or duty officer

Decide what should be done.

Liz Wilcock and
Sheila Collins

Reference books

The ABC of Child Abuse edited by Roy Meadow (B M J Publishing Group) 2nd edition pub 1993 75pp

Child Protection: Everybody's Business by M Macleod (Community Care/Childline) pub 1997 36-page report

Useful addresses

National Society for Prevention of Cruelty to Children (NSPCC)
42 Curtain Road
London EC2A 3NH
Tel: 0207 825 2500

Childline: 0800 1111
Childline is the free, national 24-hour helpline for children in trouble or danger. Trained volunteer counsellors comfort, advise and protect children and young people. Professionals wanting to see their range of publications and posters should send for a catalogue to: Childline, Freepost 1111, London NW OBR.

Barnardo's have a role to play in child protection, offering support through projects at home, at school and in the community. For more information, contact them at Tanner's Lane, Barkingside, Ilford, Essex IG6 1QG. Tel: 0181 550 8822. They also publish books which may be of interest, such as *What Works in Child Protection?* and *What Works in the Early Years?* Publication enquiries should be addressed to: Barnardo's Child Care Publications, Barnardo's Trading Estate, Paycocke Road, Basildon, Essex SS14 3DR. Tel: 01268 520224 ext 267.

National Children's Bureau publish various titles on child protection, though they tend to be for social workers. However, some may be relevant for staff development in child care settings.
For example: *Developing Good Child Protection Practice* by Sara Noakes and Barbara Hearn Price £17.50

ISBN 1 900990 28 8.
Write to their Library and Information Service for a publications catalogue at 8 Wakley Street, London EC1V 7QE. Tel: 0207 843 6000.

Chapter 4

Unit M7: Plan, implement and evaluate learning activities and experiences

About this unit

This unit is best done towards the end of your qualification because it gives you the opportunity to pull together all the activities you have done for other units such as C10, C11, C3 and C5, which deal with the promotion of children's sensory and intellectual, language and communication, physical and social and emotional development. You will have already planned, carried out and evaluated individual activities for these areas of development, and you may have included work plans which you have been involved in preparing for your setting. In this unit you will show how you can fit them all into the overall process of planning the curriculum for young children, and how you cater for individual children within your overall plan. The unit is also closely linked to C16 – 'Observe and assess the development and behaviour of children' - because in order to plan effectively for individual children's needs, you must observe them first. If you have observed individual children and made recommendations for supporting their learning or development, you will be able to use that evidence, too.

Values

If you have a look at the values statements for this unit you will see that you need to be aware of most of them when planning your curriculum. You must show that you are taking account of the gender, racial origins, religious, cultural and family background, disabilities and individual needs of the children in your care, and that you are helping them to appreciate the cultural diversity of the world they live in. This doesn't mean simply doing an occasional topic on a religious festival, but ensuring that in everything you do, you help children to value differences and treat each other with respect.

You need to have a good knowledge of the current thinking and practices on teaching and learning, especially the Early Learning Goals at the Foundation Stage for children aged three to the end of their Reception year and the National Curriculum at Key Stage 1, for children from Year 1 (age 5 plus) to the end of Year 2. Your setting will probably have at least some of this documentation. If not, your local library will have copies. You will find a summary of both in this chapter. You will find the *Curriculum Guidance for the Foundation Stage*, published in May 2000 to support the Early Learning Goals,

helpful in planning a curriculum appropriate to young children. If you are working in an infant school, you will also need to be aware of the national literacy and numeracy strategies.

This unit will help you to show how you have become a reflective practitioner, able to think about why you are including particular activities and experiences, what benefit the children will gain from them, how you are able to adapt your plans to take account of individual children's needs and how you are constantly evaluating and improving your practice.

There is a wealth of information in the articles in this chapter on different approaches to the early years curriculum, such as High/Scope and the Montessori method, and the value of different areas of curriculum, such as 'The value of music'. We suggest that you read through these articles before you start your evidence. If you already carry out long-term planning for your setting, use the information to check that you are covering everything you need to in the most appropriate way. If you are not used to planning, use them to help you decide what to include.

Step Forward Publishing produces a whole series of planning books called *Planning for Learning* which cover a range of topics, such as 'All About Me' and 'Clothes', and will help you to plan for all aspects of the Early Learning Goals. These will be helpful when writing your medium-term plans based on topics.

Getting started

In this unit you will need to show that you can:

◆ Plan a curriculum to facilitate children's learning and development

◆ Develop individual learning programmes for children

◆ Implement planned learning activities and experiences

◆ Evaluate planned learning activities and experiences

Have a look at the elements and see what you feel confident about, where there are things you may find difficult to achieve, or where you have insufficient knowledge. If you are a childminder you will be able to show how you implement particular activities to cover different areas of learning, and how you cater for the individual needs of the children of different ages over a period of time, within a long-term plan. However, it may be more difficult for you to show how you implement a more formal curriculum plan. If you belong to a childminders' network, where childminders and their children meet on a regular basis, you may find it useful to put together a long-term plan for those sessions as part of your evidence.

If you are in a school, the class teacher will probably do all the planning. She may involve you in the planning or you may not be involved at all. In this case, you may need to plan a curriculum knowing that you will be unable to carry it out. Discuss with your class teacher whether you could plan and carry out a topic within the overall curriculum plan. If this is not possible, you will need to show how the activities you do with the children fit in with the teacher's plan, and evaluate how effective they were in achieving their aims.

Don't forget!
Check your cross referencing sheet for evidence in other units - you may have a lot of evidence of short-term planning, implementation and evaluation but no medium- or long-term plans. You will also have some child observations which you can cross reference.

Element M7.1 Plan a curriculum to facilitate children's learning and development

Key issues
The notes at the beginning of this chapter have already pinpointed the key issues, so check back on those and read the recommended documentation in your candidate handbook before starting your planning. You need to take account of the information you have gathered about the children, through observation and assessment, and through consulting with parents, colleagues and other professionals. You have valuable resources in your local community, such as those listed in the notes for this element, so do include some opportunities for using these. You need to show that you have short-, medium- and long-term plans.

Remember
how important play is when you are planning for children's learning.

Which evidence?
Plan how you will gather your evidence. Your assessor will not need to observe any part of this element, because it is all about the planning stage. If you have been involved in planning the curriculum for your setting, include some examples of your *curriculum plans*. Write a statement to say how you were involved in the planning - did you attend planning meetings, were you responsible for a particular area of learning? You need to show how you used information about the children to ensure that the curriculum is appropriate. Did you carry out any *child observations*? Do you have *developmental records* for each child? Have you consulted parents? Did you have a meeting with colleagues?

Have a look through the evidence from the other units and include examples of *activity plans*. They will probably only be short-term plans, although you may have included medium-term which covered, perhaps, a week's topic on food or a festival such as Diwali or May Day. If you have not done any medium- or long-term planning, arrange with your supervisor or colleagues to plan the next month or term, or even longer if possible. If not, do a plan of what you would do if you were in charge. Use the documents we recommended at the beginning of the chapter as a guide, and make sure you cover all the different areas of learning. Don't forget to include plenty of flexibility so that there is time for children to choose free activities. Check that your evidence has covered all the PCs and range. A *reflective account* of how you organised your planning will help you to do this.

One idea for a medium-term plan is to use a topic as a starting point. Brainstorm all the activities and experiences you could include to cover the different areas of learning, based on the Early Learning Goals and then expand on the ones you decide to include, and how they will develop the children's learning. You don't need to give as much detail for each activity as you provide in your activity plans, but you need enough to show what the activities will involve. For your long-term plan you should use the Early Learning Goals as a starting point, or the National Curriculum if you are working with children over five years old. For each curriculum area, identify which activities and experiences you will provide for the children over a period of, say, a term, showing how you will promote progression in their learning, and allow for the different stages of development of the children.

Try to reflect work with children of different ages in your plans, to show that you are aware of how to plan for different stages of development

The *knowledge evidence* statements for this element are 1, 2, 3, 4, 6, 7, 8, 9, 10, 11, 12, 15, 17, 21, 22, 29, 30. Many of these should be evident in your plans and other evidence, but if there are gaps, write a short assignment to cover them. For points 6 and 7, you need to show your knowledge of the curriculum guidelines currently in use, which we have already identified earlier in the chapter. Note that some of the points cover the whole unit, so make sure you cover the other aspects of the unit at the same time. You will find many useful articles at the end of this chapter.

Element M7.2 Develop individual learning programmes for children

Key issues

Within your curriculum planning, you also need to plan for individual children's needs, because each child will have different skills, interests and abilities. You need to be aware in this element of the needs of children from different cultural backgrounds, and children with disabilities or additional needs (including very able children), when planning individual programmes. Observation and assessment is the key to planning for individual needs. You will find the chapter on C16, 'Observe and assess the development and behaviour of children', in Book 1, especially helpful for this element. There is a section in that chapter on developing an individual education plan which is particularly focused on a child with special educational needs but has a strategy which could equally well be used for any child.

If you don't already know, find out from your supervisor or discuss with colleagues what your setting's strategy is for assessing different aspects of the children's development, and for using assessments to plan for individual children. It's important that you consult parents about their children's abilities and interests, and this may be built into your setting's policies and procedures. For instance, you may keep a daily diary which staff and parents contribute to, or you may have more informal conversations as parents drop off and collect their children

All schools must have a system of baseline assessment to assess children's abilities before they start work on the National Curriculum Key Stage 1. Many early years settings will have adopted an assessment system, too. Your setting will probably keep developmental or assessment records on each child, and this will form the basis for identifying individual needs. You need to build time into each day to focus on particular children - you won't be able to focus on every child every day but should aim to cover every child over a period.

If you operate a key worker system you will find it easier to manage, because you will be responsible for a smaller group of children. You will be able to observe each one closely, and plan for their individual needs by adapting activities if necessary or giving them extra support in areas where you know they are less confident, or you can follow a particular interest of an individual child. For example, you know how important it is to encourage children to have an interest in books, because it gives them a good foundation for learning to read. If you find that a particular child never goes into the book corner but loves playing with cars and lorries, make sure that there are books on vehicles set out near the play area, which will spark an interest for this child.

Which type of evidence?

Your assessor does not have to observe this element because, again, it is centred on planning. Cross reference **child observations** you have already carried out to show how you have planned to help individual children to develop further skills or deal with difficulties you have observed. If you have evaluated your observations well, you should have several examples of this. If they don't give enough detail, expand on them by writing an **individual plan**, and check that you cover the PCs for the element through your evidence. Cross reference from C16 any examples of your setting's **assessment or developmental records** you have helped to produce and any **individual learning plans** you have done. Write a **reflective account** of times when you have planned an activity or experience to help a particular child, or spontaneously followed a child's interest in a way that led to further learning. You often do this without thinking when you are playing with a child.

Don't forget!
Refer to the knowledge evidence statements and include what you need to when you write your other evidence, to save having to repeat things.

The **knowledge evidence** statements for this element are 1, 3, 4, 9, 11, 12, 13, 14, 15, 17, 20, 22, 30. You should have covered much of this in your evidence for other elements.

Element M7.3 Implement planned learning activities and experiences

Key issues

This element is about how effectively you carry out activities and experiences with the children, making sure that you are aware of health and safety issues in the materials and equipment you choose. Think about the level of supervision necessary in order to enable children to make choices and work as independently as they are able, whilst at the same time giving appropriate support to children who need it. You also need to show that although you are working consistently within the curriculum plans of the setting, you are flexible enough to take advantage of spontaneous learning opportunities as they occur.

We cannot stress too much here the importance of giving young children the freedom to play when you are planning the curriculum. If you have read the guidelines on the Early Learning Goals you will have realised how much emphasis has been put on play. Young children learn by having the opportunity to try things out for themselves, to practise skills, to explore, to experiment, to make mistakes in a non-threatening situation. It's not appropriate for young children to be sitting filling in worksheets, or watching adult-led activities for long periods. Adult-led activities should include full hands-on involvement of the children. If you have to do a large part of an activity yourself, the activity is not appropriate. If children are having to wait long for a turn, the group is probably too big. It's better to repeat activities with small groups, and the younger the child the more important this becomes.

There is no difference between work and play for a young child. The important thing is that you structure children's activities and experiences so that they make progress in their learning, you evaluate their learning through frequent observation, and you support their learning through your appropriate involvement and interaction.

You may find the model below useful when you're thinking about how to balance the different aspects of planning, implementing and evaluating your curriculum. It shows how closely interlinked planning, implementation, observation and evaluation are, and how you need to take account of individual needs within your planning.

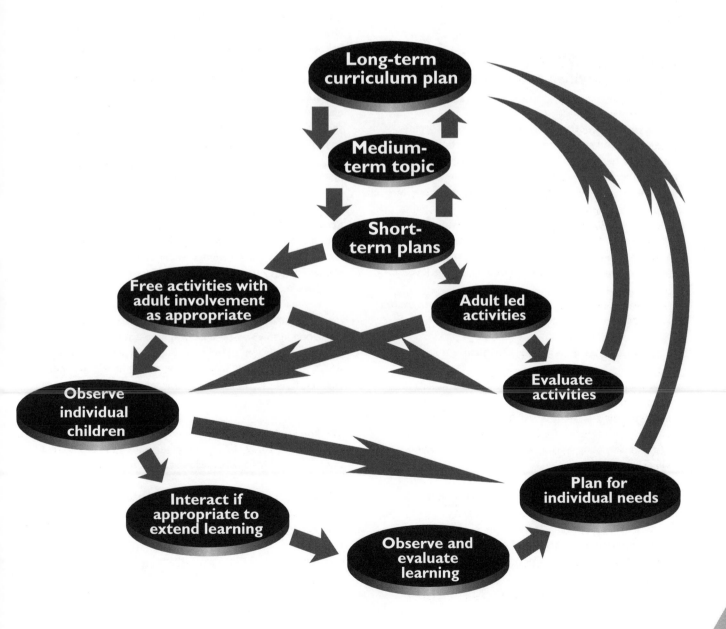

Which type of evidence?

Your assessor will need to **observe** all of this element apart from the last PC which is about your responses to unplanned learning opportunities. She may not have been present when an opportunity arose. You will probably be able to **cross reference** the whole of this element to activities your assessor has already observed for C10, C11, C3 and C5. You should not need to find any additional evidence. If there are gaps, write a **reflective account** to cover these and any areas of knowledge you need to.

The **knowledge evidence** statements for this element are 5, 6, 7, 8, 15, 16, 17, 21, 22, 23, 24, 25, 26, 30. You should have already covered all but numbers 5, 16, 23, 24, 25, 26 in M7.1. Check whether you have covered this evidence in your planning and evaluations of the activities you carried out in the other units.

Element M7.4 Evaluate planned learning activities and experiences

Key issues

You need to be constantly evaluating children's learning experiences and seeking to improve the practice in your setting. You can do this by observing the children taking part in the activities you have planned and carried out and evaluating whether they met your objectives. You also need to reflect on your own involvement, and how well you contributed to the children's learning through your interaction with them. As a staff, you need to discuss the whole curriculum you offer to children and how appropriate the activities and experiences are. Ask yourself these questions (with colleagues if you can):

Have we got the right balance of free play and structured activities?

How much choice do we allow children?

Do we involve them in planning where appropriate?

Are there any activities which are not achieving anything?

Are we reflecting equal opportunities and cultural diversity in the curriculum?

Do our plans cover all the areas of learning and development?

Is my involvement in activities helping the children's learning?

Do my questions encourage children to extend their thinking and language?

Do I encourage children to stick at an activity and give them help where necessary to enable them to succeed?

Are we aware enough of individual children's needs?

Are we observing and assessing children on a regular basis?

Are we providing adequate support for children with additional needs?

Are we keeping the parents well informed, and involving them in planning where possible?

Which type of evidence?

Your assessor does not need to observe this element but she will want to see evidence of your **evaluations of activities and overall planning**. You will have already cross referenced some of the plans you have evaluated for other elements in this unit, so see what is appropriate as evidence for this element. Most of the evaluations you have done will be for short-term plans, so evaluate the plans you included in M7.1 and M7.2, using the questions above. You may find it useful to refer to the Early Learning Goals and the guidelines (or the National Curriculum) when evaluating your curriculum plans.

When you have carried out your evaluation, write a **reflective account** including the conclusions you have drawn and how you aim to modify your planning and implementation in the future. Look at the knowledge evidence requirements for the element and try to reflect on them while you are writing your reflective account.

It will not be so easy for some of you to carry out a full evaluation in this way, because you have not been able to implement your long-term plans, but there are many questions which you can answer about the work you have done with the children, how they fit into an overall curriculum plan and your own effectiveness.

The **knowledge evidence** statements for this element are 2, 6, 7, 8, 18, 19, 20, 27, 28, 30. The evaluations you have carried out will probably have covered most of these points.

The following pages have some helpful reading on the value of play and different activities, how to plan and some examples of different approaches to curriculum planning and delivery.

Gay Wilkinson explains the content and requirements of the Foundation Stage

The Early Learning Goals

The Government announced its intention of revising the Desirable Learning Outcomes within the paper *Excellence in Schools*. Following consultation by the Qualifications and Curriculum Authority (QCA), the Government published the *Early Learning Goals* in October 1999. These replaced the age-related Desirable Learning Outcomes (DLOs) from September 2000. From this date all settings registered with their local Early Years Development and Childcare Partnership (EYDCP) to receive nursery grant funding and schools with nursery and Reception provision have been inspected according to the Early Learning Goals (ELGs).

When publishing the *Early Learning Goals* the Government also announced its intention of issuing more detailed curriculum planning guidance to support practitioners in implementing the new goals. This guidance, called *Curriculum Guidance for the Foundation Stage*, was published in May 2000 and circulated to all providers.

Foundation Stage

The Early Learning Goals cover six areas of learning and reflect the Government's intention not only to continue to expand free nursery provision for all four-year-olds but also for all three-year-olds. Accordingly the Government has now established a Foundation Stage that precedes Key Stage 1 of the National Curriculum. This stage begins when children reach the age of three and finishes at the end of the year during which children become five. This final year of the Foundation Stage is commonly referred to as the Reception year since most children are admitted into the Reception class of a primary school at some point during this year depending upon the

admission patterns adopted by individual schools. The goals set out what is expected for most children by the end of this Foundation Stage and lead into the National Curriculum that all children are required to follow from Year 1 of their statutory schooling. The Early Learning Goals, within the context of the Foundation Stage, are therefore an important measure in promoting curriculum continuity between the different settings that children may attend in the early years as well as with statutory schooling. They also provide a sound basis for all children's future learning within and beyond school. The six areas of learning are as follows:

- Personal, Social and Emotional Development

- Communication, Language and Literacy

- Mathematical Development

- Knowledge and Understanding of the World

- Physical Development

- Creative Development.

Practitioners are reminded that, although the areas of learning are described separately, this does not mean that young children's learning is divided up into areas. Rich, stimulating and appropriate experiences may provide children with opportunities to develop skills, thinking and competencies across several areas of learning. The *Early Learning Goals* booklet emphasises that neither the areas of learning nor the goals are a curriculum by themselves but, together, they provide a framework for long-term planning throughout the Foundation Stage.

Both the *Early Learning Goals* booklet and its related curriculum guidance clearly define those factors which should ensure that all early years educational provision is of high quality by setting out a statement of principles that take account of both research about teaching and learning in the early years and what practitioners during the consultation said were important issues when providing for young children.

The principles underpinning high-quality provision

- The experiences and activities provided should build on what children know and can already do. They should enable children to feel that they are learners and therefore to want to go on learning. This will protect them from experiencing early failure.

- No child should be excluded or disadvantaged because of race, culture, religion, home language, family background, special educational needs, disability, gender or ability.

- The curriculum should be carefully structured, planned and organised. The structure should contain three strands: provision for the different starting points of children (building on what they already know and can do), experiences that match the different levels of need and 'planned and purposeful' activities that give real opportunities for teaching and learning both indoors and outside.

- Children learn both through play and in other ways and the planned curriculum should take account of all these processes. Children do not make a distinction between play and work and neither should practitioners when talking about or describing activities with the children.

- Opportunities for children to be involved in activities planned by adults and those they have planned and initiated for themselves.

- Opportunities for children to work for regular sustained periods of time without constant interruption and time to complete both adult-set and self-initiated activities.

- Opportunities for children to work in large and small groups.

- Adults who spend time with the children listening to their ideas, talking to them and taking a real interest in what they are trying to achieve - 'practitioners must be able to observe and respond appropriately to children, informed by a knowledge of how children learn and develop'. Effective education needs practitioners who understand that children develop rapidly.

- Adults who understand that teaching and learning is a partnership between themselves, the children and their parents. In order to ensure that all children feel secure and valued, practitioners must establish and maintain positive relationships with parents - 'children, parents and practitioners must work together in an atmosphere of mutual respect'.

Putting the principles into practice

The guidance states that these important characteristics of the curriculum form the basis from which all the elements contained in the guidance document have been developed. To help practitioners understand these principles fully there is a detailed section on putting the principles into practice. The text is presented in a helpful format with exemplification. The examples of how these principles have been put into practice in a range of different settings including a reception class, playgroup, pre-school and a childminder are placed in coloured boxes alongside the relevant good features points.

Both the *Early Learning Goals* booklet and the guidance emphasise the importance of responding positively to diversity. Practitioners are reminded of the different experiences, knowledge, skills and interests that each child brings to an early childhood setting, whether at three, four or five, all of which will affect both their ability to learn and how they learn. Some will have experienced living in a richly cosmopolitan society whilst others will have lived in a community that only reflects their own culture, religion and language. Some children may have personal experience of living with someone with a physical or learning disability and others may be coming to terms with a particular need of their own. There may be some children who have not experienced these sorts of differences until joining an early years setting for the first time. Some children will already have a rich understanding of a wide range of stories whilst others may have little experience of books. There may be some children who are fluent talkers in the language they hear spoken at home but who are in the very early stages of learning to speak English. Practitioners are reminded of their need to be aware of current legislation relating to diversity and that in developing and implementing their curriculum they should plan to meet the needs of all children within their care so that each child can make the best possible progress.

Stepping stones

To provide further help to practitioners in planning the guidance identifies 'stepping stones'. These are a series of learning goals in the Foundation Stage that lead towards achievement of the Early Learning Goals. They embody the key principles set out in both the *ELGs* booklet and the guidance itself. Each area of learning has its own set of stepping stones and these vary in number between and within areas of learning. In some cases several ELGs within an area of learning are grouped or clustered together and share a set of stepping stones, sometimes one goal stands alone with its own set of stepping stones. The stepping stones and their accompanying features are presented in tabular form for easy reading. They offer a detailed description of each area of learning and are designed to act as significant signposts of children's progress. Their purpose is to help practitioners understand what learning, which will lead towards achievement of the Early Learning Goals, actually looks like for young children throughout the Foundation Stage. They show the knowledge, skills, understanding and the attitudes that children need to learn and develop during this stage in order to achieve the Early Learning Goals and

therefore act as a basis when practitioners are planning the curriculum for the children in their setting. They are not age-related. However, to help practitioners use them they are presented in a hierarchical order wherever possible, with those that generally describe three-year-olds placed in a yellow band, those that generally describe four-year-olds in a blue band, those that generally describe five-year-olds in a green band, with the Early Learning Goals themselves in a grey band.

It is important when using the stepping stones to remember that all children are uniquely different - the principle of diversity. The quality of the experiences they have had before the Foundation Stage varies enormously. Children's progress in achieving the various stepping stones will reflect this

diversity. They may achieve some of the later stepping stones in one area of learning whilst still developing confidence in some of the earlier ones. They may achieve some stepping stones very quickly whilst others take much longer. By the end of the Foundation Stage some children will still be

Communication, Language and Literacy

The 20 goals for this area are in line with the *National Literacy Strategy: Framework for Teaching* objectives for the Reception year. The numbers of goals reflect the importance of language and literacy to children's learning across the whole Foundation curriculum. They are grouped together under six headings as follows:

Early Learning Goals for language for communication
- Interact with others, negotiating plans and activities and taking turns in conversation
- Enjoy listening to and using spoken and written language, and readily turn to it in their play and learning
- Sustain attentive listening, responding to what they have heard by relevant comments, questions and actions
- Listen with enjoyment, and respond to stories, songs and other music, rhymes and poems and make up their own stories, songs, rhymes and poems
- Extend their vocabulary, exploring the meanings and sounds of new words
- Speak clearly and audibly with confidence and control and show awareness of the listener, for example by their use of conventions such as greetings, 'please' and 'thank you'

Early Learning Goals for language and thinking
- Use language to imagine and recreate roles and experiences
- Use talk to organise, sequence and clarify thinking, ideas, feelings and events

Early Learning Goals for linking sounds and letters
- Hear and say initial and final sounds in words, and short vowel sounds within words

- Link sounds to letters, naming and sounding the letters of the alphabet
- Use their phonic knowledge to write simple regular words and make phonetically plausible attempts at more complex words

Early Learning Goals for reading
- Explore and experiment with sounds, words and texts
- Retell narratives in the correct sequence, drawing on language patterns of stories
- Read a range of familiar and common words and simple sentences independently
- Know that print carries meaning and, in English, is read from left to right and top to bottom
- Show an understanding of the elements of stories, such as main character, sequence of events, and openings, and how information can be found in non-fiction texts to answer questions about where, who, why and how

Early Learning Goals for writing
- Use their phonic knowledge to write simple regular words and make phonetically plausible attempts at more complex words
- Attempt writing for different purposes, using features of different forms such as lists, stories and instructions
- Write their own names and other things such as labels and captions and begin to form simple sentences, sometimes using punctuation

Early Learning Goals for handwriting
- Use a pencil and hold it effectively to form recognisable letters, most of which are correctly formed

Personal, Social and Emotional Development

The 14 goals for this area underpin the whole Foundation Stage curriculum. They are divided into six categories. Practitioners will find this categorisation useful both when planning the curriculum and when making assessments of children's progress. The goals are as follows:

Early Learning Goals for dispositions and attitudes
- Continue to be interested, excited and motivated to learn
- Be confident to try new activities, initiate ideas and speak in a familiar group
- Maintain attention, concentrate and sit quietly when appropriate

Early Learning Goals for self-confidence and self-esteem
- Respond to significant experiences, showing a range of feelings when appropriate
- Have a developing awareness of their own needs, views and feelings and be sensitive to the needs, views and feelings of others
- Have a developing respect for their own cultures and beliefs and those of other people

Early Learning Goals for making relationships
- Form good relationships with adults and peers
- Work as part of a group or class, taking turns and sharing fairly, understanding that there need to be agreed values and codes of behaviour for groups of people, including adults and children, to work together harmoniously

Early Learning Goals for behaviour and self-control
- Understand what is right, what is wrong and why
- Consider the consequences of their words and actions for themselves and others

Early Learning Goals for self-care
- Dress and undress independently and manage their own personal hygiene
- Select and use activities and resources independently

Early Learning Goals for sense of community
- Understand that people have different needs, views, cultures and beliefs that need to be treated with respect
- Understand that they can expect others to treat their needs, views, cultures and beliefs with respect

working towards some or all of the Early Learning Goals, some may have achieved them, whilst others may have exceeded them. If all children are to make the best possible progress they are capable of there is no substitute for practitioners knowing where children are in their learning and development so that the next step that is planned is appropriately challenging but achievable. This can only be achieved through working closely with parents and through regular and careful observation and assessment. To assist practitioners in assessing progress the stepping stones are accompanied by examples of children in action so that practitioners will have an understanding of what learning might look like for each stepping stone. These examples will help practitioners to identify when either individuals or groups of children in their setting have achieved the knowledge, skills, understanding and attitudes inherent in each stepping stone.

Gay Wilkinson

Physical Development

The eight goals for this area are grouped together under five headings:

Early Learning Goals for movement
- Move with confidence, imagination and in safety

- Move with control and coordination

- Travel around, under, over and through balancing and climbing equipment

Early Learning Goals for sense of space
- Show awareness of space, of themselves and of others

Early Learning Goals for health and bodily awareness
- Recognise the importance of keeping healthy and those things which contribute to this

- Recognise the changes that happen to their bodies when they are active

Early Learning Goals for using equipment
- Use a range of small and large equipment

Early Learning Goals for using tools and materials
- Handle tools, objects, construction and malleable materials safely and with increasing control

Mathematical Development

The 13 goals for this area are in line with the *National Numeracy Strategy: Framework for Teaching* objectives for the Reception year. They are divided into three categories:

Early Learning Goals for numbers as labels and for counting
- Say and use number names in order in familiar contexts

- Count reliably up to ten everyday objects

- Recognise numerals one to nine

- Use developing mathematical ideas and methods to solve practical problems

Early Learning goals for calculating
- In practical activities and discussion begin to use the vocabulary involved in adding and subtracting

- Use language such as 'more' or 'less' to compare two numbers

- Begin to relate addition to combining two groups of objects and subtraction to 'taking away'

Early Learning Goals for shape, space and measures
- Use language such as 'greater', 'smaller', 'heavier' or 'lighter' to compare quantities

- Talk about, recognise and recreate simple patterns

- Use language such as 'circle' or 'bigger' to describe the shape and size of solids and flat shapes

- Use everyday words to describe position

- Use developing mathematical ideas and methods to solve practical problems

Creative Development

The five goals for this area cover the aspects of imagination and personal expression. The importance of creativity to successful learning is emphasised in the aims, as is the opportunity that being creative allows children to make links between one area of learning and another.

Early Learning Goals for exploring media and materials
- Explore colour, texture, shape, form and space in two or three dimensions

Early Learning Goals for music
- Recognise and explore how sounds can be changed, sing simple songs from memory, recognise repeated sounds and sound patterns and match movements to music

Early Learning Goals for imagination
- Use their imagination in art and design, music, dance, imaginative and role play and stories

Early Learning Goals for responding to experiences, and expressing and communicating ideas
- Respond in a variety of ways to what they see,   hear, smell, touch and feel

- Express and communicate their ideas, thoughts and feelings by using a widening range of materials, suitable tools, imaginative   and role play, movement, designing and making, and a variety of songs and musical instruments

Knowledge and Understanding of the World

The 11 goals for this area are grouped together in six categories:

Early Learning Goals for exploration and investigation
- Investigate objects and materials by using all their senses as appropriate

- Find out about, and identify, some features of living things, objects and events they observe

- Look closely at similarities, differences, patterns and change

- Ask questions about why things happen and how things work

Early Learning goals for designing and making skills
- Build and construct with a wide range of objects, selecting appropriate resources and adapting their work where necessary

- Select the tools and techniques they need to shape, assemble and join materials they are using

Early Learning Goals for information and communication technology
- Find out about and identify the uses of everyday technology and use information and communication technology and programmable toys to support their learning

Early Learning Goals for a sense of time
- Find out about past and present events in their own lives and in those of their families and other people they know

Early Learning Goals for a sense of place
- Observe, find out about and identify features in the place they live and the natural world

- Find out about their environment and talk about those features they like and dislike

It is helpful for professionals working with children in the Foundation Stage to know something about the next stage in their children's education. Gail Wilkinson offers some background information

An overview of the
National Curriculum

The government controlled National Curriculum was introduced, and became law, in 1988 as part of the Education Reform Act. Its intention is to give parents, teachers, pupils, employers and the wider community a clear understanding of what young people will learn at school and provide a framework within which all these partners can support them. Since its introduction changes have continually been made as people have come to a better understanding of, and agreement about, what should be taught. Most recently the curriculum was revised and updated in the year 2000 and all state schools in England were required to teach this from September 2000.

The National Curriculum is the set of guidelines that says what every pupil in school should be taught. It sets out the syllabus and content that every child should study until he or she leaves school. The curriculum has clear aims:

❏ To provide opportunities for all pupils to learn and achieve

❏ To promote pupils' spiritual, moral, social and cultural development and prepare all pupils for the opportunities, responsibilities and experiences of life

Pupils in state schools (schools that are publicly funded and therefore do not charge fees) are legally required to follow the National Curriculum. This also applies to special schools that are within the state sector.

The National Curriculum is organised into four stages of education known as Key Stages:

Key Stage 1 – pupils aged 5-7 - Year groups 1-2

Key Stage 2 – pupils aged 7-11 – Year groups 3-6

Key Stage 3 – pupils aged 11-14 - Year groups 7-9

Key Stage 4 – pupils aged 14-16 – Year groups 10-11

In 1999 a new stage was introduced for children aged between three and the end of the year in which they become five, commonly referred to as the Reception year since most children are in school at this age. From September 2000 the term Foundation Stage has been used to describe this phase of education.

The Foundation Stage curriculum is made up of six areas of learning. These six areas are designed to provide a foundation for and lead into the National Curriculum at Key Stage 1:

Personal, Social and Emotional Development
Communication, Language and Literacy
Mathematical Development
Knowledge and Understanding of the World
Physical Development
Creative Development

For each of these areas there are a number of Early Learning Goals that set out what most children are expected to achieve by the end of the Foundation Stage. Adults working with Foundation Stage children are required to assess children's achievement against these goals at the end of the stage. The Early Learning Goals are broadly equivalent to Level 1 of the National Curriculum. The achievement of children beyond the Early Learning Goals can be described using the level descriptions of the National Curriculum.

The National Curriculum prescribes the number of school subjects to be provided by schools and specifies for each one:

❏ What pupils should be taught in each subject – **programmes of study**

❏ The knowledge, skills and understanding which pupils of different abilities and maturities are expected to achieve by the end of each key stage – **attainment targets**

The subjects in the National Curriculum are separated into what are described as core and foundation subjects.

Core subjects: English, mathematics, science and information, communication technology

Foundation subjects: History, geography, art, music, physical education and design technology, personal, social and health education (PSHE) and citizenship. From the beginning of Key Stage 3 a modern foreign language must also be taught.

Although schools are required to teach Religious Education this is not one of the subjects of the National Curriculum and arrangements for drawing up an agreed syllabus are made at local education authority level not at national level.

Key Stage 1 pupils, in school years 1 and 2, work through the subject programmes of study as shown in the chart overleaf.

The attainment targets set out the knowledge, skills and understanding that pupils are expected to reach when that part of the programme of study has been completed. For all attainment targets there are a series of level descriptions, in other words, each attainment target is divided into eight levels. Level 1 is the first one that pupils would work towards achieving and

English

Speaking and listening
Reading
Writing

Mathematics

Using and applying mathematics
Number
Shape, space and measures

Science

Scientific enquiry
Life processes and living things
Materials and their properties
Physical processes

Information, Communication Technology (ICT)

Working with a range of information to investigate the different ways it can be presented
Explore a variety of ICT tools
Talk about the uses of ICT inside and outside school

History

Changes in the lives of themselves, their family, and others
People's way of life in the more distant past, either locally or elsewhere in Britain
The lives of significant men, women and children taken from the history of Britain and the wider world
Past events from the history of Britain and the wider world

Geography

The study of two localities
- The school locality and its surrounding area that is within easy access
- A locality in the UK or abroad that has different physical or human features that contrast with their own school's locality
Explore a range of starting points for practical work

Art and Design

Work collaboratively with others or by themselves on projects in 2-d/3-d and on different scales
Use a range of materials and processes
Investigate different kinds of art, craft and design

Music

A range of musical activities that integrate performing, composing and appraising
Respond to a range of musical and non-musical starting points
Work on their own, in groups of different sizes and as a class
Hear a range of live and recorded music from different times and cultures

Design and Technology

Investigating and evaluating a variety of familiar products
Practical tasks that develop a range of skills, techniques, processes and knowledge
Designing and making tasks that use a range of materials, food, items that can be put together to make products, and textiles

Physical Education (PE)

Dance activities
Games activities
Gymnastics activities
Swimming activities (optional) and water safety

PSHE and Citizenship

Developing confidence and responsibility and making the most of their abilities
Preparing to play an active role as citizens
Developing a healthy, safer lifestyle
Developing good relationships and respecting the differences between people

---

most pupils are expected to achieve Level 2 by the age of seven. Each level description describes the types and range of achievement that pupils working at that level should demonstrate. They provide the basis for teachers to make judgements about pupils' achievement at each level and give a picture of pupils' progress as they move through the curriculum. Pupils' progress is tested, using national standard assessment tests (SATS) at the end of: Key Stage 1 (age seven) Key Stage 2 (age 11) and Key Stage 3 (age 14). At Key Stage 4 national qualifications are the main means of assessing attainment in National Curriculum subjects.

In addition to the National Curriculum the Government has put in place two strategies that are designed to raise standards in all primary schools in England. These are the National Literacy Strategy and the National Numeracy Strategy. Frameworks for teaching literacy and mathematics have been published to support each of these strategies and these provide detailed objectives for planning and teaching the sections of the English programmes of study for reading and writing and all sections of the programmes of study for mathematics for pupils aged five to eleven. As well as putting in place the Framework for Teaching Literacy schools must also make sure that they cover the programmes of study for speaking and listening for Key Stages 1 and 2. Schools that fully implement the Framework for Teaching Mathematics will fulfil their statutory duty in regard to the National Curriculum subject of mathematics for Key Stages 1 and 2.

It is important to remember that the National Curriculum does not prescribe how teachers should teach. For example, although the National Curriculum is described as separate subjects many primary schools do not teach these separately, apart from literacy and numeracy and sometimes the other two core subjects of science and information, communication technology. As long as the requirements of the subject programmes of study are met then how schools choose to plan and deliver the curriculum is up to them and their governors.

For those interested in reading more fully about the National Curriculum, all schools keep copies of all the official publications. If you are not based in a school, your local library should keep copies.

Margaret Edgington is worried that the emphasis on curriculum content in the early years has put the focus on what children learn at the expense of how they should be learning.

Are we forgetting **how** to help children learn?

A group of two- to three-year-olds is being asked to join up the dots to make letters of the alphabet. Another group of three- to four-year-olds is doing maths worksheets. In these examples, both of which I have witnessed in early years settings, the children's body language and facial expressions are giving a clear message that they are not enjoying what they are doing. Some children look worried and others are saying 'Can I go now?'

Qualified staff, who have received training in child development, know that:

❑ Two-year-olds are not physically capable of writing letters and cannot relate to abstract symbols in any meaningful sense.

❑ There is an emotional dimension in learning - young children need to be motivated and feel that they are engaged with something enjoyable and personally challenging, which gives them the opportunity to experience a sense of achievement rather than failure.

However, over the last few years early years workers seem to have lost their confidence in what they know to be developmentally appropriate practice. The emphasis on curriculum content and on Early Learning Goals has put the focus on what children learn in some cases (like those above) at the expense of how they should be learning. In particular, the high priority being given to literacy and numeracy by the Government has caused some workers to panic and to feel that 'work on paper' is the only way of approaching this. Some argue it is what parents want - even though there is growing evidence that many parents are unhappy about the pressure their children are under at such an early age.

There is now an urgent need to revisit research evidence which indicates clearly what helps children to develop and learn most effectively, and how positive attitudes to learning can be promoted. The following points should help early years managers and workers to ensure that their practice has not drifted off course.

Supporting and extending young children's learning
Recognise that children need to feel secure and confident.
Transitions from home to nursery and from room to room can be stressful and staff need to plan carefully for the settling in period. This involves considering what children need to learn in order to be well settled and consciously planning to promote this learning.

High priority needs to be given to children's personal, social and emotional development, their physical development and their ability to communicate needs and feelings. If children feel anxious or unsure, they will not be able to take advantage of the full range of experiences on offer.

Bilingual learners, who are still developing skills in the language used in the nursery, need particular support if they are to feel comfortable and confident in the setting.

Make connections with children's home and community experience.
All children need to find images and resources which make them feel they belong and that their cultural identity, religion and language are valued. This requires adults to look at the nursery through the eyes of each child. Children need to see that what they are learning connects with the real world and adults need to embed new learning in real life practical contexts.

Maths and literacy development can be promoted through well-planned and resourced role play settings such as the home corner, shops, offices, baby clinic, cafes. In these settings children can draw on their experiences and have a go at being a reader, writer or mathematician: making and writing down appointments or shopping lists; referring to telephone directories, diaries, menus and recipe books; and working out how many items will be needed for the dolls' party. These meaningful contexts motivate children because they enable them to feel competent and to show adults what they know. When adults are playing with the children they can model writing shopping lists or following a recipe book or calculating how much food will be needed. In this way they extend children's ideas.

Outings (for example, to the post office, farm, park, mosque) can consolidate or extend children's experience as can visitors to the nursery, such as a father bathing his baby, a police officer or fire fighter.

Engage children in active learning processes in and out of doors.

Young children need to be actively engaged both physically and mentally and to make choices and develop skills as independent learners. They need to explore using all their senses, experiment using their bodies and a range of tools/implements, observe and imitate others, practise and refine developing skills, initiate and tackle their own challenges and become totally involved in what they are doing. This requires a well organised environment with accessible equipment where children can select the resources they need to develop their own ideas. Too often children are passive recipients of an adult-led curriculum - doing as the adult tells them or shows them rather than exploring or thinking for themselves. Rather than inappropriate worksheets, young children should be given many different opportunities to represent their ideas in their own way. These opportunities include representing with objects (such as blocks, shells, collage materials), with their own body (such as clapping, stamping, dancing), with marks or pictures (such as drawing and early attempts at writing) and talk (such as recalling their own past experiences, acting a part in role play and story telling). Older children, who understand that a symbol can represent an idea, can be encouraged to represent using their own symbols. For

example, they could be encouraged to write down the score when they play skittles or basketball, or write a message to a friend. Adults should not insist on one correct way - children might record skittles scores using drawing of the skittles or a tally system, rather than by recording numerals.

It is essential that all adults understand the importance of outdoor learning, that they ensure that a wide range of learning opportunities is planned and that they enable children to spend sufficient time out of doors to work in depth.

Give high priority to language development.

Speaking and listening skills provide the foundation for reading and writing. It is no coincidence that, amongst older children, the fluent readers and writers are also the most articulate. Children need opportunities to develop their listening skills through adults encouraging them to notice sounds in the environment, through playing listening games, and during story and circle times.

Children also need to be listened to. They need encouragement to express themselves verbally in a range of ways (this includes sign language), for example expressing feelings and needs, recalling their experiences, reasoning, predicting, imagining, telling

stories, acting in role. Adults can record children's stories, and accounts of their experiences, to enable them to be authors. Some of the most popular books in nursery book corners are the ones where a shared experience has been recorded in book form, such as 'The day the fire engine came to visit'.

These experiences provide a firm foundation for literacy, because they enthuse children about the spoken and written word and enable them to see that their contribution is valued. Adults need to ensure that there is time in the daily routine for informal talking and listening to all children.

Share the curriculum with parents/carers.

All parents want their children to reach their full potential. What they do not want is for their child to be switched off learning at an early age. Early years workers need to make time for parents and carers to talk about their hopes and fears. They also need to share some of their own observations of working with children. It is vital to explain how the curriculum is approached, and why it is so essential to promote positive attitudes to learning at an early age. Staff can help parents to support their child at home during everyday activities such as sorting washing, shopping, setting the table, writing letters or lists. In this way parents and staff can work together to protect children from the pressure which can result from misguided attempts to 'get children on'.

It is essential that staff teams regularly review their practice. Two questions could provide starting points for discussion:

- **How consistent is our practice with what we know about child development?**

- **Which attitudes to learning does our practice encourage?**

Margaret Edgington

The term schema is used by many early years professionals. But what does it mean in the day-to-day life of a setting? Cath Arnold explains and shows how you can use schema to develop your work with children

Using schema in learning

Children are learning all the time, not just when their parents or educators are teaching them. Children (and adults) learn by doing. We can help children to learn most effectively by noticing what they are doing spontaneously. Then we need to help them to connect what they are doing with what they are interested in learning and with what we know they can learn.

Children are part of families

The world of each young child begins within their own family. Everything a child does, or becomes interested in, connects with the lives of the people they know. So, knowing about the important people in the lives of young children helps you to understand what it is that each child wants to learn. Listening to and sharing information each day with a child's carers is one way of finding out what a child wants to know about.

The pattern in children's investigations

When you watch children's natural actions and investigations, you notice that their behaviour is not random. There is a pattern to each individual child's behaviour. We call this pattern in children's behaviour 'schemas'. Tina Bruce (1996) gives us this explanation of 'schemas':

'Schemas are patterns of linked behaviours which the child can generalise and use in a whole variety of different situations. It is best to think of schemas as being a cluster of pieces which fit together.'

Rather than seeing young children 'flit' from one thing to another, you can see young children 'fit' ideas together (Athey, 1990). When you know what children are trying to find out, you can help them.

What a schema looks like

A schema is fundamentally a pattern of behaviour. When young children are exploring the world, they are trying, through their explorations, to discover how things work. Some of the patterns children use are:

❏ trajectory or lines (jumping, running, climbing, banging, throwing, painting up/down or side to side, lining up cars, blocks or other objects);

❏ transporting or carrying objects or oneself from one place to another;

❏ enveloping or covering themselves or objects (with paint, clay, sand or other materials);

❏ rotating objects or themselves;

❏ enclosing objects, space or themselves;

❏ filling a variety of containers with a variety of materials;

❏ connecting objects together or themselves to other people or objects;

❏ going through a boundary (for example, train through tunnel, water through hose, self through defined space;

Schemas may be dynamic or moving, like a jump or throw, or static, like a building or line.

How schemas help us

Each child is an individual and will use schemas in their own way. Some children use one pattern very obviously, others use a cluster or will be less obvious in their use of schemas. As educators and parents, you can try to spot the schemas that children are using.

If you spot any patterns you can help children to learn more by:

❏ supporting their actions with language and resources. For example, only certain objects rotate. You can introduce a variety of objects to rotate when a child is interested in rotation. You can offer the vocabulary to match the child's actions, such as 'I see you are making it spin around.'

❏ helping them to extend their ideas. For example, showing them a globe when they are interested in rotation can lead to an interest in other countries, cultures, languages or even the solar system. Nathan's story makes this explicit.

Nathan following his own interest

Nathan starts nursery at almost three and has a strong trajectory schema. He enjoys stories and role play. Nathan begins to use resources in the writing area each day to make guns or swords, which he uses in his role play. (The writing area is an area where a variety of materials are available for children to use in their own ways. There are pens, pencils, paper, envelopes, scissors, sticky tape, glue, elastic bands, paper clips, hole punches, stampers and ink pads, a calculator and rulers.) It is important to Nathan for his props to be strong. He tries out different types of paper. We add lollipop sticks to the resources. He uses these and becomes very skilled at using the sticky tape and the dispenser. The adults at home and at nursery support his creativity by:

❏ making sure suitable resources are available to Nathan each day;

❏ helping him learn to use them, for example demonstrating how to use the sticky tape dispenser;

- giving him time to carry out what he wants to do (he often spends two hours of his nursery time each day constructing props before trying them out);

- offering him language to support his investigations, for example 'fix', 'connect', 'length', 'strength' (knowing the language helps Nathan to think more deeply about what he is doing);

- telling him stories which include ideas about swords, guns and other weapons, such as 'Robin Hood', 'King Arthur' and 'Hercules';

- extending Nathan's ideas by using open questions and comments, such as 'What about this paper?', 'Would this be strong enough for a sword?', 'How are you going to connect it?'

- checking out with Nathan how he wants his prop to look, for example 'Is this long enough?'

Nathan begins to intersect (cross) two trajectories to make handles for swords and triggers for guns.

Nathan bends his trajectory and makes it into an enclosure. He connects string to it and calls it a 'lasso'.

On another occasion, he makes several swords or guns and connects each to the next and constructs an enclosure around his waist.

It is easy for us to see the connection between Nathan's investigations and his future formal education. He will learn to add on and to measure circles with a long line (tape measure). We can help him by offering the language to describe his actions. The language and actions will help Nathan to discover and understand the concepts of adding on and measuring. (Comments like 'I see you're making it longer' and 'It fits all of the way around your waist now' are really helpful.)

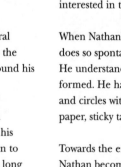

Nathan becomes interested in making shields in order to block the trajectory of his sword.

Nathan's parents realise the importance of his investigations. They provide him with similar materials and support at home. He is thinking, planning, making, trying out and playing with his props most of his time both at home and at nursery. He does not have to wait to try things out. He can learn much more than if 'creative play' was for an hour each week.

At nursery Nathan chooses to spend a lot of his time in the writing area. There are number lines on the writing table. This is another trajectory which goes from less to more. In his own time, Nathan becomes interested in the numbers.

When Nathan begins to draw and write, he does so spontaneously and without pressure. He understands how conventional letters are formed. He has already constructed lines and circles with his whole body and with paper, sticky tape and other materials.

Towards the end of his time at nursery, Nathan becomes interested in the human body. He can speculate 'If you didn't have any bones you'd be flat'! After looking at a three-dimensional body book at nursery, Nathan asks lots of questions at home. When his parents ask which bit of the book he likes best he says 'The ribs'. He stands tall and feels his own ribs. He likes the fact that they are in lines and knows that ribs protect other

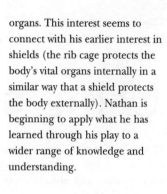

organs. This interest seems to connect with his earlier interest in shields (the rib cage protects the body's vital organs internally in a similar way that a shield protects the body externally). Nathan is beginning to apply what he has learned through his play to a wider range of knowledge and understanding.

What we can learn from Nathan's constructing

No other child will learn in exactly the same way as Nathan, but we too can apply what we have learned more generally. Other children may bend trajectories and make them into enclosures and you will look out for that in future. Parents and carers know children best. If we truly want to help children to learn, then we must find ways of sharing information with their parents or carers regularly. In Nathan's case we were able to chat daily with his parents. Other ways of keeping in contact:

- through home/school books;

- phone calls;

- sharing videos of children;

- through keeping a diary of what a child does at home;

- through sharing photos.

Spotting schemas provides a focus for what information to share. Many children, particularly boys, first explore their schemas in a dynamic form. As educators, we must pay attention to and equally value schemas that appear one minute and are gone the next. It is essential to capture children's movements by writing descriptively, filming or taking a series of photographs.

Last, but by no means least important, is the deep involvement and high self-esteem of a child who can choose and feel supported in their choices by both carers and educators.

Cath Arnold

Penny Jordan, from the St Nicholas Montessori Centre, gives an insight into the philosophy of Montessori teaching and explains how it is put into practice

The Montessori method

The Montessori philosophy is based on the scientific observations of Dr Maria Montessori who was born in Italy in 1870 and who died in Holland in 1952. Dr Montessori originally qualified as a medical doctor. Her work in this area led her into the field of education, at first with children who experienced learning difficulties and then with children with normal learning abilities.

Dr Montessori observed that education begins at birth and that children experience periods of special sensitivity during which there is a specific eagerness to learn.

The Montessori classroom accommodates children of mixed ages and is designed to meet the children's needs at times of peak interest. The Montessori method of education is an alternative type of education which harnesses the child's natural ability to learn. It is not a modern unstructured method based upon the whim of the child or the teacher, but a proven scientific method which offers concrete experiences and materials to explain abstract principles.

Dr Montessori's observations revealed that children:

❑ Learn through movement, particularly through the actions of the hand which is linked to the development of intelligence.

❑ Enjoy learning in an environment prepared to meet their needs.

❑ Learn best through education which is offered through the senses.

❑ Learn to write, read and compute at an early age.

❑ Respond to educational opportunities in an environment which is prepared to meet their special sensitivities for learning.

❑ Reveal a spontaneous self-discipline within a prepared environment.

The Montessori teacher is trained to:

❑ Assist each child to realise individual potential.

❑ Observe in a scientific manner.

❑ Present the Montessori curriculum competently at times of maximum interest and be aware of National Curriculum requirements and the inter-relationship with the Montessori curriculum.

The Montessori curriculum

This is based on Dr Montessori's principles of education within a structured environment. The curriculum aims to support all aspects of the child's personal and social development. The main curriculum areas are:

Daily living skills

Aim: To provide foundations for learning.

Centred around:

Care for the environment;

Care for oneself as an individual;

Care for others in the community.

Education of the senses

Aim: To develop skills for learning.

By observing, understanding and exploring the world through the senses, the child acquires the skills of classification, discrimination, evaluation and sequencing.

Language development

Aim: To develop the four aspects of language: oral, aural, writing and reading.

The skills developed include self-expression, listening, communication, writing and reading.

A characteristic of Montessori teaching is the phonetic method which is used to teach the sounds of the letters of the alphabet followed by word building exercises which lead to phonetic reading, then total reading. Grammar is introduced at phonetic reading stage.

Number concepts

Aim: To provide a concrete understanding of the concepts of number and mathematics in the environment.
The child progresses through an understanding of number to the structure and processes of the decimal system.

Science and exploration of the wider world

Aim: To provide experiences in all aspects of the natural world including the plant and animal kingdoms, people, events and cultures.

This section of the curriculum integrates activities in the above four sections.

Children are provided in this area with the opportunity to experience and create in areas relating to our different cultures - art, craft, drama, music, dance, physical education - which enable them to develop their imaginative responses and their creative self-expression.

The outcome is children who are developed in a balanced manner in the cognitive, physical, social, emotional and spiritual areas; children who are decision makers, who are confident and independent and are capable of progressing onwards with their potential realised; children who have gained a firm foundation in the skills outlined in the five curriculum areas and who have acquired a very broad general knowledge and an eagerness for further knowledge; children who are prepared for the next stage of development.

A typical Montessori day

The Montessori staff will arrive dressed neatly and colourfully so that they add to the attractive environment of a Montessori classroom, for Montessorians believe the environment encompasses not only the inanimate objects in a room but also significant people in the child's surroundings, including the teacher.

The preparation of this environment plays an important part in the philosophy we follow. The staff will ensure the Montessori didactic materials are set out appropriately on clean shelves. In the practical life area cotton wool, cloths, water jugs might need to be replenished. They will not change the positioning of the different materials as we believe children feel more comfortable when they know where to find everything.

The classroom will have a practical life area, a sensorial area, a cultural area, a language area and a mathematics area. The teachers will make sure these are neatly and appropriately arranged. The snack table will be set up, the flower vase put ready to receive the blooms brought in by a child as will the equipment needed for the pupils to clean and feed the classroom pet.

As the children begin to arrive, a smiling teacher will shake hands with each pupil at the door as they come in, encouraging him/her to look into her eyes as the child says 'Good morning'. A second teacher will be inside encouraging the children to make their own choice of how to start their day from the material set out within the environment.

Following the teaching of Dr Montessori, there now begins the 'work cycle', a two to three hour period when the children are left to make their own choices and to follow through any number of learning experiences. Initially, the teacher will present the material to the child before observing the child's own attempts from which may be drawn an understanding of that child's level of development. Children may work alone, in pairs or in groups that evolve from their own level of interest in an activity.

With only one piece of material available the children learn to wait their turn and share. They know to return each piece of material to the correct place on the shelf ready for the next child, thus learning to respect each other and the environment. The pupils might work at tables or on mats on the floor. They know when they leave a table to push in the chair quietly, they know to roll up the mat and replace it in the stand provided. As time passes each child finds a level of involvement and concentration, staff are quietly presenting or observing and a feeling of calm and peace pervades the room.

There is no 'snack time' as such. A pupil chooses when he or she needs a break, finding their drink and biscuit or fruit on the snack table. There will be two chairs; if they are both occupied the child will quietly wait to sit when one of his or her peers leaves a chair empty.

If possible, activities such as gardening will take place outdoors within the work cycle. It is more likely, however, that as the work cycle ends the children will move into a circle where they will discuss some of the activities undertaken during the morning, their own news, or maybe sing songs and listen to a story. The group will then move into the garden for a period of free play. At home time the children will again shake hands with their teachers as they say 'Good-bye'.

Penny Jordan, Director of Development, St Nicholas Montessori Centre, London.

High/Scope nurseries are not only doing well in their Ofsted inspections but also feature positively in prominent early years research. The Director of the High/Scope Institute explains their philosophy

What is **High/Scope?**

The High/Scope approach requires no special equipment or environment and is based on more than 30 years of longitudinal research and practice. The approach centres on the recognition and support of the unique differences in children aged between two and six and develops their self-confidence by building on what they can do.

Staff encourage children to become decision-makers and problem-solvers who can plan, initiate and reflect on work chosen by themselves; who work effectively individually, with other children, and with adults, and who develop skills and traits which enable them to become successful students as they grow older. High/Scope also encourages managers to place more value in training and encourages parents, caregivers and teachers to extend their expectations for children and themselves.

High/Scope is the only programme which has been subject to a 30-year internationally recognised study. Children involved in the High/Scope programme in Michigan in 1962, and who are now aged over 27, have been followed. They grew up to break out of their cycle of deprivation identified by high drop-out rates from school, high juvenile delinquency and low academic standing by using the life skills and positive attitudes to learning and society generated by the High/Scope programme they attended.

The approach began more than 30 years ago in Michigan, USA, and its curriculum model is now used in more than 20 countries and training initiatives have been successfully implemented through official High/Scope Institutes operating in the UK, Mexico, Finland, Singapore and the Netherlands.

The central principles of High/Scope are illustrated by the Wheel of Learning (above). These principles guide all High/Scope practitioners in their daily work. Their work is also informed by working closely with

parents based on the principle of family inclusion and the unique culture of the child.

Active learning
Through active learning - having direct and immediate experiences and deriving meaning from them through reflection - young children construct knowledge that helps them make sense of their world. The power of active learning comes from personal initiative. Children act on their innate desire to explore - they ask and search for answers to questions about people, materials, events and ideas that arouse their curiosity; they solve problems that stand in the way of their goals; and they generate strategies to try.

The key experiences
The High/Scope curriculum identifies 58 developmentally appropriate key learning experiences. These experiences occur naturally throughout the time children are in the setting each day. Staff regularly make anecdotal observations on the children's learning experiences and this forms the basis for planning and evaluating. Thus the process towards meeting the Early Learning Goals occurs in a way which meets the needs of the children and is based upon their interests and prior learning.

Adult-child interaction
Active learning depends on positive adult-child interaction. Guided by an understanding of how pre-school children think and reason, adults practise positive interaction strategies - sharing control with children, focusing on children's strengths, forming authentic relationships with children, supporting play, adopting a problem-solving approach to social conflict and using encouragement rather than a child management system based on praise, punishment and reward. This interaction

ASSESSMENT
• Teamwork
• Daily anecdotal notes
• Daily planning
• Child assessment

ADULT-CHILD INTERACTION
• Interaction strategies
• Encouragement
• Problem-solving approach to conflict

ACTIVE LEARNING
Initiative
Key experiences

DAILY ROUTINE
• Plan-Do-Review
• Small-group time
• Large-group time

LEARNING ENVIRONMENT
• Areas
• Materials
• Storage

style enables the child to express thoughts and feelings freely and confidently, decide on the direction and content of the conversation, and experience true partnership in dialogue.

Learning environment
The High/Scope curriculum places a strong emphasis on planning the layout of the pre-school and selecting appropriate materials. An active learning environment is organised to enable children with ongoing opportunities to make choices and decisions.

The daily routine
Adults also plan a consistent routine that supports active learning. The routine enables young children to anticipate what will happen next and gives them a great deal of control over what they do during each part of their day. High/Scope provides an open framework, that is one which provides for a balance of child and teacher initiation. The part of the daily routine which is initiated by the adult is small group time which usually occurs after the conclusion of the unique plan-do-review cycle.

The plan-do-review process
During the plan-do-review process children learn to create and express intentions.

Firstly, in a group or individually, and supported by an adult, children plan what they wish to do and their planning becomes increasingly sophisticated as children become conversant with the process.

Secondly, children generate experiences based upon their plans. Children need time for trial and error, generating new ideas, practising and succeeding. Personal independence is the key to active learning by self-motivated children. Time is given for children to act on their intentions at 'work time'.

Third, children reflect on their experiences at play. A high quality curriculum must provide occasion for children to reflect on their experiences with increasing verbal ability and logic as they mature. The time set aside for this process is called 'recall' or 'review'.

When these three components are systematically experienced by children they develop a strong sense of self-control and self-discipline. This control is real power, not over other people or things, but over oneself. Understanding what is happening in the environment, realising that those around us are genuinely interested in what we say and do, and knowing that our work and effort will often lead to success, is the type of control that promotes personal satisfaction and motivates productivity.

High/Scope in the UK

High/Scope UK was the first Institute outside of America, and over the past decade use of the approach in Britain has increased dramatically. The role of the High/Scope Institute is to provide materials and training for those working across the early years caring profession who wish to use the approach. Since 1986 more than 100 professionals in the early years sphere have become Endorsed High/Scope Trainers, training members of their own organisations and others across the UK to become practitioners. (Over a three-year period 1992-94 it was estimated that 17,000 practitioners were practising High/Scope and 250,000 children have experience of the approach each year.)

For a free booklet, *A Brief Introduction to the High/Scope Approach,* and publications directory, send an sae with 60p stamp to the Institute at Copperfield House, 190-192 Maple Road, Penge, London SE20 8HT.

Reference

Educating Young Children, Hohmann and Weikart (High/Scope Press 1995).

Serena Johnson, Director of the High/Scope Institute.

Sue Hedley, a teacher in charge of a 26-place nursery unit attached to a primary school in South Tyneside, shares her experience of High/Scope practice and discusses what it means for the children, parents and staff on a day-to-day basis.

Our day begins when the children run eagerly into nursery and are greeted individually by each adult. Then we follow our daily routine. The daily routine helps the children to understand and predict the order of events in their day, developing their concept of time. Knowing what to expect gives children a sense of control and a measure of independence which makes it easier for them to direct their energies to the task in hand, encouraging and developing intrinsic motivation. The children have the opportunity to start their day with their own interests and ideas and are asked 'What do you plan to do today?' Children share ideas and projects with their friends and therefore learn to negotiate, collaborate and develop independence. My children love to plan because their ideas belong to them - they are in control - they know and decide when and where the plan will be started and when and where it is completed.

High/Scope believes in a responsive teaching style. From my own experience and observations children soon become bored when working to someone else's agenda. The work may have little relevance to their thoughts, areas of cognitive concern or ideas they may have come to nursery with that day. They also have little ownership of such activities and their persistence and engagement will be low level. In contrast to this I have wearily walked up my path to

nursery after a full day visiting the local farm and the children have asked 'Mrs Hedley - can we plan now?'

Once the children have planned the area/areas they would like to work in, they go and 'do' their plan. The children might plan to work in two or three areas and put the product of their plans or an artefact related to their plans (a model, a book or a drawing/painting) in their group base area on a recall table. These will be ready to discuss at recall time. Work time lasts approximately 45 minutes to one hour when a warning signal for tidy-up time is given by one of the children. Everybody has the responsibility of tidying up the area they have worked in and when they have finished, to go and help somebody else. After tidy-up time we have recall time. They ask each other questions about their work: 'How did you get the tube to stick?', 'What is that bit there?', 'What do you like about it?', 'What did you give the baby to eat in the home area?' The development of language and literacy skills is spontaneous, meaningful and rapid.

The rest of the daily routine consists of snack time, outside time, circle time and small group time. Small group time is when the teacher plans an activity for a key experience focus. This provides the balance in the daily routine between adult and child initiation and all the children participate. The activity will be planned with the active learning ingredients in mind: materials, manipulation, choice, language from the child and support from the adult. Small group time is an excellent time to assess the children's emerging skills and abilities.

For me the High/Scope approach cares about how children learn. It has a fundamental philosophy of respect for human thought and development.

Sue Hedley

Forest Schools have been an integral part of early years education in Denmark since the 1980s. Now England has its very own Forest School in Bridgwater, Somerset. Alison Oaten offers an insight into their philosophy and what it means in practice

An insight into Forest Schools

The Forest School at the Children's Centre, Bridgwater College, was set up as a result of a visit in 1995 by nursery nursing students to Denmark, where Forest Schools have been an integral part of early years education since the 1980s. While they were there students observed children from five to seven years of age being escorted to local woodland and allowed free exploration of the outdoor environment.

The benefits to the children were so impressive - the children grew in confidence, independence and learned to appreciate the natural environment - that we decided to think about how we could apply the Danish Forest School principles to our pre-school children, aged three and four, who attended the children's centre.

and direct you to their way of thinking! After a few weeks of following dutifully written lesson plans, we decided to abandon them and let the children dictate to us what they wanted from this new experience.

Over the first hurdle
The first hurdle was to find someone who was willing to work with groups of young children in the outdoor environment on a regular basis. We approached a lecturer who had vast experience and knowledge of outdoor education and of working with students with learning difficulties. Working in the early years was new to Gordon Woodall but he was willing to try a new challenge.

Forest School was set up in a basic and different way to the Denmark culture, but we decided to start small and grow with the experience!

We began by taking small groups (six to eight children) onto the college sports field next to the children's centre. Slowly and surely we extended the time we were out and enjoyed the freedom of being outside. Being British and aware of education expectations our Forest School leader felt that there had to be a structure to the sessions. He soon learned that young children bypass planning

Thinking on our feet!
We had to think on our feet and be prepared - as always - to make instant decisions, adapt and adjust to their knowledge and learning. It became obvious that by taking them out of the nursery, in all weathers, they responded very differently to the way they did within their familiar nursery environment.

We involved second year students studying in the early years department of the college, so the ratios of staff to children could be high and we could offer a greater adult input and support. Many of the students found the situation difficult to relate to now that the children were out of the secure environment of a classroom.

Our very own forest
With the success of our first year behind us, we looked to expand and develop the provision. We were able to lease a woodland and a minibus and take the children to our very own forest for their Forest School

sessions, accompanied by second year nursery nurse students, a keyworker, Forest School leader, and a member of the children's centre management team.

Each year the opportunities for the children, staff and students changed and improved. At present, all the students who will join in Forest School sessions go on a compulsory three-day residential which helps to prepare them not only for the activities they will be supporting the children in doing but also to experience life outdoors for themselves!

All children aged three and over who attend the children's centre are given the chance to take part in Forest School. Attendance is not compulsory, but once parents have decided to sign their child up, every effort is made for that child to remain within his or her group. Group dynamics and trust soon evolve and a change within the group can have a major effect on the remaining children.

Before the first outing, a parents' evening is held to emphasise the benefits of going to

A typical activity

Building a house of sticks was part of our 'Three Little Pigs' nursery theme. The children were asked to find sticks taller than themselves and as wide as their arms. They searched the woodland to find the right building materials and for about 30 minutes they were carefully building a house of sticks using a fallen tree as a support and balancing their finds on it.

The children worked steadily as individuals within a small group, talking continuously with their carer and their peers about what they were doing, how and why.

When the house was completed to their satisfaction the children hid in their new shelter while members of staff role-played the story with them.

Forest School and for parents to voice any concerns they may have. Some children are given priority of attendance - these include children with particularly challenging behaviour or identified as having additional or specific needs. From taking part in Forest School, children such as these have been observed to develop control over their behaviour, improved concentration and independence and develop their social and emotional skills. Other children previously timid and lacking in confidence within the normal nursery environment have become confident in their own abilities within the forest and are seen to move away from reliance on adults.

The children quickly learn the boundaries within which they must work. They respond to the sense of freedom and stick to the few rules laid down for their safety.

We go out in all weathers, all year round, exploring and learning from the seasons and environment changes. Suitable clothing can be provided in order for the children to get the most out of messy opportunities. Nothing can be more pleasurable than seeing a child who has been actively encouraged to get dirty and muddy by experimenting in puddles, mud and shallow streams which can sometimes be out of bounds. Our woodland is secure - it is in the middle of fields and is entirely fenced. Because of this security, it is possible to encourage the children to move away from adult interaction and become more responsible for each other and for themselves. A central camp fire and semi-permanent shelter for wood storage have been built in the woods. An old lock-up cabin acts as a secure storage unit for the tools and equipment.

The curriculum

The curriculum of the individual Forest School sessions varies considerably for a number of reasons - weather conditions, level of staffing, group dynamics, moods of the children. Although a year's curriculum is set, the weekly results and personal achievements vary considerably.

The child's family receives a Forest School report which highlights their activities during that session and identifies which Early Learning Goals have been met. This information is shared with their keyworker, parent/carer and kept in their Celebration of Achievement file. All parties are invited to make any comments regarding that session's work, child's comments, observations, and so on.

Children's progress will be at different rates and individual achievement will vary. However, all children should be able to follow a curriculum which enables them to make as much progress as possible towards the outcomes.

Every single one of the ELGs is worked towards throughout the year of the child attending Forest School. The child's knowledge and understanding of the world, language, mathematics, creative, physical, personal and social development underpin the whole Forest School philosophy. Just match the example above against the ELGs and see!

Using adult equipment

Children are taught how to use full-size adult tools such as saws, tenon saws and pen knives safely. They are also shown how to light and deal with fires in a controlled supervised environment. We believe that by using adult equipment, showing and preparing children in this way, they will act in a mature and sensible way if and when they are faced with the situation again, perhaps unsupervised. Parents are often amazed at what we do - but how often do children have the opportunity these days to see and learn about open fires? How many families have a workshop/shed where children can learn and experiment with wood?

Bringing the experience indoors

We now extend the Forest School experience into the nursery by bringing activities into the classrooms and garden. For example, before our annual camp we put up a tent in the nursery, children build an imaginary fire and role play Forest School skills. The benefits of this is that younger children now join in - often preparing them for their turn in Forest School.

At the end of the academic year, all the Forest School children, families and staff are invited to come on a two-day/one-night camp in which the children can show the skills they have learned over the year - stick whittling, sawing, fire lighting, safety procedures, shelter building. By this time, the parents are amazed at how physically capable, confident and trusting their child has become.

Over the last year, all children's centre staff have undergone some Forest School training. Others have chosen to take it further by studying for a EDEXEL (BTEC) Forest School Leaders Award/Forest School Assistant Award, which is presently running at Bridgwater College.

All of us who have been involved in our Forest School are excited and proud of its developments and progress to date. We have worked towards many positive changes, particularly in the children's social outlook, their developing self-esteem and growing independence. We have reaped the benefits of the children's social interaction skills within the nursery. All these are now evident when our children are assessed against the baseline assessments.

In the past, children used to be able to experience that sense of freedom which then influenced their lifelong learning. At Forest School our children are able to experience that now.

Alison Oaten

For information on Forest School training please contact: Norma Frood, Information Officer, Bridgwater College, Bath Road, Bridgwater, TA6 4PZ.
Telephone: 01278 441270

The city of Reggio Emilia near Parma in Northern Italy has 22 pre-school centres for children aged three to six, and 13 infant toddler centres for children under three. What makes it so special? Heather Shannon reveals the influence it is having on her nursery

Learning from **Reggio Emilia**

In 1945, after the devastation of the Second World War, a group of parents in Reggio Emilia, a city in Northern Italy, decided they wanted to build their own school.

Loris Malaguzzi (1921 - 1994), a middle school teacher, was so inspired by the courage and motivation of these parents, that he changed his job so that he could teach in the first centre, Villa Cella. It was through his charismatic leadership and inspiration that more parent-run centres grew. In 1963, city funding was provided for a new centre and by 1967 parental pressure had led to all the parent-run schools coming under the administration of the municipality of Reggio Emilia.

Learning for everyone

The centres are characterised by the profound attention they give to learning on the part of all involved - parents, children, professional staff and the wider community. All are seen as educators.

Reggio Emilia educators show their genuine respect for children by valuing all aspects of their development. Children are viewed in terms of their strengths, not weaknesses, and are given credit for their enormous capacity to learn. The results are seen in the aesthetic environments of the schools, the spirit of co-operation between staff, parents and children, and especially the quality of the creative work.

Source of inspiration

I first learned of the work of the Reggio Emilia infant toddler and pre-school centres

from a German nursery headteacher who had visited our day nursery in Jesmond. She was so inspired after visiting the centres in Reggio Emilia that she had convinced her parents and staff to close down their nursery until they had totally restructured it on the same lines. It seemed a drastic way to achieve change, but I felt her descriptions of this imaginative and child-centred nurturing environment deserved further exploration. I was, therefore, delighted to discover that an exhibition called 'The Hundred Languages of Children', celebrating the creative work of the Reggio children, was to be hosted at a local museum.

'The Hundred Languages of Children'

I was astonished by the vitality of the children's work in the exhibition. The children had recorded their experiences, perceptions and thoughts through photographs, creative writing, drawing, painting, collage, mobiles and models.

I was particularly interested in the photographs of the youngest children. Amongst the many beautiful images was one of a very young child, about 18 months old, sitting on her own in a cut-out circle of paper on the floor, painting around herself, totally engrossed. The photograph portrayed freedom and child-centred learning. Having felt uneasy about the direction pre-school education was taking in light of the introduction of the ELGs, the image was a confirmation of the experiences I thought all children should have access to in a nursery.

I bought one of the publications at the exhibition, *The Little Ones of Silent Movies*. The photographs in it tell a story of young children in a busy day nursery in Reggio Emilia. The images show how the children had enjoyed a picture story about a fish. The story is extended into a real trip out for the children and their carers to buy their own goldfish. The awe and wonder they experience in having a live fish in the nursery is beautifully captured.

The children's own ideas are observed and expanded through the use of shadow puppet playing using fish puppets.

The photographs also explore the tension of young children learning to play together. One child throws a big toy fish out of the window. The children are sad. Fortunately, with the help of the carers, they retrieve the toy and unite it with its friend, the small living goldfish.

These photographs not only document the rich behaviour patterns of children, but capture what early childhood exploration of personal and social development is all about.

Exploring carefree play

The exhibition organisers had set up a project to involve ten early years providers in the region. This project would provide an artist to come and work in the settings, following the Reggio approach to developing children's creative thinking.

I asked if we could take part, having an artist to work with our Busy Bee group of children aged from 18 months to two years.

The project, which was well documented and photographed, explored the children's carefree play for five daily sessions over a week. Our 65-place day nursery is in a big Victorian house. We set the project up in one of our large rooms and cleared away the toys. We found it valuable to have the right environment, with protective polythene on the floor and all the creative materials to hand. This gave the children the opportunity to experience free play without the normal restrictions associated with messy play activities. Staff were freed up to concentrate on observing the children and giving them support, instead of trying to keep the children 'under control'.

We took video recordings each day and used our observations of what the children seemed to be enjoying/exploring as a basis for discussion to plan for the subsequent sessions. On the first day, the children explored body painting, on day two, free painting, day three, sand and water play, day four, fabric painting and day five, working with paint and cellophane.

Benefits for all

The benefits of the week's project were not only measurable for the children, but for the staff and parents, too.

'Our goal is to build an amiable school (and also a hard-working, inventive, liveable, documentable and communicable school; a place of research, learning, reflection and revisiting), where children, teachers and families can feel at home. Such a school requires careful thinking and planning concerning procedures, motivations and interests. It must embody ways of getting along together, of intensifying relationships among the three central protagonists.'

Loris Malaguzzi, Reggio Emilia

❑ The children had great fun. There were no conflicts between them over the week. They enjoyed the relaxed carefree atmosphere and had been able to join in or not as they chose. From the video footage we were able to observe a noticeable difference in the children's readiness to participate in carefree play from the first to the last of the five sessions. They had enjoyed the sense of ownership of the direction of the play, and had taken part in the clearing up each day.

❑ The staff benefited from being involved as a team in a shared project. They felt more positive about different aspects of their work, including the role of observer. They felt more confident about working with different media, paint and so on.

❑ Parents showed a great interest in the project. They had watched the video and it had been a good talking point, and issues surrounding allowing children greater freedom had been discussed.

Following our participation in the project, I attended a conference in Reggio Emilia and had the chance to visit some of the infant toddler centres to see for myself what makes these centres so special.

A philosophy not a method

We did not learn a new model for teaching but we shared a pedagogy which had evolved to value education in a holistic way. This was not going to be a method for early years practitioners, or a curriculum framework for developmentally valid education. Rather, we shared an experience firmly rooted in the culture of Reggio Emilia, which would not easily transport to another culture. To bring the message back to my nursery would involve bringing back a concept. Before making any changes, we would need to examine our own values and beliefs and how we would involve staff, parents and children in implementing a Reggio Emilia approach to working in a creative environment, and documenting and sharing our work.

For us, starting from scratch is not the way forward. Any changes to practice should not be cosmetic, but must be justified on the basis of what is good practice. The Reggio Emilia approach is a philosophy, not a method, which has the love and value of children and their families at the centre of its practice.

We have made a beginning, by making observations of children's play and interests central to developing a programme to support their learning. In a society of demands and frenetic activity, we are learning to slow down and listen to children and value their ideas instead of pushing ours.

Heather Shannon

Next time someone suggests a planning meeting for a topic, be positive, be inspired and be motivated because good planning makes our job of working with young children worthwhile, says Pam Taylor

Positive planning

The Early Learning Goals make it clear that children must have first-hand experiences of activities within the six areas of learning. We have to supply good practice that involves: observing, planning, assessing, record-keeping and working closely with parents. It is all there in black and white - but what they don't tell us is how to go about implementing it all in the day-to-day organisation of the nursery!

The answer? Planning. The whole crux of good practice revolves around good planning. If both adults and children are motivated by what they are doing the learning process becomes easy for the child and enjoyable for the adult.

The challenge

Planning is challenging. Start by putting yourself in this situation: a friend gives you five chickens. You are very grateful, but your freezer is full. What do you do? Well, the last thing you do is give the family roast chicken dinner five days on the trot! Needless to say they'd rebel! You'd think of five different ways of serving chicken - with chips, risotto, casserole, the list goes on and on. Yet how many of us go to our workplace each day and put out the same old equipment in the same place and in the same way? What we should be doing is thinking about how we can use our equipment to link it to our topic and present it in a more interesting way to the children at the planning stage. It's often easy with water, sand and role play, but how can you make the book corner, blocks or construction toys more interesting?

Have you thought about putting dolls or teddies in the book corner so that the children can pick their favourite story and role model the teacher reading the books to the teddies? How about putting a familiar book on a table with some props so they can re-enact the story using the pictures of the

book as prompts for the story line. Put two chairs at the table and you will soon have two children engrossed in reading, speaking and listening skills and thoroughly enjoying their play.

Mix the large construction blocks with the cars and garage for building a motorway if your topic is transport and journeys. The children will soon use their imagination and build tunnels and ramps and bridges to extend their play.

These things need to be thought of at the planning stage because they need to be role modelled by an adult to extend creativity and language before being left as a free play activity.

The rewards

Providing interesting activities through the topic brings its own rewards. Rewards come from seeing the pleasure on children's faces when they master a new skill that you have taught them; by seeing the anticipation on their faces as they guess what you might be bringing out of the magic box; hearing their conversation based upon the structured play activities you introduced throughout the week; parents asking you about an activity you did with their child because that child has talked non-stop about it since leaving nursery yesterday!

Rewards are often unexpected and make all the effort of planning worthwhile. If we feel rewarded it inspires and motivates us to try something new, to be adventurous. It brings us back to that first stage - the challenge of planning a new topic. What are your children interested in? What can you plan that will interest the children and provide

plenty of learning opportunities under the six areas of learning and, just as importantly, be meaningful, manageable and enjoyable?

Planning for a purpose

The curriculum is about the child - it consists of all the activities that promote the intellectual, personal and social, physical, emotional and spiritual development of children. It needs to be broad, balanced, differentiated, relevant and progressive, celebrate diversity and ensure equal access for all children. For young children learning is made up of child-initiated and adult-initiated first-hand experiences. The adult's role is to support and extend children's learning through a well-planned curriculum. Planning is necessary to focus on the learning goals, enabling you to move children forward through play. But where do you start?

The planning process

Planning is a complex but necessary task. It involves the planning of activities both indoors and outdoors and the management and development of staff and helpers within the pre-school setting. Planning is a cyclical and continuous process and should be collaborative between all adults. Certain questions need to be addressed:

- ❏ Who needs to be involved in planning?
- ❏ Who is ultimately responsible for planning?
- ❏ How will planning be recorded?
- ❏ By whom and when will planning be monitored and evaluated?

Who needs to be involved in planning?

In an ideal world every member of staff within a setting would be involved at every stage of the planning. Unfortunately, this is not always practical. Staff need to know why they are doing an activity and what the expected learning objectives are. An inspector will ask questions about what you are doing and why. Staff need to be able to respond confidently with the knowledge that the activity has been planned thoroughly and that they understand what they want the children to experience.

All staff need to be involved in choosing the topics for the year and the initial brainstorming. If they have been able to contribute at this stage they are far more likely to be motivated and enthusiastic about what is going on. The next stage - the medium-term planning and schemes of work - is often left to the supervisors or managers to complete before bringing it back to the other members of staff for discussion and agreement. All staff need either their own copy or easy access to the planning. This should be kept in the staff room or as a file in the store cupboard.

Planning is usually split into three areas: long-term, medium-term and short-term.

Long-term planning

Long-term planning ensures children get a broad and balanced curriculum over the period of at least a year. You need to consider the ways you are covering the specific interests and needs of the children, anything that might be happening locally that you might want to include in your planning and any particular strengths in the form of knowledge, skills, contacts, resources, and so on, that could be used to

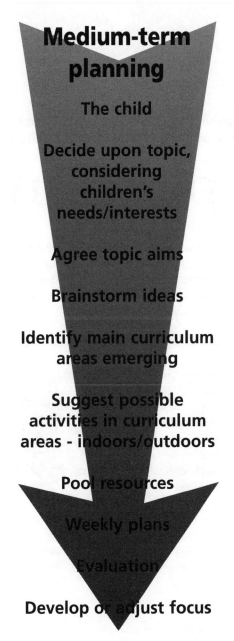

Medium-term planning

The child

Decide upon topic, considering children's needs/interests

Agree topic aims

Brainstorm ideas

Identify main curriculum areas emerging

Suggest possible activities in curriculum areas - indoors/outdoors

Pool resources

Weekly plans

Evaluation

Develop or adjust focus

full advantage of both staff and children. You need to plan for all the areas of learning in an integrated way if you are to ensure breadth and balance. This means decisions must be made early enough for all the above to be considered and discussed by all staff members thoroughly before final topics are chosen.

Medium-term planning

This ensures continuity (a focus on learning objectives over a length of time) and progression (how one activity leads onto another) through the six areas of learning over a term or half term, depending upon how you plan your topics. Without planning for continuity and progression you are not allowing children to develop through a balance of child-initiated and adult-initiated experiences. Children need opportunities to

repeat and practise in different contexts to consolidate their learning. The planning process allows you to support and extend their learning through all experiences available to them in your setting and in the local environment.

Remember to start with what a child 'can do' rather than 'can't do' and plan for progression from that starting point. For example, a child starts pre-school able to hold a book - how do you move them forward over the year? You include them in activities which involve choosing a book and holding it the right way. You show them how to turn the pages correctly one by one and from front to back. You read the left page before the right, go from left to right, top to bottom, and show how pictures tell the story of the book but the print contains a message, and so on. The child needs time to consolidate each stage before you plan to move them forward by focussing on a certain aspect in your planning.

At the medium-term stage it is an ideal time to use the seven-week overview sheet showing week by week activities over the six learning areas (see page 84). This allows you to see at a glance how you are introducing your topic and developing it over the half term. From this sheet you can write up your schemes of work.

Schemes of work

A scheme of work tells the inspector what, why and how you are doing an activity. It will link the activity to the ELG and tell you how it is to be resourced, for example:

- ❏ **What?** (activity) - using scales in the role-play shop

- ❏ **Why?** (ELGs) - to develop children's understanding of weight/use language such as 'heavier' or 'lighter' to compare quantities

- ❏ **How?** (organisation) - initially through adult-led play then free play

- ❏ **Resources** - shop, fruit and veg, balancing scales, money, till, paper and pens, bags, baskets

Always keep the why?/ELGs simple - it's no good listing everything you can think of to do with weight. Two achievable outcomes are better than a list of six non-achievable ones!

Short-term planning
This can be done weekly or fortnightly, depending upon how your team prefer to work. All staff should be involved and it's a good idea to get together at a set time, agreed by everyone.

Short-term planning allows you to focus on and address the needs of groups or individual children through differentiation, specific skills to be taught or observations that need to be made. You are identifying what children know and how you can move them forward.

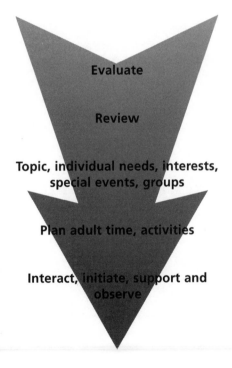

Evaluate

Review

Topic, individual needs, interests, special events, groups

Plan adult time, activities

Interact, initiate, support and observe

This is the time to allocate staff to activities and check resources. You should also evaluate how the planning for the week has gone and identify areas that need addressing as a result of this week's activities.

You need to check that all children have had the opportunity to join in the main activities even if they are not in every day. By keeping weekly activity and observation sheets you can identify certain days that certain children need to be encouraged to take part

in the focused activities. Use this time to discuss differentiation - how you plan to allow all children, including those with special needs, to have the same experiences as the other children. Differentiation allows each child to start from where they are and move forward. Think of all the different stages a child is at using scissors. Some can't hold a pair of scissors and therefore need one-to-one input. Others can snip but can't cut through, others can cut through but not around. If you have identified the different children at each stage you can allocate time and adult help to move each child on either by giving help on an individual basis or in a small group. These are the types of things that need to be discussed, identified and planned for at your weekly/fortnightly meetings.

Evaluation
This should be done weekly to identify or adjust what needs to be done next or to identify individual children with specific needs. You should also evaluate the topic at the end of the term as a whole, in other words how successful it has been, what the children particularly liked doing and what you feel didn't work as well as you'd hoped. This is always useful when you come to repeat the topic in the future.

It's sensible to keep an ongoing planning file at hand - this could include:

- Long-term planning
- Termly/half-termly topic planning covering the six areas of learning (medium term)
- Detailed schemes of work for each of the six areas of learning (medium term)
- Weekly/fortnightly planning sheet showing activities, objectives, resources, organisation, differentiation (short term)
- Observation and evaluation notes
- Jottings for future planning

Planning for assessment
We are all now expected to keep records of children's attainment and progress. These records are examined during inspection and should be available to the children's parents. Use planning to identify what activities you need to provide to develop a particular child or group of children further. Ongoing

assessment allows you to monitor in all six areas of learning providing you with useful information about a child's development and progress as a learner.

Assessment should be 'a process of observing children when they are actively involved in learning experiences' (*Promoting Quality* 1998). The two most popular ways of making assessments are when working with an individual child or small group or by on the spot or 'catch as you can', for example 'Playing a number game with Jack he was able to recognise and correctly name the numbers one to five' or 'Whilst in the writing corner Katja wrote her name using some letter shapes'.

Planning for assessment allows us to keep up-to-date ongoing records of the children in our setting, highlighting things like children who may be being overlooked or certain areas of the curriculum being left out. It is vital that assessments are not tests and are made through everyday planned activities within the nursery session.

Planning for play
All children's learning should be in the most natural way - through play. We plan for play by structuring an activity so that as the children enjoy themselves they are, through the experiences offered to them, learning without even knowing it!

If you had outlined in your planning that you were focussing on the circle shape and the mathematical language big/small, then you could structure the playdough activity to give the children experiences which involved both these outcomes. You could put circle shape cutters in two sizes on the table for the children to make birthday cakes. Whilst an adult was playing with the children at the table the language would be used naturally through questioning and conversation. This could be extended (differentiation) for the more able child by adding candles for them to count onto the cake, or for the less able child just concentrating on the shape of the cake rather than the size.

Pam Taylor

Medium term weekly planning sheet	Personal, Social and Emotional Development	Communication Language and Literacy	Mathematical Development	Knowledge and Understanding of the World	Physical Development	Creative Development	Home/ School
Week 1							
Week 2							
Week 3							
Week 4							
Week 5							
Week 6							
Week 7							

Play should be taken seriously! Julie Fisher and the Oxfordshire Early Years Team explain why and what you can do to make sure the opportunity is not missed

A play policy for the early years

Whether you are four or sixty four being playful is a crucial learning strategy. Playing with bricks, boats, balls or bytes gives the learner opportunities to explore, test ideas, take risks and enter imaginary worlds. For young children this process is particularly crucial. They have had so little experience of the world that almost everything is new, excites their curiosity and invites them to be playful.

A rationale for play

Play is one of the key processes, along with exploration and talk, through which children become competent, confident and independent learners. It is important to all other areas of learning because without the opportunity to play with materials, environments and ideas children will not develop those crucial ways of thinking and knowing that emerge from uncertainty and problem-solving. Through play children learn to be artists, writers, mathematicians and scientists. They learn to make sense of things in ways which strengthen their rapidly developing repertoire of skills and understandings. New brain research, from Oxford University and the Carnegie Commission in New York, demonstrates that if young children do not have certain key experiences in their lives, they lose the capacity to fully benefit from those experiences for ever. If young children are denied play, they may lose the capacity to be playful at critical times in their lives when learning demands it.

Progression

Play is not just for young children. There is a progression in playful behaviour which shows itself just as clearly in an adult learning to understand new technology as in a four-year-old learning to use a new construction kit. Playing is part of the human struggle to understand the world. If that behaviour is

Aims of a play policy

❑ To raise the awareness of all those involved in the setting of the importance of play within the planned curriculum.

❑ To involve staff, children, parents and managers in planning provision for play.

❑ To identify and plan the necessary space and resources to facilitate high quality play.

❑ To ensure that play provision and practice reflect the differing needs, interests and cultural backgrounds of individuals.

❑ To provide equality of access to play.

❑ To clarify the role of adults in supporting and extending children's play.

❑ To establish systems for planning and assessing children's learning through play.

❑ To put in place a framework for monitoring and continuously improving the quality of play within the setting.

absent then a child - or an adult - has lost one of the most powerful mechanisms for being an intuitive and innovative thinker and learner. When play does not progress in its complexity, then it can become an arid experience. It is all too easy to provide the same play environment without challenging whether it is relevant to that group of children or whether it is challenging them as learners. It takes a skilled adult to know when and how to extend children's play - either through the provision of different resources or by intervention with appropriate questions.

Why have a policy?

Having a policy for play helps establish its status in the early years curriculum. When adults work together to commit something to paper it sends a clear message that this issue is important to the setting. Writing a

policy together will encourage practitioners to share their understandings, beliefs and knowledge about play. This will strengthen their own expertise and the expertise of the setting as a whole in promoting play as integral to its practice. The process of debating aims, principles and processes of play is likely to help staff become clearer about their views and more effective in their planning and assessment of children's play experiences.

Creating a policy

There are various ways of creating an effective policy and the following suggestions may be of help in getting started.

1. Arrange a staff meeting to make sure that everyone understands the purpose of writing the policy and that, from the beginning, they have ownership of the process and the outcome. At this staff meeting, make some decisions about the following issues:

(a) What is your definition of the word play? Play has many definitions and none of them are definitive. What matters is that as a staff you come to a 'working definition' and feel able to share this with others - parents, governors and managers - when you talk about play.

(b) Agree your aims in writing the policy. What and who is it for? How do you hope it will affect your practice?

(c) Decide on the principles which will underpin your policy and practice. What statements would you want to make about play that will help you justify your commitment to it as central to your curriculum provision?

(d) Discuss any other issues you want to include in your policy for example:

- ❏ the provision of an outdoor area for learning through play;
- ❏ the use of space for play;
- ❏ the provision of resources;
- ❏ adult support for children's play;
- ❏ planning for play;
- ❏ equal opportunities for play;
- ❏ the observation and assessment of play.

2. Write a first rough draft of the policy, including all the elements which you think are important. The draft will be revisited and refined throughout the process of evaluation and discussion about current provision and practice.

3. Agree a strategy for auditing existing provision and practice. Before a policy can be written it is important to find out, for example, what condition resources are in, whether all areas of play provision are well used, whether planning for play addresses all aspects of the Early Learning Goals, how adults support and extend children's play and what assessments are made of children at play.

4. Discuss the outcomes of the audit. What is practice like now? What is there to celebrate? What areas need development? At this point it is a good idea to revisit the first draft of the policy as you will have a clearer idea about whether you have included all the aspects that are important to you.

5. Prioritise the areas for development. Which needs to come first in order for other aspects to follow? Which can be easily managed and which will take more time or further money?

Prioritising is crucial because time and money are always limited and the more limited they are, the more important it is to ensure that they are spent on the most important things.

6. Plan who will do what - and by when. Involve everybody and be very clear about what everyone's precise task will be. Write this down - it's easier then to check on what has been achieved. Who will be responsible for making a long list of possible new resources? Who will draft a booklet for

parents about play? Who is to visit the nursery down the road to look at their record-keeping for play?

7. Implement your plan. Make sure that everyone is keeping to their allotted tasks, are clear about what they are doing - and are getting on with it! Give a long enough time for the jobs to be done, but not so long that people's enthusiasm goes off the boil.

8. Evaluate the results of your efforts. Have all the changes been implemented? What impact have they had on the quality of children's play and the quality of their learning?

Have all the aims of your policy been met? Have all your principles been adhered to? If you feel satisfied that the policy has given you a rigorous framework for development, then now is the time to remove the word 'draft'! Otherwise, revise the policy in the light of your experience.

9. Improve. No policy should ever be written in stone. Both policy and practice need to be constantly revisited to ensure that provision is always improving on previous best. The policy should be reviewed to see if it continues to challenge all staff to provide the best possible play experiences for children. The quality of practice should be monitored, through observation of children and adults in action, to ensure that what is

written down in the policy is actually happening in practice.

Involving a range of people

Once staff have agreed a framework for their own policy it should be shared with other staff - such as classroom assistants or lunch-time supervisors - and with governors or managers, in order that they are familiar with and come to understand the policy. When all those responsible for a setting understand the value of play, then the adults working in the setting are more likely to get their backing and support.

Many settings find it valuable to include parent consultation at this stage, so that parents' concerns, comments and enthusiasm can enrich the process. Early years staff may find that they are challenged by parents about the value of play. Often parents need to understand the difference between play in the home and play in the setting. Spending time and energy agreeing the main points for a play policy can give staff invaluable opportunities to articulate their rationale, knowing that if the same question was asked by a parent that they have rehearsed the answers rigorously and thoughtfully. It is also important for the unity of the setting that if the parent were to ask the same question of a different member of staff, that they would get much the same answer.

These are some of the areas and issues you need to address when writing your own play policy

Model play **policy**

Definition

Play is the natural way in which children learn. It is the process through which children explore, investigate, recreate and come to understand their world. Play is an activity in which everything that a child knows and can do is practised or used to make sense of what is new. Play cannot be directed by adults. An adult can support, enhance or extend play, but the moment they interfere or dictate its progress then it ceases to be play.

A rationale for play

Play is a vital component of children's lives, without which their potential for healthy, mental and physical development is undermined. It provides the mechanism for children to gain mastery over their world and is an important medium through which skills are developed and practised. Play is essential for physical, emotional and spiritual growth, intellectual and educational development and the acquisition of social and behavioural skills.

Principles of play

❑ Play is an intrinsic part of children's learning and development.

❑ Play has many possible but no prescriptive outcomes.

❑ Play challenges children and offers them the chance to learn in breadth and depth.

❑ Play draws on what children already know and can do and enables them to master what is new.

❑ Play enables children to apply existing knowledge and to practise their skills.

❑ Play offers children opportunities to explore feelings and relationships, ideas and materials, connections and consequences.

❑ Play empowers children to make choices, to solve problems and to be independent in their learning.

❑ Play encourages children to struggle, to

take risks and to become resilient as learners.

❑ Play can be supported and extended but not interfered with by adults.

❑ Play presents no barriers to children because of their culture, language, abilities or gender.

Planning for play

Your play policy needs to make statements about the following issues:

Long term

❑ How will adults plan for space, both indoors and outdoors, to be maximised for learning through play?

❑ What resources are necessary, both indoors and outdoors, to support play activities across all the ELGs?

❑ How will you demonstrate that children have equality of access to a broad and balanced range of play during their time in your setting?

❑ How do you demonstrate that you are clear about the potential learning (understandings, skills, knowledge, attitudes) in all areas of play provision in your setting?

Medium term

❑ How does your planning ensure that children's play this term/week, builds on and extends that which they have already experienced?

❑ How will adults' time be planned to ensure that play is observed, supported and extended where appropriate?

❑ Who will be responsible for planning additional resources for play for a particular theme/topic/experience?

❑ How will parents be helped to understand the learning through play which you have planned?

Short term

❑ Can adults explain clearly why a particular play activity has been planned on a particular day?

❑ Is your planning sufficiently flexible to

Using the model play policy

This model play policy is not an attempt to write something that will suit every setting. It is offered as a starting point for staff debate. Each setting will need to amend and adapt the policy in order for it to meet their own particular needs. We suggest that each section is discussed, debated, changed and customised to suit your community, your age range and your setting.

ensure that the spontaneous needs of children can be addressed/incorporated in your provision for play?

❑ How will the play needs of individual children, as well as the group in general, be identified and planned?

Observing and assessing play

In order to plan effectively to meet the learning needs of young children through play, the policy needs to confirm:

❑ that observation of children at play is critical in order to have evidence from which to plan for their current needs and abilities;

❑ that observations of children at play should be recorded as part of the ongoing evidence of children's development;

❑ how observations of children at play will be shared and discussed between all adults in the setting in order to inform decisions about what is to be planned in the short and the longer term;

❑ that observations of children at play should inform any summary of judgements about children's current abilities to pass on to parents or before transfer to another setting;

❑ how adults' time is to be planned in order to record both planned and spontaneous observations of play.

Evaluation

The play provision in your setting needs to be evaluated in order to establish that it is meeting the learning needs of your children. It will be necessary to track how individual children as well as groups of children make use of the planned play experiences.

Long term

❑ Do children use the full range of play provision offered?

❑ Does any area need to be made more stimulating or challenging?

Medium term

❑ Are children making progress in their play - whether it is through exploration, consolidation or extension of skills and understandings?

❑ Are adults enhancing the quality of play?

Short term

❑ Are the needs of individual children being met by the planned play provision?

❑ Have staff made sufficient observations of play to provide evidence of children's learning and development?

Practical considerations

The following are some suggestions of practical considerations to address in your policy. You will need to add to and extend these in order to set your own standards for high quality provision.

Space and resources

❑ The availability and use of space both indoors and out.

❑ The provision and planned development of resources for learning indoors.

❑ The provision and planned development of resources for learning outdoors.

Time

❑ The time given to play activities within the planned curriculum.

❑ The time given to children to remain at play without interruption.

❑ The time created to observe and assess children at play.

Adults

❑ The knowledge and skills that adults need to support and extend children at play.

❑ The knowledge and skills that adults need to observe and assess children at play.

❑ The training opportunities available to staff to develop their expert understanding of the place of play in children's learning.

Julie Fisher and the Oxfordshire Early Years Team

How does play in educational settings differ from play in other contexts? The Oxfordshire Early Years Team looks at the critical role of adults in establishing and sustaining high quality learning through play

Supporting children's play

Most early childhood educators would agree that play should have a central role in the early years curriculum. But increasingly, many feel that play is being squeezed out of children's experiences and that it is harder than ever to justify play as a significant part of the educational day.

What does high quality play look like?

Play is one of the most crucial ways in which young children come to make sense of the world around them. Through play, children acquire understandings, skills and strategies that will be the underpinning of all their future educational and life experiences. Play provides children with their first experiences of the astonishing range of their body's capabilities. It develops imagination, curiosity, ways of communicating and social competence . . . and all in contexts which children find absorbing and fun!

High quality play challenges children. It excites and stimulates them. It has purpose and relevance to what they want to know and what they want to achieve. It is an active process that demands the involvement of their body and their mind in a search for answers to the endless questions they pose for themselves. High quality play enables children to progress through exploration and investigation to mastery and control of resources, the environment and their experiences. It is the process of play that matters more than the end product. What children try out, do, refine and adapt in the process of play offers learning opportunities unparalleled in more adult directed learning.

Giving status to play

The problem with a great deal of play in educational settings is that it is reduced to the 'second division' of classroom activity. It is an activity that is done once the 'work' is finished, it is under-resourced and is not assessed as rigorously as more adult-directed learning. When play is reduced to this status in a setting then the quality of play suffers. If play is a key process of learning then it must be at the heart of children's educational experiences. It should form an integral part of the process of teaching and learning and be treated with the respect it deserves.

There is a fine line between intervening and interfering. When adults interfere with play they can take it over, dominating both the process and the outcomes.

It is the adults in the setting who determine the status of play within that setting and their belief and enthusiasm which will raise the profile of play amongst fellow practitioners, parents and children. When adults understand the powerful nature of play then the learning environments they create and the experiences they plan all harness this most natural and effective process of learning.

Preparing an appropriate environment

An appropriate environment for play is one that attracts children to a range of play opportunities. It needs to be inviting, stimulating and cause children to ask such questions as 'What is this?', 'What does it do?' and 'What can I make it do?' The environment should reflect the breadth and balance of the early years curriculum, providing opportunities for personal, social and emotional development; interaction and communication in a variety of situations; mathematical and scientific understanding; creative, imaginative and physical challenge. All of these experiences should be planned to take place both indoors and outdoors so that play can be extended and enhanced as children move from one environment to the other. An appropriate environment for play should include a rich variety of good quality resources.

It is important to remember that resources need to be selected with an awareness of the equality of access and opportunity which they provide for children. They should be appropriate for both boys and girls, for example providing dressing-up clothes that encourage boys into the role-play area. They should reflect a wide range of cultures that have been introduced to children in meaningful ways, for example Chinese cooking utensils as part of Chinese New Year celebrations. They should also be appropriate for a range of special needs, interests and circumstances. No child should feel excluded from an activity or experience because the resources available reflect a cultural, gender, social or ability bias.

Planning for learning

Although children learn spontaneously through play it is the role of the adult to ensure that in an educational setting play is planned for in a rigorous and systematic way. This does not mean that children do what adults tell them in play situations but rather that adults select equipment and resources and give children experiences that enable them to play in purposeful and meaningful ways.

In their long- and medium-term planning, adults identify what it is that they want children to learn. These stages ensure that children receive their curriculum entitlement and that their learning progresses. It is at the short term stage of planning that the detail of the activities and experiences are identified in order to ensure that the needs of individual and groups of children are being met. Well planned play experiences cut across artificial subject boundaries and empower children to use and apply a whole range of skills, strategies, knowledge and understanding in contexts that are relevant, challenging and absorbing.

In a nursery school the adults had identified that the older boys needed more experience of role play, to improve their relationships with other children. A visit to the fishmongers in the local market sparked imaginative play of the highest quality as children, dressed in boaters and aprons, wrote a chalkboard of 'daily specials' and weighed and costed lobsters, crabs, eels and whelks. The boys, stimulated by the male role models in the fishmongers, took an active part in the recreation of the market stall. The adults had given the children a purposeful stimulus, the appropriate resources, good role models and the time and space to interpret their experiences in meaningful ways.

for long enough before intervening. It can be all too easy to misinterpret the play that is taking place and to make assumptions about what it is that children are doing and why. Adults need to recognise that even if they have provided resources for a purpose, for example climbing apparatus to develop children's physical co-ordination, that children might just turn this apparatus into a den because at that moment it meets their needs and interests to do so! This does not make the play worthless but rather shows the creative and fertile imaginations of children. The appropriate response to this scenario is to observe and record what children are doing and learning in their play and, in the light of what is seen, to readjust the short-term plans.

Observing and assessing play

If play is to have status in a setting then adults must observe and assess what children are learning in ways that are as rigorous and systematic as they are for any other activity. There are things that adults learn about children when they are playing that they will not learn from observing more adult-directed activities. Very often adults need to stand back and watch and wait in order to see the rich variety of understandings and skills which children at play reveal. As adults watch children at play important questions will arise, such as, 'Are the children involved and absorbed?', 'What are they doing?', 'What are they learning?', 'Do I need to intervene at this moment?' 'Do I need to plan for something more challenging in the future?' Having made such observations it is important to record those which give evidence of significant development in order to show progress in learning. Then, adults are in a position to make use of their observations and records in deciding what play opportunities need to be provided in the future.

Interacting and intervening in play

There are times when children need the time and space to play uninterrupted. The role of the adult here is to have provided resources, experiences and stimuli so that as children play independently, everything possible has been thought about and planned for to ensure the experience will be of good quality. Even when children play independently they should not be abandoned! Adults may be involved with other children but still keep an eye on what is happening in the home area or the sand play and, perhaps, make sure that those children playing uninterrupted have the opportunity to talk about their independent experiences later in the day.

But there are times when the quality of play will be increased through adult intervention and interaction. The skill of the adult is in judging when this is appropriate. There is a fine line between intervening and interfering. When adults interfere with play they can take it over, dominating both the process and the outcomes. This mistake is usually made when adults have not observed

The role of the adult in supporting children's play is demanding and challenging. It requires great sensitivity and great skill. It rests on a deep knowledge of how children learn and an appreciation of what they are learning in situations which are usually far more complex than they may appear. If play is of high quality then it takes sustained observation and skilled interpretation before all its many layers are revealed. Those who undervalue the place of play are frequently not sufficiently knowledgeable to appreciate how remarkable play is as a vehicle for learning. All of us in early childhood education must do what we can to understand and promote the power of play.

Julie Fisher

Outdoor play means different things to different people. For some it is a time for children to let off steam and for staff to have a break. For others the nursery garden is at the heart of children's learning, a place where children can develop their minds as well as their bodies. What does outdoor play mean for you?

The value of **outdoor play**

Outdoors offers unique learning experiences which cannot be provided indoors. It is an ever-changing space which provides new sights, sounds and sensations. Nature can be experienced at first hand and living things observed in their natural habitat. It offers space and freedom for children to explore and investigate, to imagine and create and to try things out. Outdoors can complement the indoors and offer activities such as painting, chalking and modelling on a larger scale. Children can play more freely with the sand and water when they don't have to worry about the mess.

We know how important the outdoors is for developing gross motor skills such as climbing, balancing, sliding and swinging but we must not ignore other fundamental areas of learning. Climbing up, over, through, on top of, inside and underneath objects builds not just physical dexterity, strength and confidence, but mathematical concepts too. Researchers such as Chris Athey have shown that whole body experience of movement is essential for young children to build an understanding of abstract concepts such as height, weight, gradient and space. Children manoeuvring wheeled toys around, for example, experience speed, distance, weight, forces, friction, energy and gradient, which are vital aspects of early scientific learning.

Movement is closely related to children's social and emotional growth. Being able to do something well makes a child feel confident, it boosts their self-esteem, and sense of well-being, giving a feeling of 'I can do it' which research has indicated is vital to later learning. Vigorous movement is also crucial for children's health and research at

Exeter University suggests that even young children are not getting enough exercise to prevent later heart disease.

Creativity and imagination can thrive outdoors. Think about how much of children's imaginative play involves movement and going somewhere. Outdoors, fire-fighters can travel to put out the fire, picnickers can get dressed up, pack their bags and go for the picnic and then return home, horses can gallop and aeroplanes fly! Dramatic play takes on a new dimension - 'The Three Billy Goats Gruff' story becomes more meaningful (and fun!) when you can really trip trap over a wooden bridge!

Today when there are fewer and fewer opportunities for safe, child-initiated play, rich outdoor provision becomes more important in fostering some of the essential aspects of childhood, such as freedom, spontaneity, joy and wonder. Outdoors can offer safe opportunities for children to take risks, try things out, to develop confidence, to express their noisy exuberance and the sheer joy of being alive!

But what about the curriculum?

Outdoors is much more than just physical learning. It should offer opportunities for learning in all areas of the curriculum. There seems to be no aspect of learning which cannot be fostered outside.

Observing insects under logs, hiding in an upturned box, measuring how long the ice takes to melt, watering the garden with the hose, listening to the tinkle of the wind chimes, digging for ancient treasure, writing price tickets for the pretend aeroplane, acting out a well-loved story, smelling the newly opened lilac; these are all part of the magic of a properly planned outdoor area. However, they are also essential ingredients of scientific, mathematical, creative, historical, geographical, and literary learning.

Outdoors, children are exercising and developing their minds as well as their bodies, providing the resources are well planned and the adults are well informed.

What should you provide?

The quality of children's experiences and play outdoors will depend on the quality of the provision. A bare piece of tarmac will inspire nobody! Think of creating flexible spaces for different types of play, for example an area for climbing, an area for imaginative and construction play, an area for digging and investigating, a sound and sensory area, and an area for growing herbs, flowers and vegetables. An area for large scale creative activities is important and wall space can be used for big painting, chalking and writing. Opportunities for transporting objects and people in wheelbarrows, trucks and carts are also necessary, as are spaces and objects where children can hide or get inside such as boxes, bushes and hidey holes. Small seats or logs can provide secluded places to talk and to watch others.

You don't need expensive equipment - children quickly tire of structures such as a fixed fire engine. Just give them some boxes, crates, tyres, small ladders and planks and let their creativity and imagination run wild - they can be a fire engine today but a bus tomorrow! Flexibility, versatility and robustness are key criteria when buying equipment. 'What can children learn from this?' and 'How many different ways could the children use this?' are good questions to ask. Scrap materials from local firms and from parents can be valuable resources outside. (See page 95 for ideas.)

What is the adult's role outside?

Research by Stephen and Corinne Hutt found that the adult role changed from being participatory indoors to being monitorial outside. Too often adults can be seen patrolling, supervising, chatting to each other or standing looking cold and bored! Does this apply to your setting? Be honest! In effective early years settings adults can be seen joining in the play, listening, talking, discussing and sharing exciting discoveries as well observing and recording what children are doing. Think of the mathematical concepts involved in this comment: 'Wow, you're right at the top of the climbing frame! You're even taller than I am now! I wonder how far you can see? Over the fence? Oh, that's a long way!'

Adults need to communicate through their behaviour and their talk that the outdoors is an interesting and challenging place. Children quickly catch on to what is considered important and what is trivial and behave accordingly. If you spend all your time sorting out disputes, arguments and turns on the bikes then children will use them for that purpose. While it is vital that children are safe, it is still possible to interact with individuals and small groups while keeping a watchful eye on the whole play area. Many settings are now choosing to abandon short rotas so that staff can spend a longer time really developing the play outside. Nursery managers need to be good role models for their staff. Enthusiastically preparing the outdoor area on a cold frosty morning can help to change staff attitudes. Issuing directives from a warm office does not!

How long should they be outside?

If we see the outdoors as an important learning environment then it is important to give it equal status with the indoors and allow children to move freely between each area for as long as possible. This is the ideal, as play can flow from one area to another, children have enough time to pursue meaningful activities and can be helped to make connections between the two areas.

Too often adults can be seen patrolling, supervising, chatting to each other or standing looking cold and bored! Does this apply to your setting? Be honest! In effective early years settings adults can be seen joining in the play, listening, talking, discussing and sharing exciting discoveries as well observing and recording what children are doing.

When the outdoors is fixed to a certain time children and staff often see it as a break, a time to run around and let off steam. Children can be seen abandoning their indoor activities as they rush for the door. Having too many children outdoors at one time is both unsafe and unproductive whereas about half outside and half inside can improve the quality of play in both areas.

No outdoor space?

Try to bring the outdoors inside with plants and other living and growing things and provide free access to climbing and energetic physical play indoors. You need to organise regular trips out to the park, woods, fields or nearby places of interest. You can prepare resource boxes of materials and games which can be taken outdoors or used in the park. But all this is no substitute for a proper, secure outdoor area. Remember that Ofsted (1994) states that 'resources include the indoors and outdoors and should reflect the total curriculum offered'. Argue, lobby, raise funds, mobilise your parents, and campaign for appropriate facilities outdoors. Children need powerful voices speaking on their behalf.

Helen Tovey

Outdoors can offer a rich range of learning experiences for the under-fives, or it can be a place for children to run around and let off steam. The difference lies in the provision and in the planning. Helen Tovey explains

Planning and organising
outdoor play

First, take a close look at your outdoor area and review what you already have. Be critical and consider what learning is actually going on outside. Track individual children and collect detailed observations of what they are really doing outside not what you think they might be doing. Meet together as a staff and ask yourself these questions. Does the outdoors:

- offer opportunities for learning in all areas of the curriculum?
- link with indoors?
- offer excitement, interest and sustained involvement?
- offer opportunities for exploratory, sensory, imaginative, physical and creative play?

Plan for the weather

In Denmark children are outside in all weathers, sun and snow. 'There is no such thing as bad weather in Denmark only bad clothes' (Cath Arnold *TES* 7/3/97) Yet in this country we tend to find any excuse not

to go outside. Ask yourself the question 'Bad weather for whom?' Young children are fascinated by changes in the seasons and weather. Snow, ice, puddles and shadows can provoke curiosity and delight and provide valuable sources of learning. Work with parents to ensure that children are adequately protected whatever the weather (particularly the sun). Make sure children have boots to wear and you have a system for pegging them together and storing them. Keep spare coats or macs for those who come unprepared (children and staff!) A collection of children's umbrellas can be useful for drizzly days. Prepare resource boxes for unexpected days. For example, a box for windy days might consist of a kite, long streamers and fabrics to tie to the fence, balloons, materials to make simple kites, bubble blowers, a pin wheel, books and stories about the wind, and so on. You can plan to be spontaneous!

Prepare the environment

The outdoors needs to be as carefully planned and prepared as the indoors. Plan to create flexible spaces for different types of play, for example an area for climbing, an area for imaginative and construction play, an area for digging and investigation, and a garden area with herbs, flowers and vegetables. A messy area for large-scale creative activities is important and wall space can be used for painting, chalking and writing.

You need space for wheelbarrows, trucks and carts as well as spaces and objects where children can hide or get inside such as boxes, bushes and hidey holes. Think about how the ELGs relate to outdoors and plan appropriate provision. Here are some ideas to get you started.

Physical Development

Try to make sure that there are opportunities for children to go over, under, through, in between and inside objects and equipment. Make provision for sliding, climbing, balancing, swinging, hanging, rolling, pushing, pulling, throwing, and catching. Ensure that there is opportunity for developing fine motor control skills, for example through handling insects or collecting small stones. Provide real tools for gardening and woodwork.

Knowledge and Understanding of the World

Provide a damp area with bushes, logs and rocks where children can investigate small creatures and insects. Provide a digging patch where children can dig, sieve the soil, find worms and insects (or if they dig deeply become mini-archaeologists and discover relics from the past).

Provide regular opportunities for growing herbs, flowers and vegetables. Artichokes, sunflowers, gourds, and lemon balm grow fast! Fix up pulleys and rope so that children can lift heavy objects or carry water or sand across the playground.

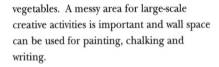

Make sure that children have access to natural materials such as sand, water, gravel, wood chips and forest bark so that they can explore the properties and behaviour of materials as they create imaginative scenarios. Lengths of guttering from a builders' merchants are a cheap resource which can be used with milk crates to build waterfalls, to transport water from one side of the playground to another and to introduce children to gradient. An old bicycle wheel with plastic cups attached to the rim makes an excellent water wheel for exploring rotation and the force of water.

Creative Development

Provide open-ended props such as boxes, crates, wheels, ladders and hats for imaginative play. Make sure that there are places where children can hide and create dens. Encourage children to use objects to 'stand for' other objects, for example leaves for food, twigs for a broom or a ladder as a lawnmower. Link imaginative play with first-hand experience such as a visit to a fire station, a garage, an airport or a garden centre.

Supplement your indoor activities with large-scale provision outdoors, for example huge paintings, large brushes, wall murals, playground chalking, large scale printing and scrap modelling.

Collect interesting stones, pebbles, shells, logs, petals and leaves for picture and pattern making outside. You can even use the fence for weaving with long strips of fabric! Wind chimes, percussion trees, bands and carnivals can all be explored outdoors.

Communication, Language and Literacy

Encourage children to act out familiar stories by providing appropriate props. *The Gingerbread Man*, *The Three Billy Goats Gruff*, *Bears in the Night*, and *The Lighthouse Keeper's Lunch* can all be extended outdoors. Provide office type materials for imaginative play so children are involved with writing messages, letters, taking orders, making appointments and writing tickets.

Use signs, symbols and logos as part of the play so that children are using print for a purpose and begin to recognise the symbolic nature of signs, for example traffic signs, directions signs, notices such as 'Way in', 'Way out', 'Pay here', 'CAUTION Hard hat area!', 'Please shut the gate', 'Parking', 'No entry'. Children quickly learn to read print which is part of their play and is meaningful

to them. Make sure that adults talk with and listen to children outside and that there are plenty of new and interesting things to talk about.

Mathematical Development

If children are able to move and travel easily through spaces they will have the chance to explore words and concepts such as higher, lower, forwards, backwards, inside, outside, far away and near, narrow and wide, on top of and underneath, up and down. Use numbers as part of the play, for wheeled toys, pretend boats, bus stops, car parks, aeroplane seats, tickets, and so on. Make simple games such as skittles (empty plastic bottles) which are knocked off a table with a soft ball. Provide an easel and paper so children can record (with emergent writing and tally marks) their name and what they have scored. Look for real opportunities for measuring, for example temperature or the height of the sunflowers.

Personal, Social and Emotional Development

Encourage collaborative as well as individual play. Try to provide wheeled toys which require collaboration and social interaction rather than individual trikes. Encourage large-scale problem-solving and construction, for example, building a fire engine or a bridge from milk crates, or trying to transport water from one side of the playground to another using guttering and milk crates. Provide small secluded areas, perhaps a circle of logs, or some seating under a tree, or a small picnic table where children can sit and talk or look at books. Children can be encouraged to care for their environment by sweeping spilt sand, puddles or leaves, to care for living things and to develop a real sense of wonder at the natural world.

Planning

First observe what children are doing outside. What are they interested in? How do they use the equipment? What are they really paying attention to? Then make provision that builds on and extends this. For example, if children are playing fire engines you might provide construction material for building a fire engine, including some hose pipes and small ladders.

With the children you might create a fire station complete with office telephone and maps, plus clip-boards to take messages. Badges and numbers for the firefighters can be made, and numbers of houses identified. You might want to make a small real fire and experiment with hose pipes and water. Water play indoors and outdoors could include tubing of different diameters with a focus on 'going through'. A trip out to a fire station or to find a fire hydrant could be planned and activities extended indoors. Depending on the size of the outdoor area try to include provision which supports learning in all areas of the curriculum, say, over a week.

Safety

Safety is paramount outside and it is important that all equipment is checked regularly for splinters, rust and repairs. Appropriate clothing and shoes are vital if children are to climb and explore safely. However, an over-zealous attention to safety by people who do not understand about children's development can result in environments which are far from safe. To develop confidence children need challenge. They need to be able to extend their range of skills, to take some risks and try things out. To be safe an environment must be challenging. Take away the challenge and we create unsafe environments for children and run the risk of creating a generation of timid children who lack the opportunity and skill to be confident and safe. We need to be powerful advocates for children and make sure that our voice is heard.

Useful resources

Expensive equipment is not always necessary to create a rich learning environment outside. Imagination, a vision of what is possible and a sound understanding of children's development is much more important. Remember that Margaret Macmillan, one of the nursery pioneers, created her own garden from a piece of derelict land!

Helen Tovey

For construction
Milk crates
Traffic cones (discarded)
Bread baskets
Tyres
Wheels
Large cardboard boxes
Packing cases / crates
Cardboard reels
Small wooden planks
Small ladders
Steering wheels

For imaginative play
Picnic baskets
Shopping baskets
Suitcases
Old blankets
Fabrics
Tents
A variety of pumps
Tool bags
Assorted helmets and hats
Jackets
Old cameras
Plastic tubing / hose pipes
Tea trolleys
Old torches / lamps
Old car radios
Earphones
Signs / notices / logos
Keyboards

Telephones
Maps
Tickets

For creative play
Pebbles / shells
Log pieces
Decorator's brushes
Buckets
Paint rollers
Large paper / card
Chalk boards
Playground chalk
Large objects for printing
Drawing boards / pens
Long strips of material
(for weaving)

Natural materials
Gravel
Sand / water
Soil / mud
Logs and bark chippings
Stones and shells
Leaves and petals

For investigation
Digging area
Small tools (real)
Magnifiers
Sieves
Watering cans
Large logs and stones
Herbs / veg / flowers
Pots and growbags

Ropes and pulleys
Binoculars
Hose pipe and sprinkler
Bird table and feeders
Guttering and pipes
Plastic beer barrels
Wheels
Water wheels
(made from old bicycle wheels)
Weather vane

Equipment
Wooden hut
Hidey holes
Stairs
Moveable ladders
A frames and planks
Slides
Wheelbarrows
Trucks and carts
Wheeled vehicles
Barrels
Tunnels
Sand pit / waterpool
Tap / hose pipe
Spare coats
Boots
Umbrellas

All materials whether bought or collected need to be checked regularly for safety and suitability.

Safety is paramount outside and it is important that all equipment is checked regularly for splinters, rust and repairs. Appropriate clothing and shoes are vital if children are to climb and explore safely.

Most good early years settings have a messy area with a water tray - or perhaps just a bowl of water - but why? What is it about playing with water that can teach children so much? And how can you help them get the most out of such regular everyday activities? Vicky Hislop asks you to stop and think

The value of water play

Water play can provide the children with a range of sensory experiences and is a valuable support to almost any topic. With enough equipment and some imagination you can incorporate it into many activities.

Those of you who are responsible for the planning and running of an early years curriculum spend a great deal of time planning new activities, making sure that the equipment is available and that the session is successful. During this process it is easy to overlook the regular activities such as water play. Even routine activities need planning for and evaluating. Using water as a teaching tool is valuable and easy - make sure you make the most of it!

Evaluate what you are doing

To re-evaluate water play you need to look closely at what you are doing, monitor its usefulness and allow for new ideas and creativity. The first step in such a process would be to do a quick survey on your current water play area.

❏ Is the floor safe? Some floors become very slippery when wet and may benefit from a non-slip mat at water play time. Some floors, especially wooden ones, may need protecting.

❏ Is the tray easy to use/ big enough/ easy to empty? You will not want to have too many children at one time playing with the water; enough room to move for about four children is usually the best size. Can you fill and drain the tray easily? Remember that you are responsible for your own health and safety and lifting trays full of water is a recipe for a bad back.

❏ Do you have enough support equipment? Changing the toys and equipment often keeps the water tray a valuable learning

experience. Jugs, strainers and buckets are useful but tend to become uninteresting on their own after a time. Plan to combine other equipment with water now and again.

❏ Are the children all getting a turn? Keep an eye out for the quieter ones who may be missing out in the hustle and bustle. Are there children with special needs who need adapted equipment?

❏ What suggestions do the staff have? Listen to each others ideas and be prepared to feed back to each other regularly. Use this information to help you in planning for improving the effectiveness of water play time - aim for as wide a selection of ideas as possible to maintain interest.

Links with the ELGs

If your activity is designed to support the children's knowledge and understanding of the world you could encourage staff to discuss:

❏ Properties of water

❏ Properties of wet and dry objects
❏ Changes and similarities in wet and dry things
❏ Displacement and volume (read *Mr Archimedes' Bath* for this one!)
❏ Communities that live on water, near water, with little water - find pictures of drought stricken communities, fishing communities, Venice, stilt houses in Borneo, Chinese junks.
❏ Water conservation and the implications of water scarcity, what we use water for, what life would be like without it.
❏ Natural water exploration - ponds, puddles, rain, stream, drains. How each forms, what purpose each serves and how to differentiate between each.
❏ The rain/cloud/rain cycle - where rain falls, why and where it goes.

A maths activity could include;

❏ Volume and shape - look at the capacity of each tub and cup in your tray, look at sponges and the shapes you can make with them. Feeling brave? Add shredded paper to the water tray!
❏ Weight (wet and dry) - where does the water

go? How can we tell it is there? Weigh a sponge dry and then wet.

- ❑ Displacement - measuring the space an object has taken up in the water.
- ❑ Changes - learning that changes can be monitored and measured.
- ❑ Describing changes - finding the vocabulary and the framework to record changes.
- ❑ Shallow/deep, more/less - opposites and similarities. Look for pattern and repetition.

Personal and social learning takes place in many aspects of the early years day but targets specific to the water tray may include:

- ❑ Working as a group, being aware of the needs and desires of others
- ❑ Hygiene, skin care
- ❑ Cleansing properties of water
- ❑ Preparation and safety
- ❑ Rules of the activity - splashing each other, sharing equipment, attention, and so on
- ❑ Wearing protective clothing - independent dressing and drying
- ❑ Water as a drink, essential to life, being responsible for our own health and aware of what is good for us

The use of as many different words as possible and the introduction of new words is a prime early years role and all activities should plan to provide for this learning.

- ❑ Describing words, finding the vocabulary to express meaning and experience
- ❑ New words - use relevant vocabulary whenever possible. Don't expect it all to stick first time but don't be afraid of using 'big' words!
- ❑ Nuances of meaning - the difference between apparently similar words such as 'tip' and 'pour'
- ❑ Widening experiences, trying out new ideas and concepts
- ❑ Water based stories and sea, river and lake legends - Neptune, Loch Ness, *The Water Babies*

Physical development is about small careful movements as well as the larger activities. Small motor skills and balance are easy to develop in a water-based activity and the developing of large motor skills in water outside on a warm day is one of the joys of childhood!

- ❑ Carrying fluids - on a tray, in a cup
- ❑ Scooping out floating objects
- ❑ Catching slippery ones - soap, plastic fish
- ❑ Controlling movements on purpose
- ❑ Rolling, floating, jumping and wading in a paddling pool

Good nursery managers know that creativity is not restricted to art and craft. It is about making the most of every opportunity.

- ❑ Use water to create shape and movement
- ❑ Mix coloured water
- ❑ Scent water
- ❑ Thicken water
- ❑ Look at colours in water, add colours
- ❑ Bubbles as an art medium
- ❑ Adding water to other art media

Staff who are working with a manager who understands the possibilities offered by water will soon come up with many and varied ideas for individual activities of their own.

Planning a new nursery?

If you are fortunate enough to be planning a new nursery or facility what about incorporating a bath or shower for all year round fun in water? What about a jacuzzi type base in the bath or a shaped one? An outdoor shower for the summer is great fun but a hose and sprinkler will do just as well - make the most of the whole activity, allowing plenty of time for dressing and undressing independently. Outdoor water play takes on a new meaning when you have pulleys, buckets, water-wheels and pipes to route the water through. There are some excellent outdoor water systems on the market which, although expensive, offer wonderful learning experiences.

Nowhere to put a water tray?

For some groups, with limited space and resources, it is simply not possible to have a water tray. Yet many come up with wonderful ideas for coping in those circumstances! The use of buckets, small bowls, washing-up bowls and sinks is widespread. Have you thought of using roller paint trays? The shallow and deep end make for some variety and allow for individual water play, but will need to be closely monitored as they are very hard to carry or move safely. They are easily stored. Little children can have endless fun pretend painting an outside wall with a cheap sponge roller, a tray and water.

It is easy to overlook playing with water. Having the tray out daily will provide much that you may not know you are missing and you will wonder how you managed when you only brought it out now and again. Make the storage, setting up and clearing away as easy as possible, plan for specific activities and evaluate their effectiveness and you will come to value the good old-fashioned water tray for the wonderful opportunities it can offer!

Vicky Hislop

Dr Benjamin Spock in his book *Baby and Child Care* claimed that 'How happily a person gets along as an adult ... depends a great deal on how he got along with other children when he was young'. Is circle time old-fashioned common sense or new psychology? Sara Stocks examines the theory behind the practice

The value of circle time

In adult therapy circle time is used in many counselling arenas. It offers a safe space for adults who have suffered abuse or addiction to talk about the issues they have faced in a non-threatening and supportive environment. The security is established by agreeing rules of behaviour within the group beforehand and by having a named leader who will maintain the smooth running of the session.

As a behaviour management tool circle time is used to guide people through difficult meetings or to help people, especially young adults, who find controlling their behaviour challenging. The theory goes that practising social interaction in a supportive environment will encourage those for whom sociability is difficult to learn. Coming to difficult decisions is easier in a formal group where the responsibility may be shared - many a committee is essentially a grown-up circle time session!

In secondary schools circle time is still a preparation for the real business of grown-up decisions. Spiritual and moral dilemmas can be faced and understood in a circle time session. In junior schools the children use the sessions to begin to express their feelings, what makes them feel good or bad and why. In infant schools the children use circle time to practise the sound of their own voice and to ensure that they understand the basic rules of communication, letting others speak and listening to others' opinions.

What then is expected of the nursery circle time? Expecting a child of three or four to be able to discuss and co-operate on the same level as an adult is plainly inappropriate.

Need for focus

Peter Lang of the Institute of Education at the University of Warwick argues that although circle time is becoming increasingly widespread in this country it is unfocused in British schools compared to other countries. That there is little theory underpinning the practice is an issue that we should be concerned about. His paper, *Getting Round to Clarity*, describes examples of the development of circle time in other countries. Americans are offered guidance on the development of self-awareness at specific ages, Italians work in small groups to improve the teacher pupil relationship and

A great deal of the most effective work on early years self-esteem and confidence will be done outside circle time but, as a preparation for more formal discussion groups, then circle time is a valuable curriculum tool and, used well, will be a benefit to all involved.

the child's self-esteem and the Scandinavians have developed clear practice guidelines for all users of circle time.

The lack of a coherent national early years policy has, it would seem, compromised the standards achieved in British settings. This does not mean that there isn't some good age appropriate work going on in our groups, but we should be aware that it is perhaps the lack of consistency that lowers the overall effectiveness of the good practitioners.

Studying child development and knowing what is appropriate for each stage is a good

place for us to begin our evaluation of current practice. Piaget's pre-operational stage (two to seven years) identifies the egocentricity of children of nursery age. Expecting an egocentric being to fully empathise with another person would, following Piaget's theory, be unrealistic. Thorndike and Skinner (child development psychologists famous for their work on conditioning - nature versus nurture) believed that the Law of Effect meant that if something good followed an action then the action would be repeated. This theory forms the basis for most behaviour modification plans and highlights the need for circle time to be a planned, positive and effective session.

Nursery groups should therefore, as a bare minimum, be able to evaluate the content of their circle time to ensure that the expectations of their group are achievable and the children are being effectively encouraged, at an age appropriate level, to become the social beings we are hoping for.

Building self-esteem

Learning what is right and wrong is an important part of the socialisation process. Circle time is one place where socialisation can be explored but the strongest influences surround the child at home and are rooted in his or her experiences of life in general. Simply including circle time in a timetable is no absolver of responsibility elsewhere in the curriculum! Feeling good enough to behave well is often a self-esteem issue.

The development of self-esteem has been studied in depth by Jenny Mosley, author of *Turn Your School Around* and *Quality Circle Time in the Primary Classroom*. Her model of

Early years circle time - Cognition through a combination of:	
Contribution	Just saying something is challenge enough for a three-year-old
Conversation	Taking turns to talk and listen
Consideration	Being aware that others may feel differently
Concentration	Sitting still and listening to another person
Co-operation	Working with/ listening to/ talking to another person
Compassion	Kindness to others
Collaboration	A coherent curriculum that has self-esteem as a mainstay

circle time is to build the self-esteem of each participant and to encourage pupils to take responsibility for the consequences of their actions. Her model claims to impact in many areas of life such as individual motivation and achievement, enhancing positive relationships, personal and social development and producing calm behaviour and self-discipline. Early years teachers will be able to take a great deal from the primary model so clearly presented by Jenny Mosley but must always remember that three- and four-year-olds are not the same as primary school children.

The early years are different. Nursery children are still learning to talk. Daring to speak out in a group is a major issue, never mind the content of the utterance! The new conversational skills that the baby, toddler and pre-schooler have absorbed are only just proving useful. Ideally the baby was listened to and her babble bursts were answered. The toddler was always loved and secure and introduced to new vocabulary as control of his tongue and mouth developed. The pre-schooler was given time to express opinion and praised for contributing. In the real world we all fall somewhere a little short of that some of the time but nonetheless our main responsibility as early years teachers is to build the child's ability to explore, express and discuss later in life. We are building the foundations, not painting the roof! Our circle time will, therefore, be different.

The management of circle time

❑ In the management of circle time praising contributions and developing conversation are key issues. Talking is one thing and conversation is another. Pre-school children often talk *at* one another. Encourage conversation throughout the day. Train staff to listen to children and to praise verbal contributions.

❑ Using trained staff is important - getting circle time wrong is worse than not doing it at all. It is always possible that you may encounter a child who discloses a serious personal issue to the group and the staff

member must be able to manage such an event. Observations of children within this situation are a useful indication of the child's general development, too. Make the most of it and have an observer as well as a leader.

❑ Verbal put-downs and unkindness damage young children. Setting up a space that you are calling safe to talk in makes you even more responsible for the safety of the child within that space. Circle time should, therefore, not be taken lightly or without research and training.

❑ A great deal of the most effective work on early years self-esteem and confidence will be done outside circle time but, as a preparation for more formal discussion groups, then circle time is a valuable curriculum tool and, used well, will be a benefit to all involved.

❑ Plan for circle time and evaluate your success or failure as you would any other session.

The final word goes back to Spock: 'Good nurseries are run by people who try to understand the children's needs, love them, give them attention, affection and freedom to develop'. Circle time is only ever going to be a small part of a much greater drive to produce the rounded personality that we are aiming for.

Sara Stocks

Links

Getting Round to Clarity by Peter Lang is featured in the *Pastoral Care in Education Journal* published by Blackwell Publishers. Details on www.blackwellpublishers.co.uk or from the Institute of Education, University of Warwick, Coventry, CV4 7AL

The Jenny Mosley web site is at www.jennymosley.demon.co.uk

The circle time e-zine (on-line magazine) gives ideas for stories and games and is at www.circletime.com

Books

An Introduction to Child Development by G C Davenport (Collins Educational)

Developing Circle Time (book and video) by Teresa Bliss and George Robinson ISBN 1 873942 85 0

The Giant Encyclopedia of Circle Time and Group Activities for Children 3 to 6 by Kathy Charner (Gryphon House)

Circle Time Activities by Grace Jasmine

Multicultural education doesn't just mean providing books which show ethnic faces — it means broadening children's perspectives. You need to examine your whole approach to teaching children about the world in which they live so that they grow up with an understanding of and a respect for different countries, cultures, races and religions, especially if you are in an area with few or no representatives of other cultures

The value of **multicultural** education

This article is deliberately concerned with those settings which do not have a multicultural intake, although all settings should be ready to take children of all cultural backgrounds at any time and give them the support, respect and curriculum they need.

A number of nurseries and pre-schools have been criticised by Ofsted inspectors for failing to reflect the diversity of cultures and faiths represented in our society. This is particularly a concern in areas with largely white populations. Some parents and teachers find it difficult to understand the need to reflect the variety of British society when there is little evidence of cultural diversity locally. Although not racist they may feel they have enough to do without introducing the complications of different religions and languages. If this sounds familiar, what can you do to make sure that you are not next to be criticised by Ofsted?

You must understand that multicultural education is not just singing West Indian nursery rhymes, although this can be enjoyable. It is more to do with creating an ethos and an understanding in all you do. Children need to realise that there are many different ways of speaking, dressing, eating, praying. Instead of finding these ways funny we hope they will learn to find them

interesting and respect them. They may not like Indian sweets, but perhaps they don't

like Pontefract cakes, a very English sweet, either. We all have different likes and dislikes and these preferences must be respected.

Multiculturalism is also not just about colour and race. Great Britain is a multicultural, multilingual, multifaith society. It is increasingly part of a Europe which has a growing sense of its own identity. Our society is made up of considerable numbers of people of African, Caribbean and Asian descent, not to mention communities from Europe, the Middle East and other countries. We should be preparing young people for a

world where many of the barriers between groups, between cultures and between nations will be broken down and where there will be respect for, and understanding of, others. All children - wherever they live - are likely to grow up to meet people from a wide range of cultural groups. The technology in schools will ensure that it won't be long before children are meeting their peers all over the world via the Internet. They need to be prepared to accept their cultural differences and be sure of their similarities as children of the human race.

Children need to grow up confident in their knowledge of their own culture as well as the cultural diversity of Britain. Only then will they be ready to combat racism in all its manifestations.

Multiculturalism should not be dismissed as 'irrelevant unless you are in an inner-city environment'. It is relevant to all settings. Knowledge of other cultures will enrich the whole pre-school environment and curriculum.

However, if multiculturalism is to pervade the whole curriculum you need to make sure that all staff, including helpers, are able to support multicultural teaching and that you provide a wide range of suitable resources. If you and your staff don't feel comfortable or confident about

Choosing the right books

All resources should include those:
• which offer a balanced view of the world, seen from many different perspectives
• which inspire the young with respect and understanding of other races, nations and cultures
• which reflect naturally and unselfconsciously a richness and
• which relate experiences common to all children and in which they share
• which demonstrate the validity of other languages and einforce the richness of bilingualism
• where children from any ethnic or cultural background can find characters which confirm their own sense of self and enhance their self-respect
• in which the illustrations have been drawn sensitively, thus avoiding negative stereotypes

kiwi fruit

star fruit

mango

pineapple

'A "good" education cannot be based on one culture only and should therefore be multicultural by definition. It should enable a child to understand his/her own society and know enough about other societies to enhance that understanding.'

Arora & Duncan, 1986

multicultural education, you should think about providing some in-service training. A good starting point is your nearest multicultural centre — most local authorities have one and they offer a variety of support from loan services to training.

Resources are vitally important. You also need to carry out an audit of your resources to identify any unsuitable books which reinforce stereotypes, for example, and to see which areas have scope for introducing multicultural equipment. This does not necessarily mean you need a larger budget just that you need to spend your money in a different way. Next time you invest in some new jigsaws, think about buying ones which depict scenes from different countries, for

example. Many resources, such as brochures or tourist posters are the cost of a stamp or a phone call.

If you don't feel knowledgeable about choosing multicultural materials, follow up new sources of information (see 'Sources of support') or simply set aside time to sit together with your colleagues and look through some resource catalogues to see the wide range of multicultural resources that are available and review your needs.

Education For All: a summary of the Swann Report on the education of children from ethnic minority groups (Runnymede Trust, 1985) 0 902397559.

Multi-cultural Education: towards good practice Ranjit Arora and Carlton Duncan (Routledge, 1986) 0710202296

Debbie Denham and Professor Judith Elkin

Reference

Books and guides

Fair's Fair
edited by Lesley Sim: an annotated list of books with positive images of age, culture, gender, disability and class (Youth Libraries Groups, 1996) ISBN 0946581185

A Multicultural Guide to Children's Books 0-12
edited by Rosemary Stones (Books for Keeps, 1995) ISBN 1871566029

Sources of support

Early Years Trainers Anti-Racist Network,
PO Box 28, Wallasey CH45 9NP Tel: 0151 639 1778 - provide training and a range of useful publications.

Commonwealth Institute Resources Centre
Kensington High Street, London W8 6NQ. Tel: 0207 603 4535 - national multi-media loan service on Commonwealth countries.

The Working Group against Racism in Children's Resources (WGARCR)
460 Wandsworth Road, London SW8 3LX Tel: 020 7627 4594 - have an exhibition collection of suitable resources and produce some useful publications.

Suppliers of multicultural books

Letterbox Library
Unit 2D, Leroy House, 71-73 Allen Road, London N16 8RY Tel: 0207 226 1633. Mail-order book club specialising in non-sexist and non-racist titles.

Picture books for the under-fives

Calypso Alphabet by John Agard (Picture Lions) - a traditional ABC with a Caribbean flavour.

Through my Window by Tony Bradman (Little Mammoth) - a simple picture book about Jo who stays at home with Dad when she is ill. She eagerly awaits Mum's return from work. This book is significant because it represents a mixed race family.

Handa's Surprise by Eileen Browne (Walker) - set in Kenya where Handa walks to her friend Akeyo's village with a basket of fruit on her head. Children will enjoy the joke when various animals steal Handa's fruit without her knowledge.

So Much by Trish Cooke (Walker) - a wonderful rhythmic story about a black toddler being visited by various relatives who all love him 'so much'.

Angel Mae by Shirley Hughes (Walker) - Shirley Hughes is a fine exponent of illustrating groups of children from a wide variety of ethnic backgrounds in ordinary everyday situations.

Anancy and Mr Dry-Bone by Fiona French (Frances Lincoln) - traditional folk tales retold in picture book format are a wonderful way for children to experience other cultures.

Why the Agouti has no tail and other stories by Floella Benjamin (Nelson) - a collection of favourite folk tales from the Caribbean, India, China and Africa. Retold in a simple style perfect for reading aloud to young children.

No Hickory No Dickory No Dock by John Agard and Grace Nichols (Viking) - a delightful collection of new and traditional Caribbean nursery rhymes.

Having fun during Diwali is the best way to help your children find out about this popular Hindu festival and develop respect for those who celebrate it, says Judith Harries

Learning about Diwali

We live in a world with increasingly easy access to the variety of cultures, races, faiths and nations through books, television, the media and the internet. To help your children appreciate this rich variety it is important to encourage them to find out about, and learn to respect, other cultures. If they can learn from your example that different ways of speaking, dressing, eating and living are interesting and valuable, they will be less likely to find them 'silly' or make fun of other children who are different from them.

It is essential that we seek to gain awareness, understanding and acceptance of each other. This objective may appear more straightforward in an inner-city multicultural area where

there are children of different faiths in the setting. All children enjoy sharing important events in their lives, such as birthdays, new babies, family parties, and celebrating different festivals.

If your pre-school is in a predominantly white area then it may prove more challenging for the staff to make different lifestyles appear real and relevant to the children but it is just as important to try. It is vital that all the staff have access to suitable helpful resources. You will need to build up a library of pictures, books, artefacts and information.

The Early Learning Goals for Personal, Social and Emotional Development include the following aims: 'to show respect for people of other cultures and beliefs' and 'respond to relevant cultural and religious events'. Having fun learning about other festivals is a good way to begin.

You may choose to start with festivals which are represented by children in your group or take a more systematic approach and look at one from each of the main faiths.

What is Diwali and why do Hindu people celebrate it?

Diwali, the festival of light, is one of the best-known and popular festivals in the Hindu calendar. It is a moveable feast that usually falls during October or November at the end of the Indian monsoon season. It combines the celebration of harvesting summer crops with the beginning of the new year, and is a five-day long festival associated with parties, dancing, and giving cards and presents. People see it as a special time to wear new clothes and clean their houses from top to bottom. They decorate their homes, inside and outside, with garlands of flowers, paper chains, tinsel and, of course, lights. They use many different lights from traditional clay diva lamps and candles, to electric fairy lights. All of these are to light the way and welcome home the young king Rama, who according to the epic poem 'Ramayana' had been forced into exile for 14 years. As a new year festival, Diwali is an important time to sort out business and pay off any debts. The diva or lights are also intended to attract the attention of Lakshmi, the goddess of wealth. If she visits the house, Hindus believe this will bring them prosperity for the coming year.

There are many good stories told at Diwali but the most popular one is the 'Ramayana' - the story of Rama and Sita. You can tell the children a simple version of this story and use it as a basis for drama and creative work.

Rama and Sita

Prince Rama and his beautiful wife Sita are sent away and hide out in the forest with Rama's brother. The wicked monster Ravana kidnaps Sita and keeps her prisoner on an

island. With the help of Hanuman, the monkey god, and all the forest animals, Rama builds a bridge over to the island, kills Ravana and rescues Sita. The happy couple return to their country and the people welcome them home by placing lights in the windows and doors to help them find their way and as a sign of celebration.

Take a theme from the story of Rama and Sita such as dark and light, or homecomings, and create work around it.

Dark and light

The story ends with hundreds of lights to show Rama and Sita the way out of the dark forest. Ask the children how they feel when it gets dark at night. This is a sensitive issue and needs to be handled carefully. Do they like to look out of the window and count the stars? Encourage their parents to take them outside and look at the night sky. Read them the story *Can't you Sleep, Little Bear?* by Martin Waddell. Have they ever felt scared like Little Bear? Do they like to have a light on at night? You could construct a role-play area of a dark bear cave with three different sized lanterns for the children to act out the story. Torches add another dimension to this activity.

This could lead into lots of activities about light. Diwali is particularly associated with candles. Can the children think of any other times we use candles to celebrate? Make simple clay candle holders or divas with the children using small candles or night lights.

You could make shadow puppets and act out the story of Rama and Sita using a large white sheet and a light source.

Coming home

Ask the children how they feel when they come home after a holiday or a day away? Is it good to see familiar things around them? How do we make people feel welcome when they return home?

You will find that there are often areas of common ground between festivals which help the children to relate to them. The theme of light is found in the Jewish festival of Hannukah, the Christian celebrations of Advent and Christmas and the bonfire festivities throughout Europe, as the days get shorter and the nights longer. Fireworks are a major part of celebrating Diwali and it usually falls around the same time of year as bonfire night. You can relate the different festivals to themes or topics that you might be covering in the nursery curriculum already, for example fireworks, light, patterns, clothes, celebrations.

If you have any Hindu children in your pre-school you have an ideal opportunity to help all the children learn about Diwali in a more direct way and it will also help the Hindu children to feel included and accepted. Invite the children, or their families, or members of the local community to come and talk about how they celebrate Diwali. You could make a wall display of the artwork you have made and hold a Diwali party.

Parties

Diwali is a time of celebration and parties. Talk about what the word 'celebrate' means? What do the children like to celebrate? What do they like most about parties?

Decorations: Homes can be decorated in lots of different ways. At birthday parties we hang up balloons. At Diwali, the houses are decorated with tinsel and lights and special patterns called rangoli. The children could make some rangoli patterns using coloured sand.

Dressing up: Do the children like to wear special clothes when they go to parties? Diwali is also a time to wear new clothes and decorate hands and feet with mendhi patterns.

Dancing: Do the children enjoy dancing at parties? There are lots of dances associated with Diwali. The children might enjoy learning a simple dandia dance when the dancers hold wooden sticks (dandia) which they have to tap together.

Good food: No party is complete without delicious food. What are the children's favourite things to eat at parties? Try sharing some traditional Indian food such as poppadoms or Indian sweets.

Judith Harries

Useful books

My Hindu Faith by Anita Ganeri (Evans Brothers Limited) ISBN 0237518961 - a basic introduction to the Hindu faith which focuses on the experiences of one young Hindu child and her family.

Rama and the Demon King by Jessica Souhami (Frances Lincoln) ISBN 07112 11582 - a picture book retelling of the ancient tale of Rama and his victory over the wicked Ravana.

Introducing Religions - Hinduism by Sue Penney (Heinemann) ISBN 0431066485 - an information book that introduces Hinduism. Uses full colour photographs and illustrations.

Celebrations - Diwali by Chris Deshpande (A & C Black) ISBN 07136640820 - the series looks at different celebrations in various cultures. This book shows the fun and atmosphere of the Hindu festival of Diwali through the eyes of young children.

Story time has a key role to play in children's development. You may want to share the ideas here with your staff, perhaps review your approach, and make sure you are devoting the attention to story time it deserves

The value of story time

Story time is a regular feature in the daily routine of most early years settings but its importance is often undervalued. One of the best ways to introduce children to words and language at a very early age is through a wide variety of stories and rhymes. By hearing rhymes from their first awareness, children are gradually introduced to words, phrases and communication. Children need a wealth of language, of stories and experience before they are ready to learn to read or communicate fully.

Stories are a natural and stimulating way of leading children towards many of the ELGs. Listening and responding to stories, in small and large groups, is a fundamental part of the Communication, Language and Literacy area of learning.

Story time brings the children together in a shared experience, providing the opportunity to develop listening skills and prompt group discussion and learning. It gives them a chance to sit back and reflect, to investigate their hopes and fears within the security of an imaginary situation, and begin to empathise with the feelings of others.

Storytelling (from memory) is an art. Story reading is an art, too. It also has added value because there is an element of sharing, of promoting the value and joys of reading, of understanding that someone else has

written these words for you as the reader or listener. The illustrations should add a further dimension in visual and aesthetic terms, as well as being visual aids to the child, at pre-reading and early reading stages. Stimulating visual awareness is a valuable part of children's pre-reading development.

Many teachers argue that story time serves a practical purpose, important in terms of personal and social development, of teaching children to sit quietly, to sit still when asked to do so and to listen, as opposed to hearing. They will have to do all of this once in school, so this is a useful starting point. However, story time must be enjoyable, worthwhile and fun to really hold the attention of small children. Forcing absolute quiet and stillness, without enjoyment, is counterproductive.

From talking to reading

Research by Margaret Clarke in the early eighties (*Young Fluent Readers*) showed that fluent readers were those that had been exposed to books, stories and rhymes from an early age. This was true regardless of social background or wealth and was likely to be connected with whether they had a parent who regularly took them to the local library to borrow a range of books. Clearly the nursery has a role to play here, too.

Exposure to rich, varied, stimulating language from an early age is important in the child's linguistic development. Children copy sounds and explore words from a very early age; the greater the richness of this language, the greater the child's adoption of varied language. Stories help enormously in this, which is why rich, beautiful language at the child's own level but pushing out their language boundaries is so important.

Children love unusual words and when they hear them in stories the context helps them to understand the meaning. (Whilst listening to *The Lighthouse Keeper's Lunch* by Ronda and David Armitage, one little boy latched on to the word 'scavenging' and went on to tell me that there were ants in his kitchen who were scavenging all the food!)
Children respond to rhythm, rhyme, alliteration and onomatopoeia, and stories

which include these features help children to tune into sounds. Giving children the opportunity to delight in the texture and sound patterns of words raises their phonological awareness. This is vital in order for them to relate sounds to individual letters and to decode the written word at a later date. Stories provide a natural link between talking and reading. There is a strong correlation between children's knowledge of nursery rhymes at the age of three and their level of literacy at the age of six.

Role models

During story time we are providing a model of ourselves as readers. We can show through our careful handling of books and our enjoyment of stories that books are very special and a source of pleasure.

Through sharing books with children in story time, perhaps by using big books, children can also begin to appreciate how books are organised. They will come to see that words and pictures carry meaning and that the written word represents our spoken words. We can talk about the front cover, the title, what they think the book will be about, the name of the author and the illustrator. We can point out that, in English, print goes from left to right and from top to bottom.

Stories like *The Jolly Postman* by Janet and Allan Ahlberg show children different kinds of writing. With its enclosed letters, postcard, birthday card, little book and mail order catalogue, this is a lovely book to encourage writing for a purpose.

Broadening experiences

Through stories, children can experience a wide range of emotions from sorrow and fear to joy, excitement and wonder. Many books, as well as traditional fairy stories, provide strong moral messages through which children can develop an understanding of what is right and wrong. They can judge the characters' actions, discuss their motives in a non-threatening situation and begin to empathise with the feelings of others. Stories from other cultures give children insights which will help them to respect different cultures and beliefs. It is important for children to see

their own gender, class and culture reflected positively in books.

Children's self-esteem can be reaffirmed in a direct way through reading them books such as *Can Do* by Joyce Dunbar and Carol Thompson. Stories such as *Courtney* by John Burningham confirm we are all different and special to someone.

Links with learning

Stories can become an integral part of most topics and can serve as an introduction to many areas of learning. For example, *Jim and the Beanstalk* by Raymond Briggs (in which Jim measures the giant for his glasses, false teeth and wig) shows children about the need for measuring and scale in an infectiously amusing story. 'Goldilocks and the Three Bears' encourages children to think about one-to-one correspondence with the bears, their bowls, chairs and beds. A sense of time is often integral to stories, whether it be 'Once upon a time ....', the days of the week in such stories as *The Very Hungry Caterpillar* by Eric Carle or the crucial stroke of midnight in 'Cinderella'.

Stories create a sense of place and help children to note similarities and differences between their own environment and the setting of the story. To improve children's knowledge and understanding of the world, compare the toys, household equipment, clothes and food in stories set in the past with those in the present day. Many stories involve going on journeys, for example 'Little Red Riding Hood' or *Going on a Bear Hunt* by Michael Rosen and Helen Oxenbury.

Stories can foster creative development by stimulating the imagination, increasing the children's descriptive vocabulary, and providing them with inspiring illustrations. Stories can stimulate children to tell their own stories.

Give them stories .... give them wings.

Sue Peasgood, Professor Judith Elkin, Debbie Denham

20 good books to read aloud

Each Peach Pear Plum Janet and Allan Ahlberg (Puffin)

Mr Magnolia Quentin Blake (Collins)

Michael Tony Bradman (Red Fox)

A Dark Dark Tale Ruth Brown (Red Fox)

Handa's Surprise Eileen Browne (Walker Books)

Oi! Get Off Our Train John Burningham (Red Fox)

The Big Blue Balloon Nick Butterworth (Hodder)

The Very Hungry Caterpillar Eric Carle (Puffin)

So Much Trish Cooke (Walker Books)

Amazing Grace Mary Hoffman (Frances Lincoln)

Alfie's Feet Shirley Hughes (Red Fox)

Rosie's Walk Pat Hutchins (Puffin)

The Three Bears and Goldilocks Jonathan Langley (Picture Lions)

Not Now Bernard! David McKee (Red Fox)

On the Way Home Jill Murphy (Macmillan)

Can't Catch Me John Prater (Puffin)

We're Going on a Bear Hunt Michael Rosen (Walker Books)

I Want my Dinner Tony Ross (Collins)

Farmer Duck Martin Waddell (Walker Books)

Can't You Sleep Little Bear? Martin Waddell (Walker Books)

Storytelling entertains children's minds and imaginations. It is a tool through which the Early Learning Goals can be reached with ease and enthusiasm while keeping the emphasis on learning through play.

The **value** of **storytelling**

In the past, storytelling played a central role in both families and communities. It was part of an oral culture where adults had the opportunity to educate the younger members of the community by telling stories and sharing their wisdom. It was usually a way of conveying a message about tradition, identity, morality and highlighting virtues such as justice, love, truthfulness, forgiveness, courtesy and compassion.

In every culture there is a traditional format which is used to tell the tale through the eyes of a main character – the hero or heroine - and follow them on a journey where they encounter many problems and misfortunes. Children identify with this character as they face various tests and obstacles in an attempt to resolve a conflict. They begin to empathise and learn as the character draws upon his or her own resources and potential. Storytelling, therefore, creates a safe and secure context in which children can explore and confront their fears and can improve their confidence and self-esteem.

'Today, children no longer grow up within the security of an extended family or of a well-integrated community. Therefore, even more than at the time fairy tales were invented, it is important to provide the modern child with images of heroes who have to go out into the world all by themselves and who, although originally ignorant of the ultimate things, find secure places in the world by following their right way with deep inner confidence.'
(*The Uses of Enchantment* B Bettelheim, 1975.)

The benefits of storytelling
Storytelling should be organised in an informal and comfortable setting such as circle time. It can be led by the teacher or adult, drawing upon the children's

comments and both their real and imagined experiences, or the children can play a more active role. Children will practise various skills including listening, using their imagination and experimenting with language. A discussion at the end prompted by questions such as 'Why do you think the character did that?' and 'How do you think he or she felt?', allows the children to empathise with the protagonist in the story and offers solutions to a conflict.

Telling stories rather than reading them gives the storyteller the freedom to be spontaneous with language according to the response of the children. Not having to hold a book means that you have your hands free to animate the story using upper body movements as well as a range of facial expressions to add dramatic emphasis. You can also concentrate on the children's responses and direct specific parts, words or expressions relating to the story to certain children. This is especially important in a group situation where children will need different stimuli to engage in the tale.

The home environment
At home, storytelling is an enjoyable activity which strengthens the parent-child bond. Some parents have a real flair for storytelling and you need to let them know that it is a worthwhile experience for them to share with their child. It is particularly valuable for parents who find reading difficult.

Storytelling provides a unique educational opportunity very different from that of television. Whilst television entertains children's eyes and ears, storytelling entertains children's minds and imaginations. It allows them to decide and imagine what colours, sizes, shapes and sounds are in the story rather than having these elements depicted for them.

Finding effective methods of communicating

Each person learns in their own way, so it is important to explore different methods of storytelling to find the language which will engage your particular children from the start.

Children gain knowledge through their five senses. If you then accept that children are more in tune with one sense than the others, the teacher or adult can try to tailor-make a story which will appeal to one or more senses. The three main senses to identify in a child are:

❑ Visual – the visual child sees the world;

❑ Auditory – the auditory child hears the world;

❑ Kinaesthetic – the kinaesthetic child feels the world.

This theory of how children and adults perceive and communicate was made by two linguists, Richard Chandler and John Grinder. Their model is useful to the art of storytelling as it gives a foundation on which to build the words and structure of a storytelling activity. It is possible to identify which method of learning is appropriate to which child.

The visual child

Visual children move their eyes directly up, left, right and straight ahead. They are usually more responsive to pictures, props and images and use words such as 'see', 'picture', 'bright', and so on. Using these words and sentences appropriate to a story, for example 'The castle looked magical', will engage children who have a visual mind.

The auditory child

Auditory children move their eyes horizontally from left to right to left, responding to sound. They are more in touch with the tones in your voice and what you say in a story. They are usually more responsive to words such as 'listen', 'tell' or phrases such as 'It sounded as if ...', or 'The castle door creaked open'.

'... storytelling entertains children's minds and imaginations.

It allows them to decide and imagine what colours, sizes, shapes and sounds are in the story rather than having these elements depicted for them.'

The kinaesthetic child

Kinaesthetic children move their eyes downwards when asked to think of a situation. They can also seem more shy or timid and usually need more time to make sense of the world around them. They will respond well to words or phrases which describe touch or feeling such as 'cold', 'hot', 'feels like ...' or 'The prince felt happy when he saw the magic castle'.

Parents and staff in a pre-school setting should be aware of these various types of learning and aim to include a variety of visual, auditory and kinaesthetic words in their stories. Extra materials such as pictures and music will satisfy the visual and auditory children, and props to touch and pass around will encourage the kinaesthetic children. Using these different techniques together in a group will encourage each child to develop their other senses whilst engaging them in the story.

A tool for learning

Encourage your staff to include more storytelling in their teaching. Storytelling is a tool through which the Communication, Language and Literacy Early Learning Goals can be reached with ease and enthusiasm while keeping the emphasis on learning through play.

Many other goals could be targeted in different areas of learning. Children can use their imaginations to transport themselves to different worlds where, as the story unfolds, they begin to create a clear and colourful picture. A story about Danny the Dolphin, for example, and his adventures in the deep blue ocean, enables children to have a greater understanding of the sea and the creatures that make it their home. Stories showing children from different ethnic backgrounds give children an insight into how different people live.

Active storytelling supports children's emotional, intellectual, physical and social development. The different ways of bringing stories alive encourage children to interact physically and not just verbally. They begin to explore situations and information for themselves at their own pace. They also work together to find clues and solve situations.

Even making sense of maths through rhymes and poems is simple and so much fun. The repetition and the rhythm enables children to grasp patterns and numbers and, what's more, remember them.

Even the most reluctant member of staff should be able to find an approach that they are comfortable with. It is important, however, that practitioners plan activities which are appropriate for the age of the children and their individual stage of development.

Stories seem to stay with children, often for years to come. The content is retained without the child being aware that they are learning and absorbing information. It is by using creativity in this way that we begin to see the true benefits of learning through play.

Emily Cannon and Kathini Cameron

Do you feel guilty when you sit your children down in front of the television? As long as you use it as a learning activity you shouldn't, argues Jenny Towers

The value of television and radio

'There are many myths about television and children. These include misconceptions about how youngsters use it, how actively they respond to it, and how much and in what ways they are changed by it. There is a bias towards thinking ill of television when the medium deserves a fair hearing. Television is not a one-eyed monster.'

The words of Gunter and McAleer (1997) serve well to set the tone for exploring the potential of educational television and radio broadcasts in early years settings.

The value of children watching television has been the subject of much debate. Some people say that watching television means other activities such as reading or physical pursuits are not followed. Others have suggested that there is a link between television and violent behaviour.

However, these arguments, and the research on which they are based, presuppose that children have free, unlimited access to television and that their viewing is not supervised in any way. Of course, under such conditions, children may well have access to programmes that might be inappropriate to their needs and experiences. They might, equally, miss out on other valuable activities if television is available 'on tap'. All these arguments seem to assume that adults, be they parents or teachers, have no control over children's viewing and that choices cannot be made about what to view and when. This is not the case. As J Atkins points out in her research for the British Association for Early Childhood Education: 'Positive use of television or of video (and let's include radio) starts with definite decisions rather than allowing children to

switch on without any thought'. Her point is the key to realising the potential of television and radio resources.

In early years settings children are unlikely to be viewing unsupervised, but to maximise the potential of television and radio resources teachers need to take on a far more active role. They need to be actively involved in the process of selecting the resource, planning for its use and evaluating its effectiveness.

Shared activity

The way programmes are viewed is of great importance. Using television or radio in an educational setting is a shared activity. When a group of children sit and watch or listen together they interact, not only with the content of the programme, but also with their peers - exchanging thoughts, ideas and experiences, both as they view and afterwards. Shared viewing is not the norm in the home setting. Recently I watched a class of nursery

children viewing an episode of *Storytime* (a television series aimed at four- and five-year-olds which introduces two stories per programme linked by a common theme). It was all about rabbits and began with the presenter and two children meeting a rabbit owner and her pets. A short documentary sequence showed the rabbits bouncing

With the wealth and range of resources available on the market today many of you may question whether television and radio have anything distinctive to offer. The answer is resoundingly YES!

round the garden and exploring their surroundings. As the sequence began the children immediately turned to one another, exchanging thoughts and experiences including 'I've got one like that' and 'Look at his ears, they're all floppy', to which one child replied 'That's called lop ears'. Such a spontaneous exchange of information can only exist in situations where children view as part of a group. The broadcast may well be enjoyable to a child viewing on his/her own, but viewing alone cannot promote this level of interchange. The sharing of experiences and the construction of meaning for these children had been a very active process which was negotiated and shared as a group.

In educational settings the teacher also becomes involved in the process by prompting prediction and discussion.

Educational broadcasts

Educational broadcasts, on television and radio, are specifically designed to meet educational needs and, in the case of early years broadcasts, to meet the requirements of the Foundation Stage. The last ten years has seen an increase in research looking at educational broadcasts and there is a growing recognition of the positive impact of these resources on children's learning.

With the wealth and range of resources available on the market today many of you may question whether television and radio have anything distinctive to offer. The answer is resoundingly YES! Both television and radio are able to bring sights and sounds from the wider world into educational settings that you cannot otherwise provide.

Using television

Perhaps the most obvious benefit of using television is the visual stimulus it offers - colours, images and movement. Information books are another powerful source of information but consider the contrast for a young child of finding out about a wild animal from pictures and words in a book, versus the opportunity to watch the animal moving in its natural habitat. This is not to say that television is a better source of information than a book, but rather that they offer different experiences which complement one another.

Think of the powerful images that illustrations convey in storybooks and the opportunities they provide for discussion and prediction. The same images can be brought to life on television, enabling sequences of actions to be linked, consequences revealed and predictions realised.

Positive use of television or of video (and let's include radio) starts with definite decisions rather than allowing children to switch on without any thought.

Television can also use special techniques to illustrate processes which normally it is not possible to see. For example, time lapse techniques can show the stages of an egg hatching and a chick taking its first gasps of air. Likewise, graphics can illustrate processes in a simple way such as the growth of a seed into a plant.

Using radio

How often do we hear ourselves saying that the children in our care 'just don't listen'? Children quickly become attuned to the voices of those around them. They learn to interpret the tone of voice almost unconsciously, sometimes barely hearing or registering the spoken words. Radio programmes provide a different voice, a voice the children will need to listen to if they are to follow the story or join in with the actions or movement. Radio separates sounds from the visual image and focuses children's minds on the words spoken and the range and quality of sounds.

Radio also encourages children to use their imagination. Because it does not offer a

visual picture of what is being said or heard, it falls to the children to create their own image. Some say that radio has better pictures than television because they are all your own!

Early years broadcasts

Television and radio programmes for the pre-school age range are designed for the needs of a young audience. Programme makers balance the need for the young viewer to experience variety with the aim to revisit concepts and consolidate experiences. Programmes for this age range include songs, rhymes and stories and regular interactive opportunities.

Educational television and radio are highly motivating, promote a sense of awe and wonder and provide a rich stimulus for further activities and experiences. However, the role of the teacher is fundamental in this learning process.

Television and radio cannot adapt to the individual needs of the children in your care. They cannot recognise when children are becoming restless or when they need more explanation. Only you can do this, because you can recognise and respond to a child's individual needs. Consequently, you have an important role to play in mediating the use of broadcasts. Just as you would read a children's book before sharing it with your group, the use of television and radio needs to be planned so that you can make the most of this valuable resource.

Young Children and Television J Atkins (part of the *Child Development* series from the British Association for Early Childhood Education).

Children and Television B Gunter and J McAleer (Routledge 1997).

Jenny Towers

Even if you don't have access to a television or video, you should be able to beg or borrow a cassette recorder to make use of radio broadcasts. Whether it's TV or radio programmes, Jenny Towers suggests how to choose them and use them

Using television and radio

A wealth of television and radio resources are available from BBC Education and Channel 4 Schools to support children's learning in early years settings. Programmes for this age range are made to help you meet the requirements of the Early Learning Goals.

The programmes are designed to inspire and motivate children, offering them experiences of the wider world that cannot otherwise be brought into the classroom. They also provide a rich opportunity to create a shared experience between you and your children. The potential is almost endless. However, it is essential for you to make choices about the kind of resource you want to use and to plan for its use effectively. This will enable you to make the most of the resource and to tailor it to the needs and experiences of your children. Your role in the process is crucial and what the children gain from the broadcasts will be dramatically enhanced if you are actively involved.

Television or radio?

Both television and radio bring stories, ideas and experiences to life for the audience but they achieve this in different ways. Television uses visual images to illustrate colour, shape and movement in ways that books, posters and words cannot. Radio focuses on the use of sounds and imagery to stimulate the children's imagination and to help them create their own pictures.

In an ideal world, your choice of resource would depend entirely on whether you wanted to stimulate the children visually or develop their listening skills and their imagination. However, many pre-school

groups may be constrained by both the equipment available and the working environment. Not everyone will have access to a television and video but it should be possible to beg or borrow a cassette recorder to make use of radio broadcasts. Whichever resource you decide to use, preparation is essential.

Choosing a series

Both BBC Education and Channel 4 Schools produce catalogues that will give you a feel for the content of each of the series. Think carefully about what you want the children to gain from the broadcast. For example, do

you want to develop a specific aspect of knowledge and understanding? If so, which aspect? Always keep in mind your intentions and the children's needs. If possible try to view, or listen to, a programme from the series in which you are interested.

Using a series

Having chosen a series, try to record the programmes and preview them in advance. (As radio programmes are broadcast between 3.00 - 4.30am, they are also available pre-recorded on cassette.) This will be time well spent as previewing allows you to think more about how to use the programme. Most series are accompanied by teacher's notes and these will give you ideas on how to use each programme with the children. The notes include suggestions on how to prepare children for the broadcast, ideas for follow-up activities that build on and develop the programme theme and a brief summary of the programme content.

Having previewed the programme think about how you will use it with your children. For example, consider:

❑ space - is it feasible to use the programme with a small group without disturbing other children who may be busy nearby?

❑ the age of the children - younger children will gain more from watching in smaller groups, allowing you to respond to their individual needs.

❑ location - as far as possible try and make sure that, when using television programmes, sunlight is not shining directly on to the screen or into the children's faces. For radio programmes, make sure the children sit facing the speakers and that these are placed at the children's ear height (the speakers are often difficult to locate on smaller models; some are located at the back of the unit).

When to use the resource

If you are using a pre-recorded broadcast you will be able to make decisions about the most appropriate time to use it. If you want to follow up the programme with practical activities, use the broadcast during the first part of the session. Bear in mind that if the children have sat and watched or listened to a broadcast for a sustained period they will need to get up and move around afterwards.

How to use the resource

Before starting the broadcast, talk to the children about the programme theme. If the programme supports a topic or theme the children already have some experience of, they will be able to contribute lots of relevant ideas. A pre-programme discussion helps focus the children's minds on the content and allows you to introduce vocabulary they are likely to come across.

When using radio broadcasts it is particularly useful to bring in a 'focus object' for the children to look at and discuss. For example, if the programme is about a stripy jumper, bring one in for the children to look at and talk about. Put the item on display to allow new listeners, and children who find it hard to concentrate, to focus their eyes on something that relates to the programme content.

During the broadcast

Your role during the broadcast is twofold. First, watch the children and look out for signs of particular interest or confusion. If the broadcast is recorded you will be able to pause and discuss issues, reiterate instructions or resettle the children. This is your opportunity to make the resource work for your group.

Secondly, encourage the children to join in with interactive elements by modelling the actions. The children will benefit enormously from your encouragement and modelling.

Your role in the process is crucial and what the children gain from the broadcasts will be dramatically enhanced if you are actively involved.

After the broadcast

Use the time after the broadcast to talk to the children about what they have seen. Encourage them to relate the programme content to their own experiences and to share these. Providing practical, hands-on activities that build on the content will allow the children to develop their knowledge and understanding of the programme theme.

(The teacher's notes which accompany the programmes include ideas for follow-up activities.)

Your own evaluation of the broadcast and the children's response to it is fundamental. Think about aspects of the broadcast that particularly interested the children. Were there times when they appeared distracted? Why might this be? Were there elements of the broadcast that the children would benefit from seeing or hearing again? Evaluating the success of the session will enable you to plan more effectively for future sessions.

Above all enjoy using the broadcasts. They are a rich, versatile resource and can be a stimulus for weeks of activities and discussion.

Jenny Towers

Planning check-list

Points to consider:

❑ What will we do before listening to/viewing the programme?

❑ How much of the programme will we use?

❑ What will we do while we are listening/viewing?

❑ What will we do after the programme?

Do you see mathematics as a hard subject to teach? It should not be — topics such as number arise naturally in all that you do.

The value of number

For many people the word 'number' or 'mathematics' immediately evokes memories of failure or feelings of unease and comments such as: 'I never liked maths at school, I just didn't understand.' 'You must be clever to teach maths.'

What is evident from statements like these is the division and the compartmentalisa-tion which has taken place in the minds of adults when they discuss or evaluate their mathematical skills. They appear to have made the decision somewhere along their educational route that you either have an aptitude for numbers or you do not. We must make sure that such an approach to the subject does not start in the early years. The pre-school period can provide a powerful and fertile seedbed for mathematical thinking and development.

Daily life
We are surrounded by number and its associated language. It forms an integral part of our daily life. How many beakers or biscuits at break time? Are there enough places on the mats at story time? Time is not specially set aside to discuss these points or even a decision made that number should be introduced, it occurs naturally. So how do we make sure that the pre-school child has no pre-conceived baggage to carry into mainstream school which will detract from their enjoyment and fun of using numbers?

Number is an integral part of the scaffolding that goes to make up the construction we term as mathematics. The supports of the construction include spatial awareness, measurement, sorting, matching, ordering and sequencing — everyday experiences offered in early years settings. No one aspect should stand alone though time can and should be allocated for the individual skills to be mastered so that the overall construction has depth and strength.

Taking control
Margaret Donaldson has identified that babies at a very early age show signs of a strong urge to master the environment, even in their helpless state. The desire does not appear to derive from anything else or to depend on any reward apart from achieving competence and control. Why does a baby repeatedly throw the rattle from the pram or gain such pleasure from knocking down a stack of tubs? It is important to remember that mathematics is embedded in all these experiences and the way in which the young child begins to make sense and take control of the world.

The right time
Can there be a right time to introduce a child to numbers? How appropriate is the rhyme 'This little piggy went to market' to a six-month-old or counting the stairs when following a 15-month-old? These experiences are invariably pleasurable to

both child and carer and are the beginnings of the acquisition of number skills.

Everyday nursery activities and routines provide rich opportunities for early mathematical development. To take advantage of the potential the environment offers it is vital that your staff have a sound understanding of cognitive development. They must know when to intervene, when to stand back and when to support a child in the gap between the 'I can do it with help' and the 'I can do it alone' stage.

A child's earliest experiences are concerned with space, moving around and handling objects of different shape, texture and weight. Goldschmied and Jackson describe how baskets containing a rich variety of everyday objects such as cones, corks, chains, material and so on, can offer stimuli when a baby can sit up comfortably and before they begin to crawl. The basic skills of matching, sorting, and comparing are introduced through the treasury of items contained in the basket.

Mathematical language
Language plays an important role in determining the level of a child's understanding. Using mathematical terms which include an explanation as well as showing a child a feature or attribute help to move closer to the child's thinking.

But Vygotsky warns that it is not sufficient to understand a child's words, we must also know his motivation. This is often difficult to deduce in children whose ability to think laterally has not yet been blinkered.

David Woods suggests that 'Conversations with young children at best give an insight into their needs, feelings, fears and attitudes'. But Woods identifies that not all adults have the natural ability to handle the demands of conversation with a group of young children effectively. It is a skill to be refined and used as a major tool of work. Children in their conversation or comments tend to identify objects or pictures in relation to their own experiences. During a story a child will often make a comment that would appear to have no relationship to the subject matter though they are obviously linking their feelings or happenings to the here and now and gaining order or sense of the world.

Parents often tell you how their two-and-a-half-year-old can count to 20 though sometimes give little credit to their offspring's acquisition of mathematical language. Nor do they understand the significance of the ability of one-to-one correspondence. It is essential that opportunities for this one-to-one correspondence are encouraged — a cup for everyone, a knife for every fork and a hook for every coat. Number names can be attached to objects which give the opportunity for the beginnings of ordinal and cardinal numbers.

Cardinal numbers are those which represent a set of things, for example five currant buns, ten buttons and so on. Ordinal numbers are used to put things in order, for example first in the queue.

Encourage experimentation with number. It is better to accept the child's own reckoning and later to count correctly in front of the child, very much the same as a correct pronunciation is offered, than to insist rigidly on the 'right' answer. Follow an apprentice approach, allowing for mistakes to be made and praise given for the effort. Allow a child to use numbers to experiment and make discoveries which are all the more valuable when the child has ownership.

Look for patterns
The boundaries of understanding of how children acquire number skills are in constant review. Is it possible to identify patterns of learning or schema that are more appealing to some children than others?

I recently described to a parent how, during observation, her 20-month-old child seemed to enjoy matching teacups to saucers in a well ordered fashion. During the conversation the child, now aged two, was busily engaged in a similar pattern of activity. She was placing, one by one, small world people into individual compartments of a toy. It was possible to identify a pattern of learning which held obvious appeal for the child and a pattern which could be used to introduce a new concept, such as counting.

Similarly, my own son, now aged 16, used to position his cars, bricks and blocks in long lines in the horizontal plane. When the opportunity came to select a musical instrument that he might learn to play no amount of encouragement to choose something that would fit into the back of the car was to any avail. He insisted on learning to play the trombone with its obvious horizontal appeal!

Symbolism work by Martin Hughes has challenged Piaget's view on children's arithmetical abilities and describes a method for introducing simple arithmetical symbolism to pre-school children. Most children aged between three and five years knew that, if two bricks were added to a box which already contained one brick, then there would be three bricks all together in the box. However, the same children were unable to answer questions expressed in the formal code of arithmetic, such as 'What does one and two make?' The opportunity for children to use computers offers and exposes them to stimuli which allows them to make this type of connection in a game type format.

Those working with the pre-school child should act as guides, leading children towards tasks where some degree of success is achieved, though not so easily that there is little satisfaction in the end result. Activities should be enjoyable and the problems to solve real as well as valued.

Ann Burton

Number resources

Books
Children's Minds
by Margaret Donaldson, published by Fontana.

Understanding Early Years Mathematics
by Derek Haylock and Anne Cockburn, published by Paul Chapman.

Early Education: The Pre-School Years
edited by Alan Cohen and Louis Cohen, published by Paul Chapman.

Curriculum for the Pre-School Child: Learning to Learn
by Audrey Curtis, published by NFER Nelson.

Education 3 to 5
by Marion Dowling, published by Paul Chapman.

Resources
The Hands On Catalogue, as the title suggests, has lots of early years resources which promote active learning — number lines, a range of story and song books to introduce concepts of counting, shape, measurement and pattern; a giant snakes and ladder floor game to name but a few. Hands On, Unit 11, Tannery Road, Tonbridge, Kent TN9 1RF. Tel: 01732 773399.

BEAM produce a mathematical resources catalogue with early years books, packs and equipment. BEAM Education, Maze Workshops, 72a Southgate Road, London N1 3JT Tel: 020 7684 3323.

The Philip and Tacey catalogue contains the Lasy construction kit. Recipe cards give detailed instructions as to the components necessary for a given design. The catalogue also contains the Unifix system. These cubes fit together and pull apart easily, more so than other systems we have tried. There are kits to aid counting, number bonds and number patterns, grids with underlay cards, rubber stamps as well as graph paper in various grid sizes for pattern making. Philip and Tacey, Northway, Andover, Hants SP10 5BA. Tel: 01264 332171.

How can you make sure that you don't miss the chance to bring number into the conversation while still making sure that children have fun?

Teaching **number**

Children are taught number so they can make sense of the world around them. They already use number, in its widest context, innately from an early age, such as judging the height/width of spaces where they might crawl. Helping a child understand number enables them to solve practical problems and gives them the taste of success and confidence to tackle the next hurdle. The ability to deal with shape, size, pattern and quantity in the pre-school environment prepares them for their entry to compulsory schooling.

All children's learning patterns are different. What suits one may be of little interest to another. Counting rhymes may appeal to one child yet another may respond more favourably to counting using building blocks as they are built into a tower. It should be possible for you to recognise, by observation, which method or pattern holds more appeal for which child or group of children.

Number work, although usually allocated a set time, often presents itself spontaneously whilst other activities are underway. The teacher with finely tuned antennae will pick up on the opportunity that a situation presents, for example 'How many pieces of Duplo track do we need to complete this circuit?'

Likewise, the spontaneous situation can often create an opportunity to reinforce concepts introduced in a formal number session. Anything that happens during the nursery day can present scope for learning. Anything that can be sorted, stacked, compared or weighed, such as buttons, Multi-link cubes or blocks, are all useful in every pre-school. Note that a child may use their own criteria for differentiation which is not always obvious at first glance.

Using counting books as a teaching aid is good for some children but might not suit everyone. However, they can be a useful diagnostic tool to assess development with number. They might help you to identify weaknesses in a child's command of number and you can then introduce an activity to provide practical experience.

Stories, songs and rhymes

Favourite tales should not be overlooked. 'Goldilocks and the Three Bears' and 'The Three Billy Goats Gruff' both provide opportunities for counting, sizing and the all important repetition. A recognisable story formula in these traditional tales enables children to anticipate the outcome.

An introduction to both ordinal and cardinal numbers can be made with tales like 'The Three Little Pigs'. A deviation from the recognised text will give children the chance to correct the teacher and bring the 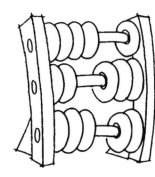 story back to the original sequence and content. Great fun!

There are an abundance of books with number as part of the story line and we all have our favourites. They enable the child to make connections without the pressure and limits of the formal setting. Some I particularly like are *Six Dinner Sid* by Inga Moore and *Ten, Nine, Eight* by Molly Bang.

Little Puffin compiled by Elizabeth Matterson offers a selection of stories, and rhymes as well as finger play and nursery games. It includes 'Five Currant Buns/Little Ducks/Speckled Frogs' and so on.

For those whose repertoire is limited, tapes such as those produced by Oxford University Press are useful aids.

Activities involving number

- ❑ Sorting small world figures and animals into dolls' house/farm/zoo.
- ❑ Fitting furniture into appropriate rooms, animals into particular area or field.
- ❑ Wooden blocks allow children to experiment with different designs and constructions. Unstable designs will need modifications and possibly create the opportunity for joint problem-solving.
- ❑ Board and card games encourage not only the taking of turns but one-to-one correspondence. Giant floor snakes and ladders with large dice is fun.

Organisation of classroom environment and routines

Number friezes should be low down on the wall to allow children to touch and count. They should be clear and uncluttered and use objects that are within the range of a child's experience, for example dog, spoon, car.

Storage should also be low, letting children be part of the management of their environment - select toys/items, put them away in a recognised space or area, rearrange furniture and assess the results, fit it into a given space and negotiate obstacles. Draw attention to the passing of time and the sequence of events. Use a clock with clear numerals and conversations that include before/after/now. Charts or displays that describe the routine or pattern of the day are also useful.

Use picture instructions when setting the table and illustrated recipes when mixing paint or preparing dough.

Opportunities for errors should be given as well as those that bring solutions.

Ann Burton

Early exploration of spatial concepts - whether it be on the climbing frame or riding a vehicle - are providing the foundation for later mathematical understanding. Cath Arnold explores what spatial awareness means, why it is an important aspect of each child's development and where it may lead in terms of later abilities

The **value** of **spatial awareness**

About two years ago, at Pen Green Nursery, we secured funding from the D/EE to build a science discovery area which would offer opportunities for children to play with sand, water, pulleys and conveyor belts.

The new area took away some of the outdoor space where children were used to riding vehicles and when it was completed, we suddenly had a spate of minor accidents involving children on vehicles outside. When we observed what was happening, we noticed that children were tending to ride down a ramp and crash into a fence. The fence was where it had always been. What had changed was the possibility of swinging around to the left and riding downhill on Tarmac.

It seems that many of the children, through their repeated experiences of using the outdoor area, had developed a sort of spatial map of the area available. This enabled them to make judgements about how fast they could safely travel and at what point they needed to change direction in order to negotiate their vehicles within the parameter of the fence.

Brain power

As human beings, we are making the most economical use of our brain power when we do some things on 'automatic pilot' (Claxton, 1998). This leaves our brains free to tackle new problems or situations. These decisions are not made consciously by us, but are the result of much practice. When something changes within our predictable environment, this stimulates us to consciously make adjustments to our actions in order to accommodate the changes.

What is spatial awareness?

- ❑ being able to judge distance, for example, how far we can reach or throw a ball
- ❑ being able to judge what will fit through a defined space, for example, understanding that a football will not fit through railings however we manipulate it
- ❑ understanding that a square peg will not fit into a round hole
- ❑ being able to make sound judgements about speed and direction, for example, slowing down and turning in order to avoid an obstacle

---

Within two weeks of using the new area, most children adjusted their actions to suit the space available to them.

Young children have a powerful urge to explore their environment actively. It is through these early explorations that they begin to build up spatial knowledge. Pat Gura (1992) says that 'Our concepts of space develop out of awareness of our own bodies'. When a baby reaches out and clutches her own foot for the first time, she is discovering where her own body begins and ends. Learning to crawl or shuffle and then to

walk enables children to see the world from new positions. The information they gain about their environment is greatly enhanced if they can see objects from different angles. Climbing trees, step ladders and climbing frames enables children to see objects and people from different viewpoints. Children can often differentiate more clearly, see where one object begins and another ends, understand how a fence divides space.

Most of us rely on sight to give us information about distance, speed and area. Children with disabilities may need help with making these discoveries. For instance, David, a child with visual impairment who attended our nursery, who had to rely on his other senses to gain knowledge of space. After seeking specialist help, we suspended a variety of objects inside a large box, so that he could begin venturing beyond the boundary of his own body (Lilli Nielson).

Mollie Davies says: 'When young children balance along walls, climb over gates, jump over streams and activate see-saws, they are developing notions of space. Through these and a variety of associated actions, they come to know about such things as height, width, distance and proximity.'

The more first-hand experiences young children have of moving within space, climbing, riding vehicles and wielding weapons, the more skilled they become at making judgements about their movements and the more confidently they move in space. This applied to David as much as to other children. The only difference for David was that an adult was close by initially and talked through what was happening until his confidence was established.

Why spatial awareness is so important

Developing spatial awareness through whole body movements is important to children's development in all sorts of ways. To explore, using the whole body, means that there is immediate feedback through the senses and this is a powerful learning mechanism. 'Crashing' into cardboard boxes when riding a tricycle and 'being told that you will crash' are very different experiences. The first has a huge impact and will be remembered. The second may not even be fully understood.

Recent research on the development of the brain indicates that the brain is plastic and constantly re-forming itself. We shape our own brains through our experiences. Experiments on animals have shown that missed opportunities can leave lasting damage. There is, as yet, no proof that human beings suffer similar damage. However, Susan Greenfield's advice about the brain is that 'activity and growth go hand in hand' and to 'not only use it or lose it, but use it as much as you can' (1997).

When we study young children, we notice that their movements become increasingly refined. Often two-year-olds walk like toddlers. By the time children reach three years, walking is easy and they are likely to be setting themselves challenges such as skipping and hopping. There is a natural progression.

Patterns of behaviour

Children are programmed to explore their environment. All young children use schemas or patterns of behaviour to make sense of their world (see pages 71-72). Many of these schemas involve exploring space. Children explore what Piaget calls 'topological space concepts' first. Bruce and Meggitt (1999, p.360) say that: 'Examples of topological concepts are: on/off, over/under, up/down, in/out, surrounding, across.'

When young children are exploring an *on top* schema, they might climb on top of every available surface. Being at the *top* of a step

ladder gives them a huge sense of satisfaction. They may also place objects *on top* of other objects. Children often represent *on top* at a symbolic level by making one thing stand for another, for example, Jack said that the block at the *top* of his tower, was the 'king at the *top* of his castle'. Children might be interested in cause and effect relationships, for example, 'If I place a marble at the *top* of the marble run, it runs all the way down'.

Later on, children develop abstract thoughts, based on these earlier first-hand experiences of being *on top*. For example, children talk about being *top* of the class or say that their favourite football team is *top* of the league.

When children make representations through role play, building, painting, drawing, dance, music, collage or in any other way, they are literally re-presenting their earlier experiences. If those experiences consist of rote learning, copying or being told about something, then children have little material to re-present and are unlikely to have gained a deep understanding of related concepts.

Where spatial awareness may lead

Young children learn in a holistic way. Children who are inclined to use their whole bodies to explore their environment can make all-round gains if they are supported in this way of learning. Athey (1990) says that 'competence generates confidence'. Tina Bruce *et al* (1995) say that 'when a child gains confidence in one direction, it affects his whole well-being'. The first point is to follow each child's lead. This results in a 'can do' approach, rather than an approach in which many children fail to measure up to the educator's expectations. The same week that Ross, aged four and a half, learned to ride a two- wheeler, he also suddenly started to draw highly complex figures and to write his name.

Curtis, who was very active in his exploration of the environment during his two and a half years at nursery, became physically strong, had good posture, balance, co-ordination and flexibility (Bruce and Meggitt, 1999). By the time he left nursery at four years seven

months, he could not only ride a two-wheeler but also perform stunts by standing on its seat.

Early explorations of spatial concepts provide the foundation for later mathematical understanding. Ideas about boundaries, position, movement, routes, distance, size and shape all underpin later concepts used in geometry like measuring the three dimensions of a figure, mapping co-ordinates and other aspects of solving mathematical problems (Barriball, 1985). Harry, aged four years, after exploring with string, could direct his parents to home using different routes, depending on the starting point. He was able to compare the varying distances of similar routes in his head and would say 'Why are you going that way? It's not the quickest.' At nearly seven years, Harry is in the top set for maths and his teacher feels that the science curriculum is 'too basic' for him. Children who have had opportunities to explore movement and position fully and freely are likely to become flexible thinkers and problem-solvers.

As parents and educators, we are pleased when young children draw or write something that we recognise for the first time. What is not always acknowledged or understood are the many actions, explorations and experiences that precede these refined movements. Bruce (1997) says that: 'It is important to remember that children will find drawing and early attempts to write easier if they also use the "doing" and "imaging" modes to the full'.

An interesting finding that is emerging from our research at Pen Green is that when children, particularly boys, begin drawing at four and a half years or later, after extensive explorations of the environment, their drawing is highly complex.

In conclusion, the research seems to be telling us that when young children have a wide range of first-hand experiences, many of which involve whole body movement and feedback through the senses, they gain a deep and meaningful understanding of concepts and are able to bring together their experiences in creative ways.

Cath Arnold

Cath Arnold highlights the importance of finding out what each child knows about or is interested in. She offers suggestions for setting up an environment to encourage children to explore space and movement and talks about the role of the educator

Encouraging spatial awareness

To promote any area of learning, we always begin with each child and with what they know and can do. Children begin nursery with a great deal of prior knowledge. If you can talk to children about even one experience they have had at home, then you are making a connection with their life outside of the early childhood setting. You can establish a starting point by:

❑ Listening to their parents and carers, and

❑ Observing each child at play.

Listening to parents and carers
We can share information with parents and carers about space and movement through:

❑ daily chats (even two minutes spent discussing how a child climbed a ladder or built a tall building that day is valuable);

❑ a note in a home/school book (if you make space and movement the focus, the parent will probably respond by including information about trips to the park, and so on);

❑ photographs are a vivid way of sharing information about something new a child has achieved at nursery;

❑ a short video sent home to show parents what their child can do in the nursery environment.

Observing each child at play
The pressure of Ofsted inspections has resulted in many settings using worksheets to show what young children know and can do. Worksheets are inappropriate for young children. They are too formal and are extremely narrow measures of ability, which rarely reflect the child's agenda. A much

better and appropriate way of showing each child's abilities is through written observations of each child's actions and language in freely chosen activities. These observations can be matched up with Early Learning Goals to demonstrate to the inspector and to the child's parents that you understand what children are working towards.

It is almost impossible to make written observations of each child every day, so you need to set up a system whereby, over time, each child is observed in turn. If one or two children are targeted to be observed during a whole morning or afternoon, you are likely to get a much fuller picture of their interests and abilities across curriculum areas. After a child has been observed and you have listened to his parents, you are in a position to make an action plan to extend his learning.

You may discover that a child rarely chooses to play outside and therefore is gaining little experience of climbing. An action plan could be to bring a climbing frame indoors and observe whether this child uses it and how skilled he is in using it.

Setting up an environment to encourage children to explore space and movement
At Pen Green Nursery, after observing children at play, we try to note any schemas or patterns in their behaviour (Athey, 1990). Some of the schemas we frequently observe are:

❑ vertical trajectory or up/down movements;
❑ horizontal trajectory or side to side movements;
❑ oblique trajectory or ramps;
❑ enclosure or surrounding oneself, an object or space;

❑ rotation or turning, twisting or rolling oneself or an object around;

❑ envelopment or covering oneself, an object or space;

❑ on top or placing oneself or objects on top of other objects;

❑ inside or being interested in the inside space of a container.

When we are planning to extend children's learning, understanding what a child is currently investigating is helpful. It can help in knowing what to provide and how to set it out in the nursery. For example, Jacob is interested in vertical trajectory or up/down movements. He needs opportunities to build, climb, use tools and weapons. This week, we leaned our eight large spades against a seat outside near the sandpit. Jacob got excited when he saw them. He could see the length of them. He set to work immediately digging in the sandpit. An extension of this would be to plant bulbs and watch them grow. He might enjoy 'Jack in the Beanstalk'.

Young children set themselves challenges and in order to do this in endless ways, they need the nursery to be set up as a workshop environment. In a workshop environment, all of the resources are available all of the time and children can choose which resources to use, how to use them and for how long.

If children are to use their bodies fully, the outdoor area must be available for them to use most of the day.

In the area of space and movement more than any other, it is important for young children to use large spaces as well as small, cosy spaces. This is where natural world resources as well as manufactured resources can help children to extend their skills. A tree in the grounds of your setting can provide challenging climbing experiences.

If the setting adjoins a school or family centre, you may be able to use a hall, gym or soft room. All of these different spaces will contribute to the children's understanding about space. If not, there may be a public park nearby. All children benefit from opportunities to run, jump, climb, ride

Useful books

Child Development and Learning 2-5 Years: Georgia's Story Arnold, C (Hodder and Stoughton)

Extending Thought in Young Children Athey, C (Paul Chapman)

Outdoor Play and the Development of Concepts Essential for the Foundations of Mathematical Understanding Barriball, D New Zealand (1985)

Recurring Themes in Education Bruce *et al* (Paul Chapman)

Child Care and Education, Bruce, T and Meggitt, C (Hodder and Stoughton)

Early Childhood Education Bruce, T (Hodder and Stoughton)

Hare Brain Tortoise Mind Claxton G (Fourth Estate)

Helping Children to Learn Through a Movement Perspective Davies, M (Hodder and Stoughton)

The Human Brain – A Guided Tour Greenfield, S (Phoenix)

Exploring Learning: Young Children and Blockplay Gura, P (Paul Chapman)

Helping Children to Draw and Paint in Early Childhood Matthews, J (Hodder and Stoughton)

vehicles and balance. Parents will know of a low wall nearby on which children like to balance.

Wooden blocks are invaluable as they 'allow for the scaling down of space, so that spatial relationships can be studied' (Gura, 1992). The maple blocks produced by Community Playthings are mathematically related to each other and are the best available. However, there are cheaper makes of wooden blocks or you can use cardboard boxes, video cases or plastic blocks.

Similarly, children can learn a great deal about spatial relationships from using construction toys, small world people, vehicles, furniture and animals. They often practise putting people on top of chairs and inside vehicles. They connect vehicles together and fill spaces with animals.

Young children need quantities of resources to manipulate, carry about and use in their own ways. These can be junk items like corks, lids, straws, material, and so on. Unless they have quantities of similar items, there is no possibility of them lining them up (horizontal trajectory which leads to measuring length), building them up (vertical trajectory which leads to measuring height) or filling a space with them (infilling

which leads to measuring area).

Role-play areas can be set up with a real world theme, for example, a restaurant. You may attract a particular child because her father is a waiter and she visits his workplace sometimes. You would know about this because of listening to her parents. The children can be involved in setting up the area. Involve them in solving problems, for example, how to make a wall and doorway. How many tables will fit in the space? What can be used for tablecloths or placemats? Allow the children to try things out to see whether they work. If the idea comes from the children, so much the better but with your knowledge of the children's home context, you may be able to suggest something which sparks off an interest in them.

The role of the adult

Having listened to each child's parents and observed their spontaneous play, you are ready to support them in their play.

John Matthews (1994) describes the role of the adult as that of 'intellectual companion' to each child. He says that 'people have a special role to play in providing the kinds of experiences which will encourage and promote development'.

Identifying schemas or patterns of behaviour helps us with what to provide. Knowledge of schemas can also help us with what to say. We can offer language to support children's actions. A comment like 'I see you are managing to balance on that low wall' or 'You are right at the top of the slide' puts no pressure on children and yet helps them to think about what they are doing.

As an adult companion, you can offer the language of blocks, for example, 'unit', 'half', quarter', 'eighth' or 'arch'. When Natasha was interested in 'twoness' it was helpful to show her that two quarters make a half and to use language alongside her actions.

Make subtle interventions, that is, be alongside a child for a couple of minutes watching carefully and trying to work out what the child is trying to achieve, before offering language or help. Think 'process' rather than 'product'. The process is important to the child. Often it is more helpful to hold back a little in order to allow a child space and time to solve a problem. If you jump in with a solution it can prevent the child from discovering that solution for herself. Children will sustain their interest for longer because you are with them.

Protecting children's work is particularly important in the block area. You show that you value their creation by taking photos or sketching their building and also by waiting for them to finish and explaining to other children that they are involved in an important piece of work.

Stories can be used to support children's explorations of space. This is where you can identify and introduce a story to a child that you think they would enjoy. Recently, when Mollie had just fetched a ladder to reach the

top of her building, she also appreciated the unfolding ladder in *Papa, Please get me the Moon* (Carle, 1986).

Allow children to explore fully and freely with as many varied resources as possible and support them by matching your language to their actions and by watching carefully for when they need help.

Cath Arnold is head of Pen Green Nursery in Corby, Northamptonshire.

Resources and ideas to encourage children to explore space

Climbing frames – if you are buying new equipment, it can be helpful to buy equipment which can be put together in different ways.

Vehicles – a variety of three- and two-wheeler vehicles and bikes, some one-seater, others two- or three- seater.

Trailers – to connect and extend the length of vehicles

Trolleys

Buggies

Wheelbarrows

Tents – you can improvise by using a clothes horse and drapes

Tunnel – or a large cardboard box with a hole at each end

Blocks – wooden and mathematically related to each other if possible, but you can improvise by using video cases, cardboard boxes or shoe boxes

Stepladder – two or three steps are enough to enable children to build higher

Dressing-up clothes – long skirts and cloaks, shields and helmets

Materials – a variety of sizes and flexibility, from sari material to carpet squares

Writing area – string, sticky tape, till rolls, wrapping paper, newspaper, scissors, tape measures (flexible and inflexible), a variety of types and sizes of paper, chalk and pencils

Woodwork tools

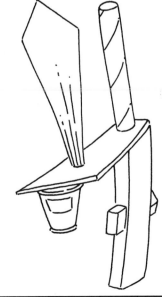

Gardening tools

Bags and containers

Buckets

Hoops

Balls – a variety of sizes and types

Small world – people, furniture, animals, vehicles with doll's house or farm or cardboard boxes

Guns, swords and sticks

Brushes

Colour pegs

Jigsaws

Construction toys

Junk

Opportunities to make guns, swords and shields and to play with them

Traditional games, for example, 'Ring-a-ring-o'-roses', 'The farmer's in his den', 'Five little speckled frogs'.

Books to support exploration of space

This area of learning covers a wide range of experiences. Gay Wilkinson singles out those aspects which relate to science, design and technology, and information technology

Knowledge and Understanding **of the World**

Science

Science for young children is all about first-hand experience - exploring, investigating and experimenting in order to make sense of the world around them; it is about making comparisons, trying out and testing ideas and considering the nature of what can be seen or what has happened as a result of their actions.

Where young children are encouraged to talk about or plan what they think they want to do and how they might do it, when they observe things closely using all their senses and note and appreciate patterns and relationships, when they use a range of tools to help them in their investigation or if they simply try out their ideas to see what happens, then they will be behaving in a scientific manner and the scientific opportunities within their play and activity will be developed.

To be able to explore and investigate confidently young children need extensive opportunities to handle materials and equipment within their play, sustained periods of time within which they can begin to try to answer some of the problems they will encounter and adults who recognise when it is the right time to intervene.

Your environment needs to be planned and organised so that it stimulates children's natural curiosity about the world around them. Are resources and materials stored at a suitable height? Are they readily accessible? Are similar resources grouped together to make it easier for children to find those which they think they need? Are there displays

of materials (natural and made) at child height which children can hold, touch, look at closely and even smell or taste which will encourage them to consider similarities and differences and pose questions?

Using displays

A display of shiny objects - mirrors, spoons, silver foil, large sequins - might prompt discussion about reflection and even lead to thinking about how the shape of the reflective surface changes the image. Children could create their own 'shiny'' display bringing objects from home or making a collection of things from within the classroom, and so extend the opportunity for further comparison and new questions. Could they sort and classify their displayed

objects according to shape, size or other criteria?

You might make a display of cooking ingredients that the children often use in cookery to encourage them to observe similarities and differences. Sugar, salt, cornflour and flour, for example, are all the same colour, but do they smell, taste or even look the same? If you were to mix them with water would they dissolve at the same rate? Ask the children to guess or *predict* how each ingredient will behave when water is added before mixing and then test to see if they were right. Do remember that children need to do these things for themselves - observation must be personal not copied.

If you are making displays which you want the children to use in this way you will need to consider what sort of guidance or help you will need to give them to ensure their safety.

The natural world

Where you have access to an outside area or garden, think about how you might develop it to help children think more about living things and the process of life. You might plant shrubs which will attract bees and butterflies for the children to observe or place some logs in one area, the more rotten the better, to encourage insects like woodlice, earwigs and spiders.

Most young children are fascinated by 'creepy-crawlies' and want to catch them. Nature viewers are useful for this. The children can watch the insects through the magnifying lid and see their shape, colour and particular features more easily without harming the insects. How might these insects eat, move, protect themselves? Why are they that colour? Why do they live where they do? For those children who are frightened or tentative about some insects using a nature viewer helps them to feel safe while allowing them to observe. Once the insect has been carefully looked at then it can be returned to its own habitat.

Birds are natural visitors to gardens and a carefully placed bird table which can be seen easily from a window will enable children to observe them all year round. Put out a variety of foods and observe which birds eat which foods. Keep a list or record in picture form the birds which are seen.

In their everyday play outside encourage the children to be aware of the weather and seasonal changes. Keep a weather diary and, if you have trees nearby, look at them at different times during the year to observe changes which could be recorded by photographs or drawings.

Could you develop an area where the children can plant seeds, care for them and watch them grow? If you plant vegetables as well as flowers then the children can harvest and eat them.

If you don't have an outside area then create one inside! Old sinks make excellent miniature gardens and are deep enough to grow most plants; old tyres can be placed on some heavy duty plastic, filled with soil or compost and planted up. Seeds can be grown in a variety of containers and even if you do have a garden you may want to grow plants in this way so that the children can observe particular aspects of growth (such as growing bulbs in water to see the root growth) or experiment to see what plants need for healthy growth (not watering some plants or keeping some in the dark).

Keeping pets
Small animals can be kept indoors - dwarf rabbits, guinea-pigs, rats, gerbils - and children can help to feed and care

for them. Where children are going to handle, move or carry an animal it's a good idea to have a large broad-brimmed ladies' felt hat into which you can put it. The animal can then be carried or held safely and there is no risk of a child being accidentally scratched. This can be particularly supportive for children who are unused to animals and a little nervous. It also prevents the animal being over-handled.

Many providers introduce the idea of life-cycles by bringing in frogspawn so that the children can observe the process of change from egg to tadpole to young frog. Caterpillars, if properly fed and kept, will pupate and eventually become butterflies or moths. The story of *The Very Hungry Caterpillar* would help the children to think about what might happen to their caterpillars and understand the cycle of change.

Sand and water
You should always make wet and dry sand and water available. You can try adding different substances to the water - bubble bath, washing-up liquid - so the children can see how the water changes. Let them blow bubbles, observing the shape and colours they see and ask them where else they have seen those colours (a rainbow). Provide made and natural objects which the children can test to see if they will float or sink. Encourage them to predict how they think an object will behave and talk about why they think this will be before they try it in the water. Have a range of funnels, containers and tubing so that the children can experiment with the water and begin to find out about its properties. If you're feeling brave, you might let them make waves and observe the effect these have on objects so that they can begin to understand the power and energy of moving water!

Most of the normal range of activities in the early years environment will provide children with opportunities to engage in the exploration of scientific ideas. Play with construction materials, for example, allows children to discover the various

properties of the materials they use. Use of modular construction kits will allow them to build a variety of models some of which may have moving parts, such as levers or pulleys, which will help them to consider forces and energy. Play on or with large wheeled toys will add to this experience. Building with large blocks allows them to think about how to make a stable structure and begin to consider how real bricks are joined together.

They can make a variety of sounds in the music corner with 'instruments' made from different materials so that they can hear differences in tone, pitch and volume. Cookery will provide not only opportunities to make mixtures which will allow them to observe how things can be changed from one state to another (creaming butter and sugar) but also to consider temperature when making something which requires oven cooking.

In addition to this basic provision you may wish to provide a range of magnets. Children are usually intrigued by their seemingly magical effect on certain materials! They also really enjoy making simple electrical circuits which allows them to begin to think about electricity. Make a collection of different sized torches for them to use to create both beams of light and shadows. You'll need to create a dark area so the torchlight is effective, perhaps the development of a cave as part of an imaginative play area!

Design and technology
Technology is about finding out about and understanding the made world, how it works and how we might influence, modify and change it. When children are using different materials and objects as part of their everyday activity they will be finding out about the different properties of the materials they handle - their flexibility, rigidity, strength, texture, porosity, what they can and can't be used for, their bonding capacity, how they can and can't be joined, the best way to handle them, whether they can be cut, folded, bent, and so on. They will

need regular and extensive first-hand experience in order to build up this knowledge. As with science, their understanding needs to be personal, not imagined, told or copied.

Does your home corner have a range of real kitchen tools within it - different shaped whisks, tin openers, timers, sieves and strainers - and are children shown how to use them safely and given real opportunities to use them within their play so that they can observe how they work? Is there a telephone they can use to make calls to real or imaginary friends? Can they build structures with large and small blocks and are they allowed to incorporate other materials, for example building a den with large blocks and using a blanket to make the roof; using a modular kit to construct a crane in the outside sand pit to move the sand from one area to another.

Children need little encouragement to create their own models. Try to provide a large table close to where all the materials children might wish to use are stored. This will allow them to encounter the problems inherent in designing and making something for a particular purpose - which material to select, how suitable it is for the purpose, how they might fit or join things together, which tools to use - and overcome them through trial and error and with helpful support from an adult. Designing and making does not always have to be three-dimensional; sewing and collage work also involves design, the consideration of different materials and the use of different joining techniques.

A woodwork bench will allow them to handle tools - hammer, saw, plane, vice - and consider the specific properties of different woods. However, if children are

to use real tools as they should, they must be taught how to use them safely and know the rules for working in that area and there should be continuous supervision of the woodwork bench while it is in use.

As well as building and making things children love to take things apart! Could you build up a collection of working artefacts - old clocks, watches, clockwork toys, radios, parts of bicycles - which children can take apart, hypothesise what individual components might do and how the object worked. Ask parents if they have any 'junk' they would like to donate. This knowledge will be incorporated into their own model making and will help them to make sense of the technological world they live in.

The opportunity to use working machines - stop-watches, tape recorders, radios, working electronic, battery-powered or clockwork toys will further develop their understanding. Throughout all of these activities it is the adult's role to encourage the children to be reflective about what they are doing, to promote discussion and help them to understand the process of planning, making and reviewing so that they will grow in competency and understanding.

Information technology
Many children will already be familiar with a wide range of programmable equipment and in some cases may be confident about using it - programmable

toys, microwave and conventional ovens, remote controlled televisions and video recorders, automatic washing machines, answering machines, calculators, radios and tape recorders. Many will have access to home computers. It is important that the early years setting builds on all these informal experiences and through well planned activities helps them to use and extend their knowledge, understanding and skills.

Practical activities such as cooking using both conventional and microwave ovens will provide them with opportunities to think and talk about what is happening and how and why they think this might be. Planning and programming a series of actions for a programmable toy such as a Turtle or Roamer will help them see how things respond to signals and what signals they need to give to get the required effect. Learning how to use a tape recorder and taping themselves, friends or sounds in the environment and pressing the buttons on a calculator will also provide them with opportunities to observe how different objects respond to signals. Many pre-schools now provide children with access to a computer keyboard and printer so that they can learn the basic skills.

Above all it is the adult's role in planning, managing and organising the learning experiences and supporting that learning through observation of the children and sensitive open-ended questioning - 'I wonder why . . . ?', 'What might happen if . . . ?', 'How do you think this will fit together?', 'What might happen next?' - that will ensure that children's scientific and technological understanding, knowledge and skills are appropriately extended.

Gay Wilkinson

Many adults think that they can't do science with children because of a lack in their own knowledge. That isn't a problem, say Carole Creary and Gay Wilson, as long as you approach science with confidence, an open mind and concentrate on the process of finding out rather than acquiring knowledge

What do we **mean** by **science** in the **early years?**

Science is all about finding out about the world and our place in it. It's about using our senses to explore new situations and experiences, discovering how things work or relate to each other, asking questions and developing ideas. This is science, whether you are three or 103!

Young children are great scientists - only we usually call it 'getting into everything'! What we as adults need to do is help children develop their curiosity and skills so that they can begin to think and work in a logical way, to begin to understand how the world works and how materials behave without destroying the awe and wonder that is so precious to childhood.

A range of experiences

Young children need to have a wide range of experiences through which they can develop ideas which they then build into concepts. The baby throwing a rattle from its pram is developing ideas about gravity. The child with ice-cream running down its chin is experiencing materials changing state. Seeing and smelling fruit and flowers, stroking a kitten or helping to care for a pet rabbit, help a child begin to appreciate the variety of life.

At first the child may say nothing, but the experiences are important because the next stage is to be able to describe these experiences. Children therefore need to develop their language skills in order to describe what is happening or what is being observed. Some children may be able to do this in a simple way but some explanations may not come until much later. Being able to describe how your trolley is moving is a long way from being able to explain the forces involved and how they are acting!

So where do you start?

Start with something the children are interested in. Don't forget, for very young children the world revolves around *me*, so that is a fairly good starting point! What are the various bits of me called? How do I move? Why do I need to eat and drink? How do I change? Does everybody have the same bits? But how are we different then?

Storybooks or poems can often be used as a stimulus to find out more about something mentioned in the story. *'The Very Hungry Caterpillar'* could start an investigation into how caterpillars change into butterflies, or how caterpillars move or what they really like to eat.

Many of the activities that go on every day in the nursery will provide a wealth of science experiences, but what you need to do is recognise the science potential in them in order to develop the children's understanding. For example, in sand and water play children are investigating the properties of materials. How is dry sand different from wet sand? What can you do with one that you can't do with the other? How do dry sand and water compare?

Outside play with large equipment provides lots of opportunities for experiencing the effects of forces. What happens to the trolley when you push it? Is it easier to push when it is full or empty? What happens if you pull it? What happens to the ball if you kick it harder?

Observation skills

Children need to learn the skills of observation. That means not just looking at things but using all their senses. What can you see? What can you hear? What does it feel like? Can you smell anything? I wonder what it tastes like? The last question is obviously to be used with discretion, but questions like these will help children focus their attention and encourage them to improve their observational skills.

Language development

Alongside questions like these must go language development. To describe objects or events you need the appropriate language. It is difficult to talk about similarities and differences between things if you don't know what words to use.

Even with very young children, try to use the correct terminology. You will always need to add a definition each time you use the new word, for example: 'The ice is melting in my hand. It is changing from a solid lump into water' or 'The sugar has dissolved in my tea. I can't see it any more. It seems to have disappeared. It's dissolved'. Using the correct language whenever possible may help to discourage the children from developing misconceptions - but do make sure that you have the concepts clear in your own mind!

Children are usually much better at spotting differences than they are at noticing similarities. They will tell you that a ball is green and an orange is orange but they won't tell you that they are both round. Again, you need to ask the appropriate questions to focus the children's observations.

Skills and attitudes

Many of the skills children need as scientists are not confined just to science. Often when doing investigations or making observations, children will need to measure or count something - is that science or maths? At first the measuring may be 'not many', or 'lots', or 'bigger than', 'smaller than', 'further than', and so on. The children may then go on to use simple non-standard measures such as hand-spans or lollysticks, cups full or lengths of string or ribbon. Later they will learn to use standard measures and become

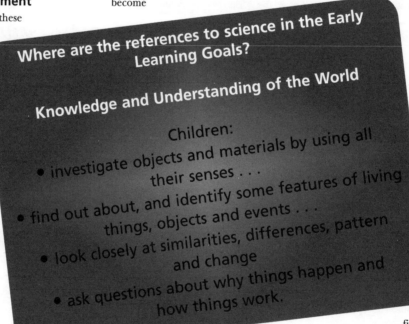

Where are the references to science in the Early Learning Goals?

Knowledge and Understanding of the World

Children:
- investigate objects and materials by using all their senses . . .
- find out about, and identify some features of living things, objects and events . . .
- look closely at similarities, differences, pattern and change
- ask questions about why things happen and how things work.

increasingly accurate with them. Investigations often mean children working together and learning to co-operate with each other. They will need to learn how to share equipment, how to listen to each other's ideas, show tolerance and take turns. They need to develop an awareness of safety - their own and other people's, and respect for living things.

Asking questions

There is no doubt that children learn through play, but when and how does an adult intervene to take that learning further? What questions do you ask? The quality of the questions asked by the adult working with children is crucial. They need to be

questions that encourage and enable a child's thinking.

What will happen if . . . ? What do you think? Why do you think that? What is your idea? These are key questions to get children thinking. Probe as far as possible. Only give answers when the children have run out of ideas. Experience will tell you when a child has gone as far as they can. Value the answers and respond with remarks such as 'That's a good idea, can anyone think of anything else?' The answers you get may also give you clues as to how children are thinking and inform your future planning.

There are times when knowledge has to be imparted, perhaps in answer to a child's question. Favourites such as 'Where does the sun go at night?' fall into this sort of category. Keep explanations clear and simple and don't be afraid to say 'I don't know, let's find out' or the magic 'What do you think?' Use the opportunity to find the answer in a book, a CD-ROM or visit the local library. It is important for children to know that information can be found in other places and that they can find it for themselves. Don't underestimate the expertise within your local community and amongst parents as well.

Ask children for their ideas and build on them. Ask them to think why some of the answers they gave are perhaps not possible. Try to keep within the experience of the children but at the same time try to stretch the boundaries of their knowledge and experience. The aim, always, is to encourage the children to think for themselves, to question and to want to find out.

Many adults believe that they can't do

science with children because of a lack in their own knowledge. This may be a problem if you're teaching GCSE or A-level students but need not be a problem for those working with younger children, as long as they approach science with confidence, an open mind and concentrate on the process of finding out rather than acquiring knowledge.

Different answers

It is important to encourage children, as early as possible, to voice their ideas. Many children come to pre-school or nursery already with fixed ideas that everything is either right or wrong - a book full of ticks or crosses! We need to help them realise that there may be different answers to some questions and that each one may be equally valid. This is particularly so when carrying out an investigation. The outcome may be different from their prediction but try to avoid saying that the prediction was wrong - it was different from what was expected. (I wonder why?) More learning can come from these unexpected results than if predictions are boringly 'right' every time. After all, if our predictions are right every time, why bother to investigate?

Young children are great scientists - only we usually call it 'getting into everything'! What we as adults need to do is help children develop their curiosity and skills so that they can begin to think and work in a logical way.

What equipment do you need?

Some simple equipment may help with some explanations but a great deal of science can be done with existing or found materials through normal everyday activities. Make sure any equipment is good quality and well maintained. Magnets that don't work or magnifiers you can't see through can be very frustrating. Sand and water play, as we have already said, is invaluable for investigating materials, as is cookery. Have a few good quality magnifiers to look closely at sand and see the separate grains or look at the difference between sugar and flour when you're cooking.

Hand-lenses are useful but children need to be taught how to use them properly. Stand magnifiers are good with young children since they are set at the right focal distance or there are some useful 'bug boxes' of various kinds on the market. Beware of toy microscopes or very small bug boxes. Children have difficulty focusing them and just become frustrated. Be aware, too, that magnifiers should be thought of as semi-consumable. A good one should last for several years but they do get scratched. Make sure they are washed and checked each time they are used and stored carefully so that they don't scratch each other. Cover a block of polystyrene with paper or sticky-backed plastic. Poke some holes in to take the handles and store them upright - helps with one-to-one correspondence too!

Collections of objects for counting and sorting according to different criteria are useful. We have found a good set of model animals invaluable.

Plastic spoons, clear plastic party glasses and plastic measuring jugs are among our essentials together with a few plastic 'cat' trays to help with organising resources. But the best resource, by far, is the children themselves.

Carole Creary and Gay Wilson

If there is one area of the pre-school curriculum that causes uncertainty and unease, it's technology. The ELGs state that by the end of the Foundation Stage most children will be able to: 'find out about and identify the uses of everyday technology and use information and communication technology and programmable toys to support their learning'. But what does this mean? Ursula Daniels explains

The **value of technology** in early years

Adults usually see technology as computers but, in the broadest sense, it also includes tape recorders, video recorders, fax machines, electronic music devices and programmable toys. Often adults use a tape recorder to play songs and rhymes, but they do not think of letting the children learn to work it themselves or to record their own voices or other sounds. Adults set a video recorder or replay a recorded television programme without explaining in simple terms how it works.

Early years settings may have access to a fax machine which is regarded as being for adult use only, and yet it's such an exciting and immediate technology for young children. They can send pictures to another school or to parents, perhaps at work, and get one back in reply. There are programmable toys which enable children to give instructions such as forward, back, left and right, develop spatial awareness, logical thinking and sequencing. So it really isn't necessary to have a computer in order to make a start with technology.

Many people would argue that even if you can afford a computer, what's the point of it anyway? Surely children should be learning through active play, not sitting in front of a screen all day! And what can three- and four-year-olds gain from trying to make sense of an upper case keyboard anyway? It is unfortunate that young children frequently tend to be on the receiving end of 'hand-me-downs'. When it comes to computers this means the primary school's ancient BBC or a parent's long rejected keyboard and monochrome television set. Both would be better placed in a museum of technology - or a skip.

The best equipment

If you're going to use a computer with young children, they will need the very best - an up-to-date multimedia system with a colour monitor, sound and a mouse or tracker ball.

I mention the last two items because there is no longer any need for children to struggle with an upper case keyboard. Other input devices are available. A mouse means a letter, word or picture can be pointed at and clicked on to make something happen. It can also be used to drag an object across the screen. So if the program is about dressing a teddy bear in suitable clothing for a rainy day, a picture of a raincoat can be dragged across the screen and placed on his body.

The conventional keyboard can be forgotten with most new software for young children.

The vision of a child working alone at a computer screen worries many people, but children can work on their own or in pairs quite happily, depending on the activity. A group might need more supervision, but so do many other activities, where work often takes place in small groups as a matter of course. On some occasions, it's not the hands-on experience that's the main focus - an adult controls the software from which a group of children are learning.

So, how can technology support children's learning? It has something to offer all six areas of learning, some more than others.

Personal, Social and Emotional Development

To further personal and social development, as with many other activities, children can work in pairs or as a member of a group, learning to share and to co-operate with one another. Technology can also support independent learning and decision-making.

Communication, Language and Literacy

In language and literacy, technology offers a multi-sensory approach - pictures, words and sounds. Talking stories and nursery rhyme books are available which let children follow a story being read to them. This helps to reinforce many basic English language learning skills such as left to right, top to bottom, in addition to encouraging listening.

Clicking on a word and hearing it spoken develops the concept that words convey meaning. Sound and animation can be an aid to interpreting pictures and understanding meaning. For example, if a dog is happy, clicking on its tail will make it wag. They can even turn the pages of the book. Whilst children also need to spend time with traditional books, a computer can present the same books in an interactive way as an added dimension.

Talking word processors can allow childen to listen to their own words or sentences being read back to them. An adult can act as a scribe for their stories, perhaps adding the words to a picture that they have created with an art package.

Software is available to tackle specific language and literacy skills in an entertaining and motivating way, for example, letter recognition where children can learn the shape and the sound of letters. Often options can be set for different levels of difficulty so that tasks can be geared to individual or group needs.

It is also possible to use a multimedia authoring package to create pages that contain any combination of images, sounds and words. The images can be drawings, clip art or photographs. The sound can be music, recorded sound effects or a voice, including the children's voices. The text can be single words, phrases or sentences. The advantage of this for young children is that it is not dependent on handwriting or spelling and can be a stimulus to the purposeful development of oral language skills. For instance, after a day out at a farm, photographs of the children and animals taken with a still video camera could appear on the screen alongside the children's own recorded voices - 'I liked the pigs best'; 'We fed the lambs'. Similarly they could make up their own story and it could be accompanied by their artwork from an art package. This type of work does unfortunately require expensive equipment which may well be outside the range of many early years settings. However, a local secondary school might be prepared to do a project with you using their equipment.

Mathematical Development
Mathematics can be represented visually on a computer. Skills such as counting, matching, sorting, sequencing and shape recognition can all be learned in a colourful, interactive environment. This supplements practical activities and is an introduction to more abstract ideas. In other words, it can provide a bridge between concrete and abstract representation. At the same time mathematical vocabulary such as 'bigger than', 'in front of', 'less than' can be developed. Animations can demonstrate the meaning clearly, a bit like a cartoon film.

Knowledge and Understanding of the World
The use of technology itself is within that part of the curriculum relating to Knowledge and Understanding of the World. Children have a natural curiosity about the world, including technology, which they take for granted. Software is available which will enable them to become more aware of their environment - creating a scene such as the buildings in a town, the contents of a house, the creatures that live in a pond or the animals that live on a farm. All they need to do is drag pictures across the screen to make the scene. There is great potential for language development at the same time. CD-Roms can open up many other areas for exploration - under the sea, outer space and life in other countries. They can hear the sounds that animals in other environments make, see videos on the computer screen of underwater scenes, find out about the way of life of other cultures.

Physical Development
Using a mouse or other input device to control what is on the screen develops hand-eye coordination and controlled movements of the hand, contributing therefore to other work in physical development.

Creative Development
Art packages provide many opportunities for two-dimensional work as an extension to other art activities. Shapes can be produced simply, changes made, whole areas of colour removed or added. Brush width can easily be altered and other effects such as spraying can be used. One program has a different sound to accompany the use of each colour - a musical painting program.

Whilst music can be created through a keyboard attached to a computer, there are many small free-standing electronic music devices that serve young children just as well in enabling them to use their imagination and express their ideas and feelings. They can play, record and re-play a series of notes. A range of different instruments and effects, including animal sounds, can be played. Some of these keyboards are specifically designed for young children.

Finally, don't neglect to talk about technology. Whilst they may not understand the technical detail, children can become aware of sensors controlling automatic doors and traffic lights, bar code readers in supermarkets, the use of cash points and switch cards. How many of their parents use computers at work? Or at home? Talk about washing machines, microwaves, video recorders - What do they do? How do we control them? Work out in simple words what the program is doing. Their attention can be drawn to the use of computers in libraries, travel agents and doctors' surgeries. Children have all heard of robots - what are they actually used for? They see weather forecasts - how do we get the images that are used in weather forecasting?

The list of possibilities is endless. And talking won't cost you anything!

Ursula Daniels

Don't worry if you don't have a computer - activities such as describing, sorting, counting and matching objects provide an important step in developing IT capability. Margaret Still explains why and shows how these activities can be taken a step further if you do have a computer

Information **handling**

Information handling is a major area in the ICT (Information and Communications Technology) National Curriculum. It is all about capturing, storing, manipulating and interrogating information.

To be effective information handlers using ICT, children need to develop many skills. They will need to be able to sort, classify and organise information in a way that can be accepted by a computer database. They will need to be able to interrogate information stored, by forming and asking the right questions. They will need to be able to analyse data that comes in the form of graphs and charts to make sense of that information, then present it in an understandable way. They will need to develop skills of predicting and hypothesising.

This all sounds very much like the work you would expect to see in a Key Stage 2 classroom - and so it is. What, you might ask, has it to do with the pre-school child?

Children are information gatherers from an early age. They find information from a variety of sources, gathering it through their senses. So that they make sense of this information they must be encouraged to talk about and describe their experiences and feelings, the objects that they use and that are around them, looking for and thinking about similarities and differences. Pre-school activities of describing, sorting, counting and matching objects are vitally important and necessary as a foundation for later information handling activities with ICT.

These skills are the basis for understanding in mathematics and science. They also form a basis for understanding ICT and provide an important step in developing ICT capability. So even without a computer you can give children activities that are a vital

pre-requisite to information handling as part of the ICT curriculum. With a computer these activities can be taken a step further.

Describing objects

Children carefully describe objects in different ways, leading to the use of a keyword. Other children guess the object described, for example:

The children bring their coats into class. They talk generally about them, what colour they are, how they are fastened, if they have a hood, and so on. In turn they think of a coat . . . I'm thinking of blue . . . zip . . . hood . . . fur . . .? It's Jade's coat!

Working with a group of about six children, you could let the children help you type two sentences into a word processor (*Wordpad* on

Windows would be good enough) describing each child's coat:

Jade
My coat is blue. It has a zip.
(highlighting the words blue and zip)

Using the 'find' or 'search' facility of the wordprocessor, ask the computer to pick out a certain keyword, thus identifying the coat associated with it.

As a paper exercise, each child's sentences can be written on a card with the keywords highlighted. With help, the children search through the cards to find the appropriate words. This will illustrate the speed of the computer in finding information.

Asking questions

(Dividing into groups - the basis for a binary tree)

Again, take the children's coats (start with only three with obvious similarities and differences).

Ask a question with a yes/no answer to divide the coats into two groups.

The children then play 'Guess the coat I am thinking of' by asking and answering the questions in turn. More coats can be added as the children are able to cope.

You can then try it using other objects, such as teddies, musical instruments, vegetables, fruits.

There are computer programs that handle information in this way but at this stage it is the process of the practical activity and the skills that are being developed that are important.

Using ICT to sort objects into groups

Children can use simple software packages that will allow them to match pictures that are the same or different by dragging them around the screen using a mouse. Such activities should not be seen as a substitute for sorting real objects on the table but a worthwhile extension of those activities that also give practice in mouse skills.

Counting the objects in each group may lead to creating picture graphs both on paper and on the computer screen.

Creating graphs

Children could investigate the way each of them travels to school. By drawing pictures of footsteps, buses, cars and bicycles they can build up a picture graph on a large sheet of paper. From the chart they can then answer questions, such as how do most

children come to school? How many people come by car/bus. The same chart can then be produced through the computer using a graphing program; clicking the mouse button on appropriate pictures in turn will gradually build up the graph on the screen.

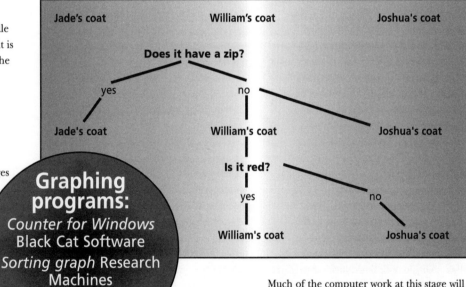

The computer will allow:

❑ multiple copies to be printed out at the press of a button;

❑ the chart to be changed, allowing for absent children to add their information when they return to school;

❑ the picture graph to be changed to a block graph (and changed back again),

showing children, visually, that one picture can be represented by one coloured block;

❑ the information to be sorted from the largest to the smallest and vice versa at the click of a button.

Producing graphs can be the result of many different sorting activities done in class - sorting beans by colour, shape or type; sorting nuts, fruits, vegetables; investigating ourselves, the colour of our eyes and hair. All these activities could lead to making paper and computer graphs.

Much of the computer work at this stage will be adult directed with children sitting around the computer, interacting with you as you question and encourage them to join in the activity. The children will contribute by adding their information to the computer as appropriate. In this way, they are beginning to learn the power of the computer.

Margaret Still

Graphing programs:
Counter for Windows Black Cat Software
Sorting graph Research Machines
Picture Point Logotron

History in the early years is about introducing the concepts of difference and change - in people, objects and places. Look at old photos, invite grandparents in to talk about when they were small. Gay Wilkinson gives details of these and other ideas

History

History is, above all, about people, how they lived and why. Young children are passionately interested in people, in particular themselves and their immediate and extended families. Whilst they are primarily occupied with the present they do have a sense of, and are often fascinated by, the changes that have taken place, both in their own lives and those of others close to them.

They love to look at and talk about photographs of themselves and other members of the family taken in the past. They love to hear stories about when mummy or daddy was little, what it was like and what they did. They ask questions about their own past and want to know what they did at particular times or recall special events that they remember.

They also think about the future; they anticipate and talk about special events that are going to happen to them such as their birthday or going on holiday.

This growing understanding about the sequence of time - yesterday, today, tomorrow; past, present and future; and their ability to both remember and predict events which have personal significance, provides a sound starting point for developing an understanding of history and some of its elements in the early years environment.

Storytelling

In planning and organising your environment you will need to take account of the natural curiosity young children have about their own history and that of others close to them and their innate interest in telling stories. Could you invite someone in to tell the story of some part of his or her own childhood?

Perhaps several children in your group will be having their birthdays around a particular period and are talking about the parties they are going to have. Could you invite a parent or other known adult to come and talk about their memories of birthdays and how they celebrated them?

As Christmas approaches we all know that children's talk is dominated by speculation about presents. Could you invite a grandparent, or other older person in the community, to come and share their memories of Christmas and the sort of presents they wanted and received or some other aspect of their childhood? Since the average life span is now much longer than it used to be there are many people well over 60 in our communities with ample leisure time. Because the last few decades have been subject to immense social and technological progress these people have experienced all sorts of changes as part of their everyday lives. There will be some who can vividly recall a time when there were few cars and most people travelled by bus, tram or steam train; when there were no supermarkets and deliveries of milk and bread were made in a horse-drawn delivery van; when they could go to a shop and buy a pennyworth of sweets. Within this group there will be some who would love to receive an invitation to share some of their memories with the children and in doing so feel that they can

still make a valuable contribution to society. You may have members of the community who can share their experience of a childhood in another country, to give the children a wider perspective.

Before any visitor talks to the children it is helpful if you talk to them first so that you can help them select the parts of their life story that you think will engage the children's attention and provide information that matches their current interests. At the same time you might want to discuss with them the size of group they think they will feel most comfortable with and any general rules you have for the children in your setting. In this way you can ensure that the experience is worthwhile and enjoyable both for the children and for themselves.

You might like to consider making tape recordings of these oral history accounts (providing that your visitors are happy with the idea!). After the visit, when you and the children are talking about what they have heard and they are trying to either recall particular information or to re-tell the story, parts of the tape can then be replayed as a reminder.

Such an activity will help them to get events in the right sequence as well as developing their own ability to tell a story, both important skills in thinking about history. If the children represent parts of the story, either pictorially, in words, or both, these can be made into a book with any additional text written by you where necessary. This can then be placed in the listening area with the tape recording so that the children can revisit the experience whenever they wish.

Toys

Such visits can often arouse children's interests in what familiar objects might have looked like in the past. A visit by a parent or grandparent to talk about the toys they played with as a child could lead to a general interest in old toys. Putting together a display of toys from a particular period alongside a contemporary collection will provide opportunities for the children to consider the differences and similarities between toys then and now and talk about significant changes. A simple collection of teddy bears would allow them to look for clues that might indicate how old different teddies might be - history is about using evidence. They could then be invited to put three or four into chronological order, starting with the oldest, and to explain what evidence they had used to determine their sequence to the rest of their group or class. It is surprising how many adults keep particular favourite toys from their childhood and many would be willing to loan them to you, especially when they are helped to understand how this will support the children in developing important concepts and skills.

There are many other familiar domestic objects in children's daily lives which intrigue them, most of which have changed over a period of time.

Themes or interests such as homes, families and ourselves, provide ample opportunities for displays of interesting artefacts. For example a collection of cookery implements would provide you with the opportunity to talk with them about what they can see, encouraging them to guess what some tools might have been used for. A collection of clothing from a specific period would give them the chance to make immediate comparisons with modern dress and they could be encouraged to speculate how particular garments might have affected the behaviour and activities of the children or adults who wore them. If possible give them the opportunity to use artefacts (where appropriate) in their own activities, for example old kitchen tools during a cookery session or in the home corner or by including some simple replicas of items of period clothing in the dressing-up collection.

Since you will want the children to be able to handle objects as much as possible do remember when borrowing things to ask if they are happy with this, emphasising that the children will be encouraged to be thoughtful and careful at all times. Where a loan is made with conditions do make sure that these are observed. If you have a local museum they might operate a loan service of artefacts suitable for young children which you can borrow. Do remember to tell them that wherever possible you need objects that can be handled. Some museums might not have a loan service but will be willing to arrange for you to take the children to visit them and let them handle and talk about the artefacts there.

Photographs

It is not always possible to give children immediate experiences which will lead to the development of an understanding of people and places in past times. Photographs and pictures are an important resource that can be used with young children to help them consider the concepts of difference and change. Look out for and collect photographs and picture postcards of your area which illustrate how it has changed over the years. Choose two which have very clear differences - changes in shop fronts, people's dress, type or number of vehicles, buildings, and so on - and invite the children to talk about what they can see and why they think the changes might have happened.

Look at the oldest picture and talk about what it might have been like to live in the area then and how people might have felt about it. What games might the children have played? How did people do their shopping? How did children get to school?

Photographs of themselves as babies, as toddlers or older provide absorbing evidence of personal change. Ask parents if you can borrow some photographs of their child which show them at different stages in their lives - new-born, crawling, first birthday, walking - and let children put their photographs in chronological order and tell their story to the group or a friend. Where it is appropriate children might attach date labels to photographs. In this way they will be introduced to the use of a time line.

Use a camera in your own setting to record different aspects of special events such as an outing and invite the children to help you to put them in the correct order in the album.

Take photographs of your setting, indoors and out, which reflect seasonal changes and use these to create a book that describes key features of the children's year, for example pictures of Christmas parties, decorations in classrooms, the arrival of Father Christmas, bare trees in the outside environment, snow on a path or playground, children wearing coats, scarves and gloves, the winter sky.

Use a Polaroid camera to record the sequence followed by a group of children engaged, for example, in building with blocks or cooking. After they have finished and cleared up invite them to recall the event using the photographs and to put the photographs in the right sequence. These can then be used to create a picture book for the book area. Children will delight in revisiting these moments in their past over and over again, recalling what they did, said and felt and will find visible evidence of their own growth and change.

All children love to hear stories read and told. You can use this natural enthusiasm to introduce them to the lives of special people in the past (remember that the past doesn't have to be a long time ago, so keep an eye on the newspaper for items that will make a good story at some time). Look for good models from different cultural backgrounds - there are many to choose from. It is important to help children begin to distinguish between fiction and fact. When telling them stories, whether created in someone's imagination, or about real events in the lives of real people, or a combination

of fictional characters in a real historical context, tell them what sort of story they are going to hear. You could begin to make an anthology of factual historical stories that you have found the children enjoy and this will provide your setting with a useful resource in the future. Remember to update it as you tell or read new stories.

Drama

Drama is a useful tool in helping young children begin to understand that people who lived at different times were real people, that they would have had the same sort of feelings as themselves, the same general wishes, fears, problems and delights.

Give them opportunities to explore events in a story that they have heard and enjoyed through either self-initiated role-play or through an adult-directed drama session. A few well-chosen props in the role-play area will often prompt them to explore particular aspects of a story they have heard, but do remember that this is their play and that they may choose to use the props for purposes other than those you had intended!

A well-planned drama session will allow you to build on the children's spontaneous play and more actively guide them towards thinking about particular ideas which will develop their understanding about the past and how people behaved at that time and why. It is important that you think carefully

about what the children might already know within their own experience and then how you can use this to create a meaningful context which will involve them in thinking about those concepts you have selected in your planning.

Language

History starts with a child's own past and they use the knowledge about their own life history and the everyday routines which bind it together to make sense of the lives and experiences of others. It is therefore crucial that they are helped to develop a language that enables them to think about and describe events and people within the context of time.

Gay Wilkinson

Learning from objects may sound like the sort of thing curators of museums do before displaying their treasured artefacts in glass cases next to technical labels. But objects can be a great way for young children to get to grips with the way life has changed over time and to become confident interpreters of historical evidence

History **through** objects

The Early Learning Goals and even Key Stage 1 of the National Curriculum are quite vague on what young children should 'learn' in history, and rightly so.
The Early Learning Goal in the Knowledge and Understanding of the World section simply says: 'find out about past and present events in their own lives and in those of their families and other people they know'. Early years history is not about particular periods but rather about developing a sense of time and the skills to make sense of the past.

History is about looking at life and how lives have changed over time, so it draws on just about all the areas of knowledge that children are developing. It's about seeing the similarities and the differences in people's lives in the past and ultimately recognising that our history plays a huge part in making us what we are today.

A sense of time
Whilst we as adults have been taught to think of time as neatly parcelled up into past, present and future, young children have a less measured view. They know when something has happened, but may be unsure

if something they are looking forward to has happened yet or not. To pre-school children, last week, last month and last year can be much the same thing. Some children may begin to try to get some measure of time. Common ways include talking about things that happened a long time ago or when they were not even born yet and learning to count the days to an exciting event. They may say 'It's only two more sleeps to my birthday' or 'It's not the next day, but the next day until we go on holiday'. This slightly fluid idea of time means that talking with children about dates or about things being 100 years old doesn't really have the same meaning as it does to adults.

How can objects help?
Time is such an abstract idea that objects are a good way of making the past more concrete, of giving children a first-hand experience. Whilst this is true, we must be aware that thinking about objects in an historical way is very different from the way children normally interact with things. They will need help to make sense of them.

Good objects to start with:
- ❑ Domestic appliances such as flat irons and copper kettles, sugar tongs, wooden butter pats and moulds, stone hot-water bottles, fire irons, toasting forks, brushes, carpet beaters
- ❑ Jewellery, such as glass beads
- ❑ An old box Brownie camera (old toys can be expensive)
  Just go and look around your local junk shop or go to a car boot sale for inspiration.

Objects have lots to offer. They can:

❑ be motivating, exciting and unusual;

❑ help children develop historian's skills;

❑ lead on to children collecting things themselves;

❑ lead on to children becoming interested in museums;

❑ spark off children's creativity.

What skills do children need to learn?
To learn from objects you need to be a detective. Children need to learn how to ask their own questions and to find ways of finding out the answers. In history, if you can't find out, it's quite all right to make your best guess based on what you already know, so any logical answer can be 'right'.

The skills involved are:

❑ **observation**
Children will need to learn to look closely at the objects. They will need to notice small details and to use all their senses.

❑ **classification**
Children will need to look for

similarities and differences between objects in the past and between past and present objects. By trying to see how a camera from the 1920s compares to a modern child's camera, they might be thinking about materials, weight, the look of the things, shapes, how it works, what each was used for, who would have had one, and so on. By comparing the 1920s camera to a 1920s light, they might begin to see how things from the same time sometimes have things in common.

❑ **making links**

Children will need to draw on what they know of their own family's past, on things they have seen outside of nursery and on things they have learned through other topics to make sense of the objects. To identify a flat iron, for example, may mean making a link to someone ironing at home or to the role-play area.

❑ **interpretation**

Children will need to feel that they are detectives, piecing together the story behind the objects. All the things they can see, feel, smell, and so on, are clues as to what the thing is and how it was used. Children should feel confident that any ideas they have will be listened to and valued. In historical enquiry, when previously unknown objects are discovered, there may be lots of different ideas on how the thing was used or who owned it.

How do you start?

Whilst many young children are capable of asking questions about things, it is frustrating for them if all the questions they ask can't be answered or involve looking in books with adults and being told the answers.

A good way to start with objects is to introduce an object through oral history or an historical story. Early years history is based on oral history or family memories and these are strong ways to connect with what children already know about and to build their sense of belonging. This is also a natural way to reflect the diversity of cultures in our community. By adding an object to the spoken history, you can introduce a new dimension and allow children to begin to

---

Questions to ask of objects:
- ❑ What is it?
- ❑ What does it do?
- ❑ How does it work?
- ❑ Does it remind you of anything?
- ❑ How is it similar or different?
- ❑ What is it made of?
- ❑ Is it very old?
- ❑ How do we know?
- ❑ Can we tell who it belonged to?

---

investigate the past for themselves.

Families often have as many treasured objects as they do memories. A session where Grandma talks about her childhood could be extended if she could bring with her an object from that time. The object can help children to think about questions to ask and they can use both their own observations and the story Grandma told to answer questions about the object. They may even be able to add detail to Grandma's story by thinking about the object and suggesting ways it might have been used, things that might have happened to it and so on. The good thing is that Grandma will be there to answer questions or fill in information if needed.

How do you make the leap to just looking at an object?

Objects don't really make sense out of context and even historians would rarely just be looking at an object for no reason. The key to helping children to be able to learn from objects is to give the investigation a meaning.

There are any number of ways you could set up your object session. It could have an art focus, a language focus, a maths focus or a role-play setting. Children could be making a book about things you use for cooking and you might include some historical utensils. Making drawings or paintings of objects with as much detail as possible encourages close observation. Use the end products to create the background picture for a new role-play corner or display them with a tape recording of children explaining what they found out about their object. You might like to write a poem together about what it must have been like to iron with a flat iron and children could tell you their ideas to weave into the poem. Or perhaps three different families have muddled up their treasures and children need to help to find which belongs to which family using clues. Clues could be photos of part of the object, tape recordings of someone talking about how they used their object or pictures in a book of something that looked a bit like theirs.

Whichever way you choose to look at objects children will be asking similar questions (see the box below). When you are talking with children about what they have done that session, try to encourage them to think about what the questions were that they were asking as well as describing what they did. If children reflect on their questions, they should have a good place to start next time they encounter an object.

Where do you get objects?

To find interesting objects ask parents, grandparents and carers, visit car boot sales, junk shops and even charity shops. Some local authorities or museums have loan collections and may be prepared to let you borrow things. Be sure if you borrow objects (on loan or from families), to teach children about handling things with care and to represent as many different family backgrounds as possible.

Try to find household objects so that young children will be able to relate them to things they know from their own lives.

Jo Graham

Geography is about people and places. When you're teaching very young children, keep activities within their scope of experience, says Gay Wilkinson. That means simple ideas such as spotting local landmarks or features on a walk to the park or meeting local people to find out what jobs they do

Geography in the early years

Geography, like history, is about people, the places they live in, the way in which their environment affects and shapes their lives and the effects they have upon that environment through the process of living. Some of the experiences that you might provide to promote the development of children's historical understanding and skills (a visitor coming to share their memories or the use of photographs, for example) have the potential to contribute to their geographical understanding or vice-versa! It is therefore important that when you are planning activities you have a clear view of which aspect of an Early Learning Goal you are seeking to promote at any one time as a main focus (although recognising the links with other areas of learning).

Near and far

The children you work with will have a range of knowledge about a variety of places, both local and further afield, developed through either routine everyday events or special family activities. In their local area they might have walked with their parents to the local shops, visited the doctor or dentist, been to the vets, the park or playground, collected an older sibling from school and visited friends' homes. In the wider community they may have travelled by car or bus to the supermarket, the cinema, the swimming pool or been to visit relatives. Many children will also have experience of places far away from where they live as a result of going on holiday or visiting friends and relatives either in their own country or abroad and will have some understanding of long distance travel. You will need to take account of such journeys when planning your curriculum, perhaps using them as a starting point.

Journeys of discovery

Children have the ability to invest the smallest activity with the excitement of great events and journeys always have a tingle of adventure! A walk to the local shops or the park provides opportunities for children to think more carefully and deeply about well-known places as well as have some fun!

If you are planning to take the children on a walk for a special purpose, do it first yourself without the children. Make sure you know about any features that you want them to notice in particular. Find out about any potential safety hazards. Be sure that the route you have planned does include the features that you want the children to think about. Brief the other adults going with you

about the main focus of the activity and what to look for with the children. You might give them a map with any special features identified.

It can be helpful to bring the children together before the walk so that you can prepare them for what they are going to be doing and why. For example, if you want them to notice particular buildings, use selected reference books to talk about the buildings in the pictures and discuss their possible use. By doing this you can be sure that every child will be able to take an active part in the walk. As they walk with you, remember that they will also want to talk about the things they see which have a special significance in their personal lives - nanna's house, the chemist's shop, the mosque, the park - as well as look for things you have identified.

Making maps

To help the children begin to understand about map-making you might take a short walk in the immediate area, choosing a route that is familiar to all the children. Before the walk, discuss with the children what they think might be the significant features of the journey, which would help to describe it to others. If possible, take a Polaroid camera with you and take pictures of these features and any others that seem significant during the walk. When you return, talk with the children about the photographs and let them choose those that they think would be the most helpful to include on a map. You could then make a simple map together with them placing the photos where they think they should go.

You can also use the photographs to stimulate the children's memories about the walk and the sequence of where things were seen, their purpose and their relationship with other buildings or objects. Both these activities would help the children acquire and use geographical language of position and location.

If you are able to obtain a blown-up aerial photograph of the area you have visited (these fascinate children) or a blown-up street map you can identify and trace the route taken with the children. Some of them might like to represent the experience by drawing a picture of things they saw on the way. A similar activity can be undertaken to represent where the children live. They can then talk about how they come to school, comparing the different routes taken by each child, and might lead to individual map-making of these personal journeys.

Treasure hunt

Mapping activities, that will involve the same skills, can also be undertaken within your own setting. Help the children observe and think carefully about this part of their world that they are very familiar with and yet perhaps never really look at closely. Use games to help them begin to explore their classroom - perhaps arrange a treasure hunt with pictorial clues that will lead them to the treasure.

Organise the children into pairs so that they have the opportunity to discuss the clues and help one another. Instead of helping them with the usual hints such as 'getting warmer' or 'getting colder' you might like to give directional hints such as 'You're facing the wrong way', 'It's on your left/ alongside/in front of you' or 'You need to make a half turn'. The children can then be encouraged to draw a map of the route they took to find the treasure, which would include significant features of their classroom, and then talk about what they did with their friends. You might consider giving a child or small group the responsibility for planning such an activity including giving the verbal clues.

Language skills

'Observe, find out about and identify features in the place they live and the natural world'

There are many resources that can be used for focused work leading to the acquisition of geographical language and understanding. For example, give two children each an identical set of model farm animals and a large piece of card which you have coloured to represent different fields and enclosures. Sit the children facing one another but put a low board or thick card partition between them so that they cannot see what each other is doing. One child then arranges their animals on the farm and then gives verbal instructions to the other child so that they produce the same arrangement. Once finished the two children check by comparing. The second child can then have a turn at giving the instructions and the process is repeated.

Resources such as blocks, play mats, Lego, toy cars, train sets, farms and model people offer countless opportunities for children to create real or imaginary road layouts and enact imaginary journeys. If you have a large area, indoors or outside, where the children can use wheeled toys, you might sometimes mark out a road system, in consultation with the children, so that they can re-enact journeys and explore through their imaginary play issues such as road safety.

Children also love to talk about themselves, their families and their homes. They will often draw and paint pictures of their house with family members and themselves. Could they make simple maps of areas in their own home - their bedroom perhaps? - and share and talk about these with other children? Such an activity might present an opportunity for parents to join in with their child's learning.

'Find out about their environment and talk about those features they like and dislike'

Sharing holiday experiences

At the end of any holiday period, but especially the summer, children are eager to share with you and their friends what they have been doing and where they have been. If possible, have large maps of Great Britain and the world as well as a globe (there are some inflatable plastic globes available which are light enough for young children to handle comfortably) and some copies of children's atlases.

Invite the children to bring in one photograph of their holiday that includes themselves. Discuss with them where they have been on holiday, how they travelled there, how far away it was, how long it took to get there, the relatives they visited, if any, and what they did on holiday. Help the children to locate their holiday venues on the appropriate map and/or globe and encourage them to speculate about the different places and make comparisons. If possible, display the maps on the wall with the children's photographs, or drawings they have made, and use string, wool or coloured tape to map these to the places visited. If they have any souvenirs from the countries they have visited, would they be willing to lend them for a display?

Parents from other cultures whose children attend your setting - and the children themselves - can be a rich resource. They often bring into your setting in-depth first hand experience of other countries and ways of life that can enhance the understanding and knowledge of all the children. Perhaps a parent or grandparent could bring in a family collection of artefacts that reflect the culture and environment of their country of birth and talk about these with the children. They might be able to help a group of children cook food from their country using the appropriate cooking utensils, ingredients and processes.

People to meet

Young children are intensely curious about other people that they come into contact with within their immediate environment. They want to know people's names and talk about the different work they see them doing, particularly when that work has some immediate impact upon the lives of themselves or other family members. Local shopkeepers or assistants, the school crossing patrol person, the local policeman or woman, the milkman, the postman or lady, the person who delivers the newspaper (the list is endless!) are all people that they will have come across and have some knowledge of before coming to pre-school. Would any of these people be willing to come and talk to the children about what they do? Are there people within your own setting - the cook, the caretaker - who could talk to the children?

You could set up a display with a range of artefacts, including clothing, which illustrates a particular job and discuss these with the children. Or set up an interactive display of artefacts representing different roles and encourage the children to sort them into appropriate sets saying why they have put certain items together. Inviting other adults into your setting presents a positive opportunity to get parents involved and is often one way in which fathers and male carers are able to see that they can make a real contribution to the curriculum.

In the local area are there particular people whose work makes a unique contribution to the community, or whose work brings them into regular contact with the children, who would be willing to talk about their work? After their visit you could set up and resource a specific role-play area so that the children can explore what they have heard and seen through their imaginative play and consolidate their understanding. For example, following a visit from the district nurse, could you create a nurse's room? What might it have in it? Which patients might visit and why? A visit by a local greengrocer could lead to thinking about the different countries that fruit and vegetables come from and identifying these on the world map or globe.

Environmental issues

Our responsibility for caring for the environment is now an important issue for everyone. Introduce the children to environmental issues by giving them real opportunities to make considered choices within your setting. Involve them in discussions about the arrangement of furniture and resources in the classroom. Are things in the right place for the work you all want or need to do? Remind them that they will need to consider not only their own needs but those of friends and the adults who support them.

Talk with them about how you might develop the outdoor area. What sort of features might be included? Could you develop a simple conservation area where grass and wild flowers could grow unchecked and insects are encouraged to visit or live? Could they be invited to design the area? What sort of impact might this have on their usual outdoor activities and on their own behaviour? How might they resolve this conflict of need? Talk about the local area

with them and the sort of things they like to do there. How well does the local area meet their needs? Go for a walk and look for good and bad features in the context of their needs. On their return let them draw designs or build a three-dimensional map of how they think the area could look. Remind them of their shared responsibility for the immediate environment - tidying up and returning things they have used in their play to their proper place is a first step into beginning to take responsibility for the wider environment we all inhabit.

Gay Wilkinson

Help children get to know their environment and begin to develop the skills needed for geographical investigation with these ideas from Margaret Edgington

Developing a sense of place

From the moment they're born children use all their senses to get to know the features of the different places they spend time in. These images they get from their senses are powerful, and many adults, when asked to remember their childhood, talk about textures, sounds, tastes and smells (as well as sights). Early years workers need to support and focus children's sensory explorations, helping them to talk about and compare the features of different places. You need to help children become more conscious of their environment and begin to develop the skills needed for geographical investigation.

Explore the immediate environment

When children start at an under-fives setting they have to learn:

- to find their way around the building and outside area;
- where equipment is stored;
- who the adults are;
- the daily routine and expectations.

You need to plan carefully so children have the time they need to adjust to being part of the new community. Storage trays and shelves should be labelled with pictures and words so children can see where things are kept. Photos of staff members with their names and roles, and photo-books or displays showing the sequence of the day, can be made to help parents and children understand the new experience.

Once settled, children can be encouraged to explore further. Indoors they can be helped to notice, and talk about:

- how the building has been built (materials used, shapes, structure);
- what happens in different parts of the building;
- who works there (there will often be cleaners, secretaries, managers/ heads, caretakers, cooks or meal supervisors)

and what equipment and skills they need to do their jobs.

You might ask children what they think about the layout of their room and encourage them to make suggestions for improving it.

During outside play children can be helped to focus on, and talk about, what they can see and hear. In a world of visual over-stimulation and seemingly non-stop noise, it is all too easy for children to switch off, and looking and listening activities are increasingly important. Questions to encourage focusing could include:

- What can you see when you face this way/that way?
- What can you see from the top of the climbing frame/through the tunnel, etc? (Encourage them to notice detail, and to compare things seen from different angles and distances.)
- With eyes closed - what can you hear when you stand there/when you are inside the tunnel or barrel?

Questions could also be posed to help children focus on specific aspects of their environment. Can they see places where you could shop/eat/post a letter/start a journey? Can they see or hear people

working/animals or birds/traffic? Can they smell anything and, if so, what do they think is making the smell?

Explore the local environment

Visits into the local community are essential to broaden children's first-hand experience - taking a small group of children is usually more productive than a large group. Although they travel around the area daily, they may not have had time to focus and may be unaware of some of its features. All local communities will include at least some of the following, each of which can be the starting point for a visit:

- shops;
- recreation/sports areas;
- parks and gardens;
- churches and/or temples and mosques;
- museums or art galleries;
- library;
- places for animals;
- transport systems (roads, bridges, railways, canals, the sea, flight paths);
- different landscapes (parkland or fields, housing development, woods, hills) - notice seasonal changes;
- people doing different jobs.

When planning a visit decide on a focus and be clear about what you will encourage the children to notice and talk about (questions adapted from the ones above will provide starting points). A pre-visit without the children is therefore advisable.

To show children that their community can be represented in different ways, adults can use and talk about street and ordnance survey maps, old and new photographs (some showing aerial views) and plans. Older children may be inspired to make their own representations using small world or construction equipment or drawing.

Margaret Edgington

'The development of geographical awareness' sounds a frightening term but we all use directional language and geographical skills in our settings if we really think about it! Start with the child and you will find that maps and plans become a natural part of your work

Using maps in the early years

When children first come to their early years setting, finding their way around indoors and outdoors is a daunting task. Where are the toilets? Which way is it to my coat peg? Where is my teacher now?

These are all questions that happen regularly within the first week. Think about these questions and about developing the children's awareness of location through using a basic plan or map of your school or setting and plan together the way to the toilets or coat pegs. This is an excellent way to introduce the idea that print, signs and symbols all have a meaning. (You can use your own appropriate signs and symbols at this stage.)

This is also an appropriate way to introduce the idea of following directional signs and symbols within the building, for example, 'Exit', 'Office this way' and will help the children become used to signs in the outdoor play area.

Using maps outdoors

Use maps outdoors to continue to develop the awareness of location of familiar objects. Make a simple map of your garden (see example) and help the children develop their matching and geographical skills and the awareness of seasonal changes, for example, 'Where is the garage?', 'Where are the carrots and

lettuce growing?', 'What has happened to the cherry tree?', 'How does it look different?' If you keep photographs showing the seasonal changes whenever you do this activity, you will be able to develop a simple book for the children to refer to when they are considering the differences.

Maps are an excellent introduction to natural science. Planned walks using a 'spring trail' or a 'bug trail' are exciting ways to follow maps around the garden looking for similarities and differences and collecting mini-beasts.

Remember to include a route to return the mini-beasts to their habitat! Most of this type of map work can be closely linked with other activities or topic work that you are doing.

When the children have become confident at using and following these maps, encourage them to make their own. For example, draw a map to show the way to the pond, going past the house and cherry tree. When you get to the pond, what can you see? Get the children to record their findings and begin to annotate their maps as an introduction to simple key work. Again use the activity to reinforce learning that is happening elsewhere in your setting.

Simple map work in the garden to develop children's matching and geographical skills and awareness of seasonal changes:
❑ Where are certain fixtures?
❑ Where are things growing?
❑ to observe - plants, trees, birds
❑ to count how many items found
Child to tick each item when found.

Find these things in the garden.

meadow

pond

garage

bird table

tree

house

vegetables

verandah

sandpit

climbing frame

tyre

plants

door

plants

gate

nursery

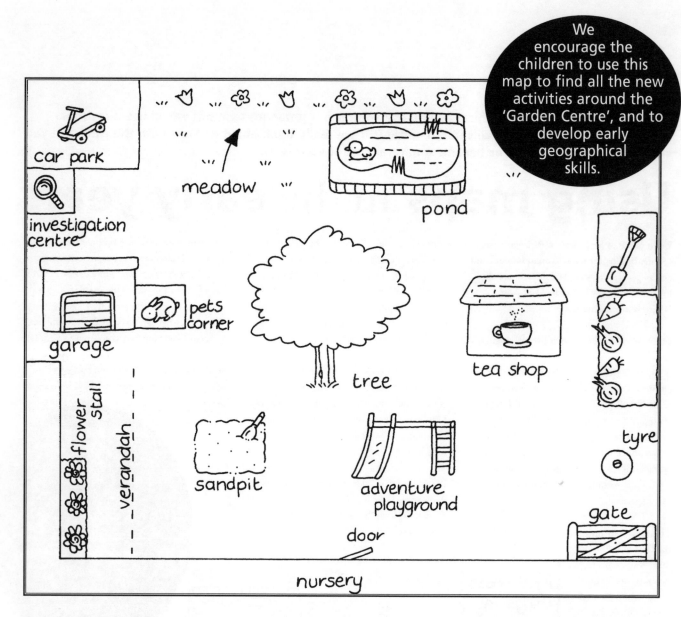

We encourage the children to use this map to find all the new activities around the 'Garden Centre', and to develop early geographical skills.

Using maps in the community

When you take your children to visit the local library, shops or church, make a map and take it with you. Look at the map before you go and explain to the children how you use the directional clues and signs which are in the environment to find your way, another excellent way of illustrating that print has a use and a meaning. When you come back, recall what you saw on the way and get the children to draw their version of what they have seen. More able children will be able to make a simple key.

Making the most of holidays

This is something all early years workers do without realising the geographical significance! Have a map of the UK or world to locate holiday destinations of children and staff. Children love to see their name on a distant unknown place or country. This helps to develop a wider awareness of the size of the world and opens up discussions on methods of travel, weather, and so on.

Train journeys are easy to follow on a map and you could consider this if you are going on a school outing on a steam train or visiting your local station for a short train ride.

A globe is a fascinating addition to your book corner along with a selection of maps and atlases and will stimulate challenging debate.

Celebrating festivals

Have a map of the world to enable staff and children to locate the country highlighted in the celebration as a starting point to your work. Where is China? What would it be like to live there?

Using maps within topic work

Certain topics lend themselves to developing mapping skills and using maps with children:

❑ The farm
❑ Journeys
❑ Garden centre - see map
❑ Supermarket
❑ Holidays

All these topics enable you to make plans and maps of your indoor and outdoor classrooms to help children develop geographical skills.

As you can see, once you get started, the opportunities are endless and a simple map exercise can cover most of the curriculum areas in one go. So be brave, get the clipboards out and use your outdoor classroom as a starting point and then you will see the benefits.

Ann Clay

Karen Hartley explores the nature of problem-solving, why it is thought to be an appropriate way of developing children's learning and the need for colleagues to have a shared understanding of the approach

The value of problem-solving

There are a number of definitions of problem-solving which all link the ability to solve problems to the development of thinking skills. The *Curriculum Guidance for the Foundation Stage* places much emphasis on children solving problems. This follows research into the way in which thinking skills are developed.

'The value of problem-solving lies in its impact on the development of our cognitive processes ie it is concerned with children organising their own learning through remembering, guessing, thinking and finding a solution that is most useful to them' (Stevenson and Palmer, 1994). The process of trying to solve the problem develops the thinking and not just the solution. Fisher has also considered the role problem-solving plays in the development of children's learning (see Figure 1) and suggests that where young children are involved in solving problems, high levels of play and concentration are evident. Ashman and Conway suggest that learning involves the organisation of newly acquired knowledge and skills in such a way that they can be stored and used when a situation requires specific information and that this is the basis of problem-solving.

What can be achieved through the problem-solving approach?

In High/Scope settings, problem-solving is a crucial feature of the curriculum. Hohmann and Weikart consider that 'problem-solving is the process of reconciling the unexpected with what they

(the children) already know about the world' and that this stimulates learning. This learning will be apparent across all areas of learning.

Burden and Williams suggest that because children use their senses when engaged in problem-solving, the physical perceptions of the problem stimulate their 'working memory'. This involves the formation of mental representations which are fundamental to mathematical understanding.

The Early Learning Goals for Knowledge and Understanding of the World require children to explore materials and events in a number of contexts which promote question-raising. Fisher suggests that through

Figure 1 (after Fisher, 1995)

involve first hand experience

foster self esteem and confidence

encourage peer interaction

utilise relevant everyday contexts

raise further problems

problem solving can

provide opportunities for language development

develop independent thinking

highlight process rather than product

encourage question raising and decision making

relate to several areas of learning at the same time

encourage critical thinking

provide opportunities to apply concepts and skills

problem-solving, curiosity is fostered and that the opportunities for decision-making promote confidence and independence of thought and action. As children have positive experiences, they develop a high level of self-esteem and 'learn to regard themselves as capable and successful'.

What makes a problem?

What about the nature of a problem? Would all children find the same problems in a situation? Will a problem always have a solution? Stevenson and Palmer say that there could be a recognised goal with a number of routes. They also point out that, conversely, something is a problem because the outcome is not clear. Problems for some children will not be problematic for others. Problems may be caused by:

❏ materials which don't behave as expected (trying to glue cardboard tubes end to end);
❏ a lack of understanding about the concepts involved (the best place to keep chocolate to stop it melting);
❏ two or more children wanting the same toy or piece of equipment (limited negotiating skills).

These different types of problem require different strategies.

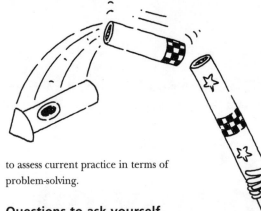

Sometimes problems arise during children's play, sometimes they may be posed by adults, either as a planned activity or when they see the opportunity to ask a question or make a comment to challenge the child's thinking. Practitioners need to recognise situations that may cause problems for children, such as:

❏ Open-ended activity - some children do not know 'where to start' when they need to join one material to another;
❏ Challenge - when an adult or another child asks a question or the child meets a situation that requires thought rather than an automatic response (could be self-initiated or posed by an adult);
❏ Unfamiliar context - a child may be using familiar materials in a situation that is new to him, for example in a baking activity;
❏ Lack of specific knowledge or skill - a child may not know that the type of surface will affect how her toy moves across the floor;
❏ When something requires a specific way of applying skills and knowledge - setting the table for snacks requires an understanding of one-to-one correspondence.

How are problems solved?

Problems can be solved in a variety of ways, often through trial and error, using existing skills and past experience or by making a plan. Fisher suggests that there are three factors to problem-solving - whatever the age of the problem-solver!

❏ Attitude - interest/confidence/motivation;
❏ Cognitive ability - application of knowledge/use of memory to make links/thinking and reasoning skills;
❏ Experience - familiarity with context, content, materials/strategies for problem-solving.

The key to maximising these factors is an informed adult who is able to see the potential for setting challenges in everyday situations (asking children to help with emptying the water tray or cleaning out the pets) and exploiting opportunities that arise through children's play (manoeuvring a tricycle around the track in the outdoor area; finding the best place to hang the dolls' clothes to dry on washing day).

You may find it useful to audit your setting to assess current practice in terms of problem-solving.

Questions to ask yourself

❏ Do practitioners have a shared understanding of the nature of problem-solving?
❏ Is there a climate where thinking creatively is the norm, where enquiry is encouraged, where individuality and autonomy are valued?
❏ Is problem-solving seen as part of the accepted teaching/learning process? Is play recognised as a way in which children learn with enjoyment and challenge? (*Curriculum Guidance* page 25)
❏ Is there a shared understanding that children who are told or shown a solution without any understanding of the strategies employed are not going to develop their learning?
❏ Are practitioners attuned to the needs of individual children so that they are able to 'read' non-verbal cues such as facial expression and gesture which indicate whether the child is thinking and needs time or is confused and needs help?
❏ Do adults see their role as that of an 'informed other' who works jointly with the child and where both share knowledge and responsibility for the task?
❏ Are adults willing to relinquish control of a situation and stand back so that children can try things for themselves?
❏ Is 'failure' seen as a potential learning experience? Are adults aware of ways in which they can support children's attempts and overcome disappointment and frustration?
❏ Does the environment support children as they solve problems - are materials and tools stored and labelled in such a way as to make them accessible to children? Is there room for children to work individually or in groups in all areas of the setting, both indoors and outdoors?
❏ Are adults comfortable with the idea of turning any activity into a problem-solving opportunity through the use of open-ended comments and questions?

Bibliography
Ashman, A and Conway, R Using Cognitive Methods in the Classroom (Routledge 1993).

Brown, S and Walker, M The Art of Problem Posing (Lawrence Erlbaum 1990 2nd edition).

Burden, R and Williams, M (1998) Thinking Through the Curriculum (Routledge).

De Boo, M ed Science 3-6: Laying the Foundations in the Early Years (Association for Science Education 2000).

Fisher, R Problem Solving in Primary Schools (Blackwell 1987).

Fisher, R Teaching Children to Think (Stanley Thornes 1995).

Hohmann, M and Weikart, D Educating Young Children (High/Scope Press 1995).

Nutbrown, C Threads of Thinking (Paul Chapman 1994).

Siraj-Blatchford, I and MacLeod-Brudenell, I Supporting Science, Design and Technology in the Early Years (Open University Press 1999).

Stevenson, R and Palmer, J Learning: Principles, Processes and Practices (Cassell 1994).

In the section on 'Common features of good practice' (*Early Learning Goals* page 11), it is suggested that practitioners should identify their training needs. An audit such as the one outlined above may be useful in helping a team determine the most effective way of developing a shared understanding of the nature of problem-solving.

Karen Hartley

Encouraging **problem-solving**

Among the aims for the Foundation Stage is the expectation that the curriculum will provide 'opportunities for all children to solve problems', both during their spontaneous play and as a result of adults' planned provision. Problem-solving is an approach not an activity and it may involve a rethink of the way in which adults work with the children.

'Through play, in a secure, learning environment with effective adult support, children can:

❏ communicate with others as they investigate or solve problems'. (*Early Learning Goals* page12)

'The parallel growth of confidence and trust enables children to take risks in their learning, to try to solve problems and to view practitioners as helpful teachers'. (*Curriculum Guidance* page 21)

There is an implicit suggestion in the above statements that finding the solution to a problem is not always the main outcome. The process of trying to find a solution and having the opportunity to share this process with interested adults and peers is more important. These statements underpin the role that practitioners play in developing children's learning. The nature of adult intervention is an essential factor in whether children have the chance to solve a problem or whether it is done for them!

The *Curriculum Guidance for the Foundation Stage* suggests that the adult's use of conversation is crucial in challenging thinking and that carefully framed questions (page 23) such as 'How can we...?' will promote children's ideas and suggestions. The practitioner's role is vital in ensuring that other key elements are in place in order to foster purposeful problem-solving including:

❏ a shared understanding of the problem-solving approach by the practitioners;

❏ effective use of space and resources;

❏ sufficient time for children to explore situations and materials;

❏ opportunities to communicate with peers and adults;

❏ a culture of valuing process over product;

❏ the use of support strategies.

Consider the following situations with these elements in mind.

Setting A
In a Reception class, three children were involved in building a castle in the sand during worktime. As the activity progressed, the sand began to become quite dry and towers were beginning to crumble - problem! One of the children suggested adding some water, which should have solved the problem, but an over-generous amount of liquid resulted in sand that became more

like mud and took on the properties of water. The nursery nurse was summoned to the scene. The children were quick to tell her that they had added too much water and that they were going to dig channels instead of building the castle. The direction of play changed completely. At the close of the session, the children were expected to clear away and tidy up after themselves. The three in the sand looked nonplussed at this stage and so the adults engaged all the children in the class in solving the problem of drying out the sand before the following day. The children were reminded that the change in the sand had occurred as a result of water being added. It was agreed that the water had to be 'removed' from the sand. One child suggested that it could just be left and it would dry ('like our paintings') but others thought that would take too long. After some discussion, the solution that gained unanimous agreement was that the sand tray should be wheeled outside and left in the sunshine because 'the sun's hot and makes things dry up quicker'.

In this play situation, there was an opportunity for the children to recognise and solve a problem of their own, that is the consistency of the sand not being appropriate for building castles (neither before nor after adding the water). The staff's belief in the value of problem-solving ensured that they recognised the opportunity to set the children another problem which was relevant and real.

The potential for learning may not have occurred had the nature of the classroom climate been different.

Firstly, the children had access to materials in the classroom and felt confident in changing the existing state of the sand to meet their needs. Although the children's action did not have the desired result (damp sand that compacts), when the practitioner arrived on the scene she encouraged them to think about the amount of water added - ideas and terminology specific to capacity were addressed in the process. Some thought was also given to a more appropriate strategy for adding the right amount of water that could be used next time! There was no sense of blame for the incident - rather a shared understanding that 'a bit at a time' might be more appropriate, so confirming the need for them to act responsibly.

Secondly, they were able to explore how very wet sand behaves like water (flowing, pouring) and to make comparisons between the damp and wet sand.

Thirdly, they were part of the discussion in which the children were encouraged to use their existing knowledge of evaporation and the part played by heat in this process. They were reminded of their previous experience of watching puddles shrink after the rain had stopped. They were expected to relate this experience to a new context in order to reach a solution. Although the staff acknowledged children's responses, asked questions and reminded the children of related experiences, the suggested solutions came from the children. In this incident, the practitioners exploited the opportunities for fostering learning in the areas of Mathematical Development, Knowledge and Understanding of the World; and Personal, Social and Emotional Development.

As the *Curriculum Guidance* reminds us, 'Allowing children to think about and practise ways of solving problems helps them to gain confidence in themselves as problem-solvers, to develop the problem-solving habit and to feel capable of responding to self-chosen challenges.' (page 29)

Setting B
Contrast the previous situation with this one that occurred in a nursery class.

As the children arrived for the session, they were encouraged to plan where they wanted to play. One child chose to go to the tactile area. She helped herself to a board, found

the appropriate container, opened it and took out all the dough. At this stage, she was by herself in the area. One of the practitioners, who had joined Laura in the area, smilingly commented on the amount of dough she had and asked her what she would do if anyone else chose to play there. Laura looked thoughtful and said, 'I've got all the dough'.

'Yes, you have', agreed the practitioner. At this point a second adult arrived in the area.

'Laura', she said, 'you can't have all that (dough)' and proceeded to set out five boards (one per empty chair), remove the dough from Laura's board and break it into six equal sized portions.

'There you are, Laura - you must share with your friends', she said as she left the area.

Laura looked at the first practitioner and said: 'But none of my friends are here yet.'

'Another opportunity lost', murmured the practitioner to herself.

It may be worth considering the 'lost opportunity' for Laura's learning. Having recognised that there was no-one with whom she needed to share the dough, the first practitioner was giving Laura a chance to practise her social skills by asking her a hypothetical question that could have led to a discussion on sharing; the number of

people who could come to sit at the table; how many boards would be needed; and what Laura would need to do to enable others to play with the dough.

As in the first incident, here was an opportunity to encourage Laura's thinking about mathematics and to develop social skills through posing a hypothetical problem. So why wasn't this achieved? Consideration of the situations may provide the answer.

A shared understanding
In the first setting, the practitioners shared an approach towards developing independent thinking which was not immediately apparent in the nursery situation. This common approach is achieved as a result of analysis of practice and by supporting each other in developing the skills needed to identify opportunities, ask meaningful questions, and stand back while children try things for themselves.

Effective use of space and resources
In both the situations described, the children had been given choice about the selection and use of materials. This is an important feature of young children's learning. Children need to have access to resources which can be used in an open-ended way and which encourage decision making. For example, children enjoy adding soapflakes to water and an element of decision making can be introduced by providing different sized bowls and a variety of whisks. 'Will the balloon-shaped whisk work in the small bowl? If not, why not? What sort of whisk would work better?'

Research suggests (Fisher, 1995) that children who are actively involved in creating their own environment have the opportunity to take real life problems such as space, noise, 'traffic' into account and appear to use the areas more purposefully in their play. This is quite easily achieved in the outside area where often large apparatus and toys are taken outside. Children could be invited to suggest suitable locations for the slide, tunnel, roadway. This could form part of the adults' planning for children to engage in first-hand experiences that encourage problem-solving - a requirement of the Early Learning Goals for Knowledge and Understanding of the World (*Curriculum Guidance* page 84). Other open-ended resources could include lengths of guttering, wooden ramps, squeezy bottles, buckets and household painting brushes.

Time

If only we had more time is a common cry! Children need it, too. How far was Laura (setting B) given time to respond to the challenge set by the first practitioner? Children need time to think about what they are doing, to find what works through trial and error (very time-consuming but can be immensely valuable), to talk about their experiences with peers and adults. Children develop their sense of time through consistent routines and the time when they are engaged in self-initiated activity and will encounter problems should be the longest part of the session. Trial and error is sometimes considered to be time-wasting but if children are given time to reflect on the experience then this will develop their learning. For example, when using a programmable toy children need time to find how far it will travel in response to the commands before they can begin to understand cause and effect. Only then will they be able to interpret a situation and determine whether it needs a higher number to enable it to reach its goal. They may appreciate clues to help them in the process of trial and error. Prompts such as 'Number four made it reach the chair; if you want it to reach the table will you need a bigger or smaller number?'

Communication

Children often describe their actions as they play and do not always appreciate adult intervention. However, using adults or peers as a sounding board is a useful way of thinking through the solution to a problem as they are doing it. Young children are not always articulate enough to explain what they are trying to do and part of the adult role is to model use of language, although communication also includes use of gesture and facial expression. Although questioning ('What will happen if...', 'Can you find a way to...?') is an important strategy in promoting problem-solving behaviour, it can be over-used and adults should use comments to prompt ('Have you thought of...?') and remind children of previous experience (as in setting A). Sometimes adults can challenge children by making a simple comment. For example, in a large circle time with a Reception class, the children were looking at toys from the past. 'I don't think I can make this work', said the practitioner holding up a clockwork toy. Immediately, half a dozen voices chorused 'I can' and for the next few minutes children were busy finding out how to wind it up and the effect of turning the key a different number of times.

Process as well as product

Recognising that how they do something as well as having an end product is crucial in developing children's 'self concept of themselves as thinkers, fostering feelings of satisfaction and pleasure at being able to think out solutions' (Burden and Williams, 1998). Therefore, practitioners need to value children's attempts to solve problems even if the outcome is less than perfect or achieved differently from the way envisaged at the outset. In setting B, Laura may not have shared the dough in even amounts but her attempts at doing so should have been praised.

Strategies

Although the *Curriculum Guidance for the Foundation Stage* emphasises children solving problems, they will need support in doing so. Fisher (1995), Ashman and Conway (1993) offer useful advice about supporting problem-solvers. Some of the strategies are evident in the first illustration (setting A).

❏ Help children identify what the problem actually is and that sometimes 'working backwards' is useful - for example asking 'What do you want to happen?'

❏ Help children consider the factors - 'What do we already know that will help?'

❏ Remind children of a previous, similar experience and what worked then.

❏ Simplify (if possible) by breaking the problem into steps.

❏ Help them to plan - it is believed that planning develops thought patterns which develop sequential thinking which is often a key to finding a solution. Those practitioners who adopt the High/Scope approach of 'plan-do-review' often find that children become confident in trying to solve problems.

What implications does this have for us as practitioners? Problem-solving is a cognitive process in which children are engaged every day - the adult's role is to ensure that curriculum planning makes this explicit through the elements described above. It is also important to model problem-solving through the adoption of the strategies outlined since this will help to develop children's understanding of the approach. By thinking aloud about what our problem is, why we're trying something and showing a positive attitude if it doesn't work, we show children that problems can be solved. The key to developing this understanding is that the approach is shared by all adults working with the children.

Karen Hartley

Nature walks sound like an old-fashioned idea but they are still one of the best ways for children to explore the natural world, acquire knowledge about plant and animal life and develop skills and attitudes which are at the core of scientific learning and development.

The value of nature walks

Since the early days of pre-school provision the natural environment has been a valued part of children's experience and learning. Some practitioners emphasise the contribution of physical exercise and fresh air to health, others the spiritual and creative opportunities presented through a nature walk. The ELGs advocate that by the end of the Foundation Stage, children will be able to 'observe, find out about, and identify features in the place they live and the natural world, and find out about their environment and talk about those features they like and dislike'.

Children are intensely curious about themselves, others and the natural world around them. They are eager to engage actively with their physical environment and are fascinated by plant and animal life. They are natural scientists who investigate, explore, ask questions, make hypotheses and seek explanations for what they observe. The nature walk is one way which enables children to explore the natural world, acquire knowledge about plant and animal life and develop skills and attitudes which are at the core of scientific learning and development.

Links with learning
Children benefit from the physical stimulus which nature walks provide. Negotiating slopes in a park or tree roots in woods or just a brisk walk all contribute to personal health and physical co-ordination. Success in completing a walk, scaling a hill, taking part in a social activity or finding interesting

specimens is also likely to promote personal confidence.

Nature walks contribute to a positive sense of self if adults encourage children to:
❑ be involved in the planning and organisation of the walk, including aspects of road safety and conservation;
❑ make lists of clothing or equipment to take;
❑ suggest things to look out for;
❑ share knowledge of what they know about the area already;
❑ predict what they might see;
❑ state preferences they have for certain trees, plants or creatures, and
❑ bring relevant story or reference books and games from home.

Children will develop a social sense of self as they co-operate with peers during the walk by holding hands, listening to others ideas, preferences and descriptions, making shared collections of leaves and seeds, and helping each other to make tree rubbings or plaster casts. They will also gain a sense of themselves in relation to the broader

community as they walk around the local area viewing buildings and meeting local inhabitants.

As children move around their locality they are physically developing a sense of space and time and learning about the proximity of buildings, roads, parks, woods and other local landmarks in relation to one another. This physical knowledge of the environment is a prerequisite to their later construction of three-dimensional 'maps' using recycled materials or bricks and blocks and the more abstract two-dimensional counterparts using pencils and paper. The foundations for later geographical understanding are being developed.

The nature walk is an ideal way in which children can learn appropriate knowledge and vocabulary in a meaningful context. They learn that the natural world is made up of a variety of plants and animals which have specific names, characteristics and habitats. Over time they discover that growth is influenced by weather and seasonal change, and that animals and plant forms are dependent upon each other for life, for example birds feed upon insects which feed upon plants for their survival. They develop early concepts about food chains. They learn the names of common birds, insects and minibeasts and specific vocabulary such as flower, stalk, petals, stamens and pollen. Children also develop the early science process skills of observing closely using all the senses, identifying similarities and differences within and between animal and plant life, describing and explaining what they see and communicating their experiences in a variety of ways using a range of modelling materials, through painting and drawing and music and movement experiences.

Developing observation skills

Children collect data about the world around them through observation. Observation is not only looking but involves all the senses:

❑ **listening** to the sound and pattern of bird song, the call of a cricket, the noise of feet trampling through leaves or along a pavement, the flow of water along a stream, through a fountain or garden hose;

❑ **touching** leaves, flowers and trees to learn about different shapes, size, textures and weight;

❑ **smelling** freshly cut grass, the dampness of the woodland after a storm and dry hay stacked in fields;

❑ **looking** at the variety of insect life, comparing body shapes, numbers of legs, styles of movement and types of habitats, observing chicks hatching;

❑ **tasting** blackberries collected from hedgerows, eggs collected from the hen on the farm and apples, plums or cherries from trees.

Note: Children should be warned NEVER to touch or eat anything from the hedgerows without consulting an adult.

When collecting specimens children should preferably wear plastic gloves and be carefully supervised by adults as some specimens can be poisonous or belong to a rare species.

Observation also involves viewing the environment from a number of different perspectives, for example the underpart of a snail as it rests on a magnifying glass looks distinctly different from the upper view of the spiral shell. As children observe they will also count seeds, plants or shells which they have collected, match specimens and use mathematical language as they find 'more' crabs than anemones, 'big' and 'little' shells and pick up 'heavy' stones.

Talk while you walk

Talking during the walk is vital to the children's developing understanding. Encourage them to comment upon, and ask questions about, the things in which they are particularly interested before providing

information which is not immediately relevant to them. Their questions are likely to be profound, for example: 'Why is the sun hot?', 'How do flowers grow?', 'Where do the stars go in the daytime?' You may need to find appropriate reference material or a resident 'expert' before such questions can be answered. However, the children can also be involved in this genuine search for information.

Developing positive attitudes

Positive attitudes towards the environment and living things can be fostered through the nature walk. Children learn to treat creatures with respect and handle them with care. They learn to overcome their physical exuberance, fear or apprehension in relation to wildlife. They discover that there are appropriate pieces of equipment such as pooters or nets for collecting live specimens and that there are equally appropriate storage containers in which to house them. They begin to understand that not everything that is seen should be collected, and that some things which are collected may be kept only for brief periods of time. They learn that specimens such as frogspawn and newts are rare and that others such as pine cones and acorn seeds are relatively plentiful. They become aware that where they walk, or the litter people leave, affects plant life and minibeast habitats. They learn that levels of noise and movement can affect bird and animal behaviour. They have the opportunity to experience and express a range of emotional responses such as fascination, joy, apprehension, awe and wonder. They learn that they are one of a range of life forms on the planet. The child's curiosity is fostered in a way that respects both the child's learning and environmental needs.

Was it worth it?

Assessing the effectiveness of a walk can be done by referring back to the stated aims identified during the planning stage. However, this does not take account of the additional learning that takes place from situations or questions which arise spontaneously - you can count on children to ask the unexpected!

The best way to assess the effectiveness of a walk is to invite children to give verbal feedback immediately following it and again a short period afterwards. (They will have made a memory trace only of those things which they found fascinating in some way.) Ask them what they enjoyed best and encourage them to share anything new they think they learned as a result of the walk. Is there anything they would like to look at again? If children have been motivated and challenged by the experience they will replay it in a variety of ways on subsequent days. They might role-play the walk, recalling the events which made most impact on them. Spontaneously produced models from wood, recycled materials and natural materials, collages, paintings and drawings will all be evidence of what children found intriguing; whether it was the bird's nest, the stream, or the woodlouse. The secret of receiving feedback from children through their spontaneous products lies in providing a range of materials from which children can choose, ensuring time for them to represent what is meaningful to them, and refraining from imposing predetermined adult outcomes upon them.

Joan Santer

Reference materials

The *Usborne Nature Trail Omnibus*

Usborne *First Nature* series: *Trees; Creepy Crawlies; Birds; Butterflies and Moths; Flowers.*

I Wonder Why Spiders Spin Webs (Kingfisher).

Animal Roundabout by Johnny Morris (Dorling Kindersley).

Watch Them Grow by Linda Martin (Dorling Kindersley).

Dorling Kindersley Pocket Guides: *Birds; Butterflies; Moths; Insects and Trees.*

First Look Birds and *First Look Insects* (Treehouse).

Stories to share

In the Tall, Tall Grass by Denise Fleming (RedFox).

Jasper's Beanstalk by Nick Butterworth and Mick Inkpen (Hodder Children's Books).

Spot's Walk in the Woods by Eric Hill (Picture Puffin).

Animal Seasons by Brian Wildsmith (Oxford University Press).

The Tree by Tim Vyner (Collins Picture Lions).

Hopper's Treetop Adventure by Marcus Pfister (North-South Books).

The Worm book by Janet and Allan Ahlberg (Picture Lions).

The Very Hungry Caterpillar by Eric Carle (Picture Puffin). (Try making a felt version of this to use with children.)

You don't have to live in the country to go on a nature walk. Joan Santer gives a step-by-step guide on what to think about before you go, suggests some places to visit and what to look out for when you're there

Going on a nature walk

Where your setting is based will dictate the focus of a nature walk and the type and variety of natural life which children may come across. There will be less variety of life in towns than countryside, but on town walks you can still look out for wall mosses, ants and beetles, weeds growing through cracks in the pavements and walls, birds such as house sparrows, pigeons and starlings, nests in sheds and garages, or even spiders' webs across doors and windows.

Where to go

Think about what might be a fruitful area to visit over time. Land which is designated to become a housing area would be interesting to watch as the building work will bring about changes in animal and plant life. Visits to such areas can be the beginning of a child's long-term understanding of human influence upon the environment. Useful contacts can be forged with members of the local community who have gardens, allotments, greenhouses or keep household pets. They may be willing to host a visit.

Here are some ideas for places to go:
- ❏ the woods
- ❏ the park
- ❏ a local garden or allotment
- ❏ the seashore
- ❏ a farm
- ❏ an aviary (check for children who may be allergic to bird feathers.)
- ❏ a greenhouse
- ❏ a stream or pond
- ❏ a disused plot of land (check for safety first)
- ❏ a riverside

There will be seasonal influences upon what you will find. That is why it is valuable to visit the same area regularly over a year so that children can observe change over time. Photographic records of walks which have been turned into home-made books will help children to recall and reflect upon their previous experiences.

The venue will dictate the size of group you can take. There simply won't be enough

room for a lot of children in a greenhouse, aviary or allotment, for example, but larger groups can be taken to the park, a farm or the woods. A suitable ratio of adults to children is necessary for all visits; one adult to two children ensures that the ideal care and attention can be given. In enclosed contexts, such as gardens, one adult to three or four children may be enough. Children should be organised into small groups, each cared for by an adult. Reinforcement of the Green Cross Code and other road safety procedures can take place within this small group.

Before you go

- ❏ Make a preliminary visit to the area before taking the children.

- ❏ Find out precisely what you are likely to see. Be willing to follow the children's interests but also know what *you* want to draw to the children's attention.

- ❏ Do some preliminary research from books, videos, CD Roms. Keep a file of ideas and information for future reference.

- ❏ Plan and discuss the walk beforehand with all staff and parents who will be involved. Ensure you all understand the planned aims and know what roles you will each play. Know which children will be your responsibility, who will carry the first aid kit and spare clothing and who will have responsibility for keeping an appropriate pace and check the timing of the walk.

- ❏ List the route and the areas of particular interest at which you plan to stop.

- ❏ Predict the appropriate length of the walk and the time it will take. (You can be more ambitious as children gain in experience. You will be amazed how far

they will walk if they are engrossed in what they are doing.)

- ❏ Collect books, stories, games and posters which can be used either to introduce the walk or as reinforcement materials afterwards. Ensure you have fiction and reference materials. (Children should have access to adult reference books about birds, minibeasts, plant and pond life and the seashore.)

- ❏ List and gather all the practical resources you will need during your walk ie magnifying glasses, pooters, containers for small creatures, fishing nets, binoculars, bags for collecting plants and seed specimens. Magnifying glasses can be carried easily if they are tied to string and children carry them around their necks. Bum bags make other practical carriers.

- ❏ Pack a first aid kit, including sunscreen for hot days.

- ❏ Inform parents and children when and where the visit will take place. Ask for information about children such as whether they have any allergies or fears relating to certain animals or places.

- ❏ Advise parents about appropriate clothing for children to wear. (Waterproof coat, wellies if it is wet.) Make sure you take a spare set or two for accidents.

- ❏ Invite parents to join you. The more individual attention children receive the better the quality of the experience.

- ❏ Prepare a pictorial plan of the walk to

show the children before you go. This can be placed on a wall with a summary of the aims and used as a talking point between peers, parents and staff.

❏ Discuss the walk with the children. Collect their ideas, revise road safety knowledge and introduce the country code. Children should learn not to drop litter, to close gates behind them and to keep to well established paths where appropriate.

❏ Take a camera to record the story of the walk if you plan to make a book about the visit.

❏ If you want to make a 'sounds' tape during the walk, take the cassette recorder.

❏ If you plan to make plaster casts of animal tracks, take strips of card, paper-clips, plaster of Paris, a container of water, a dry container and a stick to stir the ingredients.

❏ If you want children to find particular flowers, grasses, insects or trees you might find it useful to prepare mounted pictures or drawings of these on cards which the children can carry as a visual prompt.

Things to look out for

Before the walk decide where the stopping points will be to make observations or collect specimens (or even have a snack). Have a flexible structure which will enable you to respond to children's interests.

Look out for different types of plant life, trees, bushes and flowers. Differences in height, shape, size of leaves and flowers or blossom can be observed and compared. Some plants such as wild strawberries are creepers, others such as ivy are climbers. Plants can be classified as flowering and non-flowering. Children can collect grasses, leaves, seeds and fruit, observe the growth of buds on trees, compare the colours and shapes of flowers or learn about seed dispersal from dandelion or poppy heads. (For conservation purposes plants should not be dug up and only one specimen flower should be taken even when they are in abundance.)

Signs of animal life are visible in tracks on the ground, droppings, pellets, half-eaten pine cones or nuts, or gnawing or friction marks on the bark of trees. (Plaster casts can be made of animal tracks - see right). The height of scouring marks on the tree will

Insects are minibeasts which conform to specific criteria. They have:

❏ Three parts to their bodies - a head, thorax and abdomen.

❏ Three pairs of jointed legs attached to the thorax.

❏ A pair of antennae on their head for feeling and smelling.

❏ Most have a large pair of compound eyes.

❏ Most have wings.

❏ They are the only animals apart from birds and bats which fly.

Examples: bees, wasps, ants, crickets, ladybirds and butterflies.

indicate the type of animal visitor. Low marks are likely to have been made by the gnawing of rabbits, voles and squirrels, higher ones by the friction of deers' antlers. Pieces of bark which have fallen off trees can be collected but bark should never be pulled from trees as this can kill them.

Minibeasts will be found under stones, attached to leaves and on long grasses. These should be collected by using pooters and stored in transparent jars which have air holes in the lid, or magnispectors which have lids which magnify the creatures. Children will spend long periods of time intrigued by the size, structure and movement of these creatures. (Make sure you have allowed adequate time for this in your planning.) They can observe insects which are attracted to plants by their colour or smell and learn about camouflage.

The term 'minibeast' is used to describe the range of small animals such as slugs, snails, spiders, woodlice, centipedes and millipedes.

After the walk

The best way of reinforcing the children's learning after the walk is to try to replicate the experiences they have had, so they can revisit them in order to refine and extend their understanding. You might like to try out some of the following ideas:

❏ Set up an aquarium or a large sweet jar as a habitat for caterpillars. It is important if you do this that you bring with you some leaves from the plant the caterpillars were found on as this is their staple diet. You

Cover with muslin.

Cut for easy access.

Place a separate container with food inside the jar.

can do the same for a range of other

How to make plaster casts

You will need: collections of shells, small cones, seeds, leaves, Plasticine, plaster of Paris, water, a narrow strip of card, a paper-clip.

1 Press objects firmly into the Plasticine

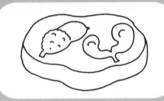

and then remove.

2 Surround impressions with a strip of

card joined with a paper-clip. Mix plaster of Paris with water until it is of a creamy consistency. Pour plaster over impressions.

3 Leave plaster to dry out. Remove card rim and Plasticine base. Paint.

creatures, but ensure you carefully recreate their natural habitat and keep them for only short periods of time. Sowing grass seed in a container has speedy and effective results.

❑ Make a wormery using a large plastic sweet jar. Place layers of soils, sand and peat inside. Put leaves on the surface and worms inside. Cover the jar with black paper or cloth and view from time to time. The worms should carry the leaves underground and their tunnels should be visible.

❑ Press flowers, grasses or leaves by placing them in a conventional flower press or between two sheets of blotting paper underneath a pile of books. After two or three weeks these can be mounted on card and covered with plastic and used for a wall display or made into a book. Alternatively they can be used for collages or making cards.

❑ Make plaster casts of leaves, shells, cones or stones by pressing into Plasticine, surrounding by a strip of card and pouring plaster of Paris over.

❑ Play back the tape recording during group time and see if the children can identify the sounds.

❑ Use the photographs to make a book or wall display.

❑ Make a feely box and each day place inside it different objects collected during the walk. Encourage children to describe then guess what the objects are.

❑ Design a garden or park. Give children a collection of objects found during the walk (twigs, leaves, pressed flowers and grasses, feathers, pebbles, sheeps' wool) and a tray (a toffee tray). Ask them to design their own garden.

❑ Make a plant 'greenhouse' using a 5-litre water bottle. Cut around the bottle one third from the bottom. Fill the base with soil or compost. Sow seeds or plant cuttings in here. Water the seeds/cuttings then cover with the top of the bottle.

Children will be able to see the seeds/plants develop. The bottle will retain the moisture providing an ideal environment for growth.

❑ Make a growth or life-cycle wheel.

❑ Make your own insect collector or pooter.

❑ Make games which will help the children to remember vocabulary or meet again the range of animal and plant life.

Kim's game:

❑ Objects gathered during the walk are placed on a tray.

❑ Children discuss and name them.

❑ The objects are covered and one is removed.

❑ The children are asked to guess which object has been removed.

The memory game:

❑ Take six leaves and make two identical rubbings of each. Cut these out and stick them to individual cards all the same size.

❑ Talk about the cards with a group of children.

❑ Turn the cards so that they face down and ask the children to take turns to see if they can turn over a matching pair.

Nature lotto:

Use pictures, photographs or silhouettes made from tracing around objects the children have collected. You will need two pictures of each object, one for the large players board and the other to be mounted on an individual square of card.

The insect game:

You will need one dice and six cards for each player.

❑ Each card will have drawn on it one part of the insect: head, thorax, abdomen, wings, antennae or jointed legs.

❑ Each card will also have marked in the top right-hand corner one number from the dice.

❑ The aim of the game is for the children to take turns throwing the dice and depending upon the numbers which arise to collect parts of the insect.

❑ The first one to complete an insect wins.

Joan Santer

Drill two holes in the lid of the jar.

Place one length of tubing through each hole.

Leave one tube. Cover the internal end of the second straw with muslin & place the art straw in the external end.

art straw

muslin

Place the lid on the jar. Suck through straw!

You will need: A plastic straw with lid. 2×20cm lengths of 7/8mm plastic tubing. A small piece of muslin. One large art straw. 1 × 6mm drill /cork borer.

Colour is a topic that we all cover in our work with small children. But why do we do it and how much can children understand? Gill Hickman questions some of our assumptions

The value of teaching colours

Many studies have been done on how babies see and what they choose to look at. In the name of science, researchers have subjected some very tiny babies to some quite peculiar tests! As you would expect, a baby's first interest is their mother's face, especially her eyes and mouth, indeed, they can imitate their mother's mouth from a few days after birth. In one test (to prove that they can perceive difference) young babies were presented with a certain pattern until they ignored it, then the pattern was changed or turned upside down and the babies showed renewed interest.

At birth it seems babies can already see colours and by 15 days old they will show renewed interest when presented with a new colour to look at, rather than another shade of the same colour. One of these tests involves shining a moving coloured light on a background of another colour and watching the baby's eye movements.

By three months, babies are found to gaze longer at a bright colour than at grey and between six and 14 months they begin to show colour preferences. Red is invariably children's first favourite followed by yellow. The ability to discriminate colours becomes more subtle in pre-school and later years. There is some evidence that boy's visual acuity is greater than girls.

The conclusion of all these studies is that babies are programmed to look at the world in certain ways and to pay attention to certain relationships.

Visual discrimination
A baby's visual discrimination develops rapidly. By three or four months they have begun to develop a sense of object constance, this includes size constancy (that mummy stays the same size even though she appears to get

smaller as she walks further away), shape constancy (that book remains a rectangle even though it looks like a trapezoid when it is tilted) and colour constancy (that my yellow duck stays the same colour even though it appears different depending on the amount of light or shadow). The more experience children have of handling and looking at objects, and later, talking about what they see, the more accurate their perceptual skills will be.

It seems ironic then, that later when learning to read children have to unlearn some of these shape constancies, for example, a cup is a cup whichever way its handle is facing, however, a b is not a d, nor a p a q although they are all the same shape with their 'handles' rotated in space.

It has been shown that five-year-old children who have difficulty recognising mirror images also have greater difficulty in learning to read.

Matching
As the child grows older, colours become an increasingly interesting part of her environment, and she naturally talks about them more and more. By the age of two or three she happily plays simple matching games with colours (Can you find a block the same colour as this one?), indeed she delights in finding matching pairs of anything not just colours. 'Same - same!' she exclaims, until parents or nursery adults suddenly start 'testing' her to see if she can name the colours yet!

Children need plenty of time to become confident at matching before they can begin to learn the colour names.

Colour names
It is probable that accurate colour perception is not fully developed until naming is grasped, so it is perfectly acceptable, indeed necessary, for adults to name colours for children from an early age. What is not acceptable is expecting children to learn colour names before they are ready. Chomsky (a well known US linguist who specialised in the links between language development and intellectual development) describes it thus, 'She needs to translate her perceptual experience into generalised rational understanding' - or in plain language, she needs to label what she experiences!

The way most children begin to use colour labels is at about 18-24 months when they choose one or two colour names they like the sound of or can say most easily, for example 'red' and 'lellow', then they 'label' everything as those colours for

a while. It is vital that children get encouragement not criticism at this stage. They have gained the general concept of colour, they just need time to acquire the specifics. It's comparable to the stage in initial language development when a horse may be called a 'dog' - well, they both have four legs! Gradually, with support and encouragement, children learn to name colours accurately. The first few are usually red, blue and yellow, next tend to come green, orange and pink. Black, purple, brown and white often come later. Obviously not every child will learn them in this order, and it doesn't matter one bit!

When children develop any new skill they are delighted and will want to repeat it again and again. Helen Bee calls this 'the joy of development'. (Helen Bee was an American child psychologist well-known in the 1950s.) How sad then if that joy becomes replaced by anxiety, fear of failure, or fear of disapproval. This can so easily happen when staff believe their role is to help children learn their colours and, without meaning to, their questioning ends up like interrogation! It is worth remembering that colour is only one particular perceptual skill, just one aspect of the child's vast arena of learning! Learning should be fun and should always be pitched at the child's level.

Colour blindness

It is worth remembering that a small percentage of children, most of them boys, are colour blind. The most common form is red/green blindness, when the child cannot see red or green clearly but sees both as a murky brown. Other children have difficulty seeing blue and yellow but this is much less common. If you suspect a child may be colour blind, a simple test could be placing a cut-out shape in red on a green background and vice-versa, and asking them what shape they can see. There is no known cure for colour blindness - people learn to cope with it in the best way they can. Teachers obviously need to be aware of it so that they don't unfairly underestimate a child's abilities.

Shades

As children grow older, at around three to four years, their perceptual abilities increase, and they become able to notice different shades of colours such as 'dark' green and 'light' brown. Adults can help children at this stage to find the correct verbal labels for what they see. Children love the opportunity at this stage to work with paints and crayons, mixing various shades and tones themselves.

Why such emphasis on learning colours?

It is probably because most children do learn to name colours somewhere between two and five years and it's a nice safe task for adults to focus on. Staff can say 'We taught them their colours' when in fact the children learned the names themselves. However, because there is so much else that is being learned at the same time, and because children are all unique with their own differing starting points, it is wrong and could be damaging to assume that all children must learn their colours before they are five years old.

In her book *The Nursery Teacher in Action* Margaret Edgington points out that adults working with young children need to remember that the most important part of their role is in helping the children's personal and social development. Adults need to encourage security, self-esteem, self-discipline and positive social interactions before thinking about helping children learn colours. What is the point of having a three-year-old who knows all her colours if she hits out when she is angry or does not yet understand about taking turns? Yes, colour is of interest to most young children and there are many, many interesting and motivating activities which have a colour focus, but it is only one part of the whole picture.

Gill Hickman

Cookery is something that most of you do as a regular activity within your setting - but do you know why? Rebecca Taylor asks you to remind yourself of its value and reappraise your whole approach to this undervalued part of the curriculum

The value of cookery

With the right planning and preparation children really benefit from cookery sessions. It gives them responsibility, helps them become more independent and they are learning a vital life skill. Hopefully they will enjoy their food more if they cook it and it is a great way of teaching them about the foods they eat and what they should eat to make them healthy. But do you and all your staff - including any parents who help on a regular basis - appreciate just how much children can get out of cooking?

It is vital that you discuss the value of cookery as a team. Get your staff to think about why we should do cookery with young children. Hopefully they will come up with arguments such as 'The children enjoy it' and 'It reinforces skills in all the areas of learning'. Here are just a few suggestions - you'll think of many more.

❑ It teaches maths through the measurement of ingredients and the children learn capacity vocabulary such as 'full', 'half full' and 'overflowing'.

❑ It is great for developing personal and social skills as the children share tasks, utensils and, eventually, the food they have prepared. They learn the importance of personal hygiene.

❑ It covers a large part of the language and literacy area of learning as the children can be shown how to follow recipes. They have to respond to verbal instructions and can be encouraged to talk about what they are doing.

❑ Manual skills and co-ordination are developed as they stir, spread, sieve and wipe tables.

❑ Cooking is a creative activity. Even if everyone makes biscuits following the same recipe, children can use their imagination to cut them out in

different shapes and sizes and decorate them how they choose. Cooking also provides the chance to explore texture and to respond to how things feel - flour as it's rubbed into butter - and smell - the aroma of freshly baked bread.

❑ It offers an ideal context for asking scientific questions such as 'What do you think will happen if ... ?' and exploring concepts such as physical changes to materials. For example chocolate melting and pasta changing from hard to soft, and jelly setting.

Once you have brainstormed all the advantages you should also consider potential negative issues and how these could be tackled. Common arguments include 'We never seem to have enough equipment', 'The children always get over excited' and 'Cooking is always done in a hurry and does not seem part of the curriculum' and, of course, 'What can we make'? Safety is a big issue to consider as you do not want any accidents.

Once you have decided as a team that cookery is valuable discuss how you can improve on each negative point. If you don't have a cooker or enough suitable equipment, then you need to think about making it a priority in your budget or as a focus for fund-raising. Can you arrange to have access to one elsewhere - the village hall, a local school?

Do you have the equipment but find the prospect of cooking with 20 four-year-olds daunting? Improving the child:adult ratio will help the issue of over excited children and reduce the chance of mess and accidents. Parents are often willing to come in and help with cooking. Going on a food hygiene and First Aid course will boost your staff's confidence and give them the knowledge to provide a safe working environment for your children. Time is crucial and cooking is often seen as an add-on activity. You may decide that for a set number of weeks you are going to timetable a member of staff in the cooking area who can work alongside parent helpers.

Think about how cooking can be linked to the rest of your work. Remember, children learn by feeling, smelling, looking, tasting and listening. Cooking is a great way of promoting these senses.

Planning

Spend some time as a team planning and writing down a session plan for the cookery activity you intend to carry out. This should include key objectives such as 'continue to develop fine motor skills when chopping', 'continue to develop social skills'. It should also include key vocabulary that all staff are going to use with the children such as 'full', 'half-full', 'empty' and 'overflowing'.

It should then list step-by-step what the children are going to do. It should list times when the oven should be turned on and include activities that can be carried out while the children are waiting for things to rise and set. Don't plan for all the children in your setting to cook in one day. Spread it over a week with a group cooking each day. Put the plan in a plastic folder so that it can be easily referred to as you are working. Put all plans in a food folder.

At the beginning of each year look at your topics and decided how they link with cookery. For example a topic on change gives great opportunities to make pasta and soup.

Above all listen to your staff and work together to raise the profile of cooking.

Role play

Extending the cooking theme to the home corner to encourage role play is always popular with young children, and it doesn't have to be a home/kitchen - it can be a cafe, a hotel, a motorway service station even. Think of contexts which will appeal to all the children in your setting.

The trouble most nurseries experience is having the right equipment for the role-play to be effective. You can buy some specialist kitchen role play products from educational suppliers, but first try asking parents for any unwanted utensils, tablecloths, napkins and cutlery. You will be surprised at what will be donated. Timers, bowls, kettles and scales are all valuable additions. It is also important for children to be able to handle real utensils and not just plastic imitations.

Most home corners do have some kitchen equipment but for those who are starting from scratch it can be difficult to choose when making new purchases, especially if funds are tight. It is a good idea to buy equipment that can be used in more than one capacity. A plastic pizza, for example can be used in maths lessons when teaching halves and quarters. When considering what to buy, think of its wider uses and durability - this way the whole nursery can benefit.

Don't forget books when setting up a cooking home corner. Multi-cultural cookbooks as well as story books with a cooking theme are all important.

Putting cookery into context

You may be lucky and have a parent who is a chef or cook and is prepared to come in and demonstrate their profession or read a story. They may be able to bring in some food to sample or do a cookery session with the children. Involving parents and their knowledge and experience of cooking is a great history lesson as well. A mum, granny and great granny will all have memories of how they cooked as a child. Great granny will talk about how toast was made over an open fire whereas the children will have toasters in their homes. Granny may talk about how food was rationed during the war and how eggs and milk were only available in dried form. If you can invite parents and relatives of both sexes and all ages into the nursery to talk and even help in cooking with the children it will really enhance your children's learning.

In Steiner settings children are given the opportunity to cook every day. In Steiner Waldorf kindergartens they believe that children learn through social activities such as cooking how to consider the needs of others. They feel that children learn in the context of an activity such as baking bread because it is meaningful and arises from the life of the kindergarten itself. Cooking allows children to actively make sense of their world by using tools and ingredients rather than expecting them to assimilate abstract information.

Food from around the world

Talk about and sample foods from around the world. You could focus on a specific type of food, such as fruits from different countries, or bread. Supermarkets have a wide selection - Italian ciabatta, Indian naan or chapati, Irish soda bread, French sticks and brioches, as well as our traditional cottage or sliced white loaves.

Or focus on the country, such as Italy. Explain how some food gets its name - spaghetti bolognese was first made in the city of Bologna and the pizza Margherita was named after the first Italian queen.

Cultures and food

Encourage the children to talk about what they would eat if they went on holiday to another country. Don't forget regional variations and recipes within the UK as well - Welsh cakes, Bakewell tarts, Scottish oatcakes.

Use cooking or examples of food to teach your children about other cultures and their beliefs. A focus on the Jewish religion can refer to cheesecake for example. Cheesecake reminds Jews of their prophet Moses. They say that Moses waited so long for God to tell him the rules of their faith that milk had time to turn to cheese.

Food is central to festivals and faiths. For example, Christmas wouldn't be Christmas without the turkey and pudding. It's traditional to eat hot dogs and jacket potatoes on Bonfire Night. Eggs at Easter are the symbol of the stone that was rolled away from Jesus' tomb. Bread and the sharing of it is an important part of many religious acts.

Food is a celebration and it is important that you include it in your nursery celebrations. You could have a sandwich and fruit salad party to celebrate the end of the year with the children making the food for their parents.

Rebecca Taylor

Young children need exercise like the rest of us. Kate Wright explains why, and how it should be done

The value of exercise

As adults we tend to interpret the term 'exercise' as meaning 30 lengths of a swimming pool, a five-mile jog or an hour's fitness session in the gym. It is a specific part of our lives. Exercise for pre-school children is their physical play. They have boundless energy and an almost obsessional need to move. In their physical play they will climb, jump, roll, crawl, wriggle - in fact they will seldom be still! They will unknowingly practise skills that they already have and develop new ones, too.

Because their bodies are different to those of adults young children must not be subjected to the rigorous training schedules of an adult. Young children have bones which are softer and can be easily damaged by too much excessive movement, which makes frequent long distance jogging totally unsuitable. Children's muscles are light and elastic so there is an inability to perform long sustained movements that an adult would practise in a gym. However, children will naturally exercise in a way that suits their developing bodies.

Why do children need exercise? Is it enough to just let them play and what role has a structured PE programme to offer our children in nurseries and pre-schools?

Why should we exercise?

Bodies are built to move and studies show that our body system works more efficiently when regularly exercised. Fitness centres and doctor's surgeries constantly advertise the benefits of exercise - these reasons apply equally to children.

Dr Craig Sharp of the British Olympic Medical Centre believes that one of the most important justifications for regular exercise from an early age is that at as early as nine years of age children can reduce high levels of blood fats through exercise. He adds that children of this age can undergo changes in their circulatory system which could lead to heart disease.

Exercise

Improves circulation

Reduces the risk of heart disease

Controls asthma

Improves the cholesterol level

Helps control weight

Increases strength, flexibility and agility

Helps bones to become stronger

Helps to manage stress

Promotes a sense of well being (perhaps that should be top of the list!)

Dr Sharp also states that one study showed that children who took little exercise may grow into under strength adults. Regular reasonable exercise may be necessary for muscle to realise its normal potential.

Other studies show that regular exercise can help control obesity, hyperactivity and poor concentration.

The more we research the more it is clear that children need exercise for healthy development and the earlier we start the more beneficial it is.

Do our children get enough exercise?

Because of the physical nature of children, many people assume that children get plenty of exercise. Generally speaking, in previous generations, this was so.

When we look at life in the new millennium it is alarming to find that the opportunities for ordinary everyday exercise for our children are becoming fewer and fewer. Time is a vanishing commodity so we strap our children into car seats, buggies and supermarket trolleys so our everyday necessary jobs and journeys can be done faster. Busy roads and dangerous pavements make the use of bikes and trikes more difficult and children no longer play the old-fashioned street games. There are fewer safe open spaces in which to play, and even a Sunday stroll is now being threatened by a trip to the hypermarket. In our homes children (and parents!) will often opt to switch on the TV, video or computer and be entertained passively.

When we let the children out for playtime at nursery, we have to realise that for some of the children this may be their first opportunity for exercise that day. It is not enough.

We cannot change what is happening at home, but we can make sure that whilst children are

at nursery or pre-school they are receiving an adequate amount of regular exercise.

A PE programme for nursery and pre-school

PE in nurseries and pre-schools is not simply an opportunity for the children to let off steam. It should be a planned educational programme which encourages all children to feel good about themselves. If we give them the foundations for a positive attitude towards fitness in the first five years then it is more likely to stay with them for the rest of their lives. PE should not be seen as an isolated subject but as an integral part of the day.

How can we achieve this?

Firstly - a nursery or pre-school does not necessarily have to have a large amount of space or specialist equipment to achieve the above aims. The ideas which I put forward should work in a nursery room where tables and chairs have been stacked to one side.

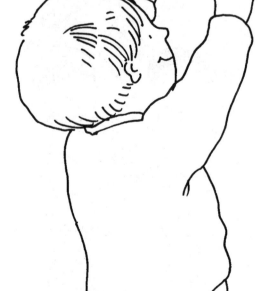

A safe, challenging and fun PE programme should aim at developing:

Physical skills
Improving: Balance, co-ordination, flexibility, posture, strength of bones and muscles, and respiration and cardio-vascular rate.

Body management
Improving: alertness, timing, ability to stop and start quickly, manual dexterity. Musical activities help improve listening and concentration, timing and co-ordination skills.

Intellectual awareness
It allows children to: think for themselves, stimulate their imaginations, solve problems.

Secondly - the children are definitely on our side. When considering how we are going to achieve the above aims we need to look at the strengths of pre-school children and how we can use them in our teaching.

❑ Young children want to be physical and have a natural joyful response to movement.

❑ Young children have wonderful imaginations. Ask a child to be almost anything and they will go into a variety of contortions until they are satisfied with the result.

❑ Young children are delighted by toys. They love to manipulate objects, throw objects, roll objects and aim at targets.

❑ Young children love music and have a natural sense of rhythm.

Thirdly - it doesn't have to be a complicated curriculum to achieve our aims. PE can be simply delivered by use of:

❑ Music (eg: action songs can help the development of co-ordination skills)

❑ Hand apparatus (even something as simple as a balloon can help with throwing and catching skills)

❑ Theme work (a wide variety of movements can be experienced through the telling of a short story and the children 'become' objects within the text. This can be linked to your current nursery topic.)

❑ Large apparatus (if available, but not necessary)

In conclusion, if we are to allow complete development of our children PE needs to be seen to be of parallel importance to academic and social skills. It should be included in every nursery programme so that all children have opportunities to use their bodies as a part of their whole development.

The aims of a PE programme are quite straightforward and staff should be reassured that it does not need a lot of specialist training but that everyone can and should make it a part of their nursery day.

Kate Wright

Exercise is something that should be happening daily within your nursery or pre-school. Because of this it is important to plan a series of sessions, looking at what you are going to teach and how you are going to teach it. Kate Wright gives some ideas

Organising **exercise** sessions

Many staff shy away from PE. Either they see it as a specialist area, they don't actually like PE themselves, or they have tried it and found a room full of children with bean bags a pretty daunting experience! Do not give up!

Gather as many resources as you can. There are a number of reward schemes on the market which present a wide variety of ideas and skills to be taught. Be careful not to make your activities competitive - all children should be allowed the feeling of success.

Look out for music - you may like to use instrumental music or action songs with specific movements. Action songs will help co-ordination skills. Old favourites are: 'Head, shoulders, knees and toes', 'If you're happy and you know it', 'Wind the bobbin'.

Try and build up as big a collection of hand apparatus as you can - children like variety! Your collection could include: balls - small, medium, large .... and even huge, balloons, bats, bean bags, foam cubes, hoops, a parachute, ropes, streamers, tap sticks and quoits. You don't necessarily have to spend a lot of money - a bean bag can be very cheaply made with material scraps and filled with bird seed from the pet shop.

Always be on the look-out for new ideas. Your collection of resources should go on for as long as you are in nursery education.

Practise together
Now, tracksuits and trainers on, get together as a group with your fellow playgroup leaders/teachers/helpers and, using our check-list of movements, go through the skills you are going to teach. There is no need to demonstrate them all because you can pick out children to demonstrate, but the more you do the more you can become involved with your PE session.

Practising with adults is far worse than participating with children because adults are far more critical, so once you have done this bit the worst is over. Aim at demonstrating good quality movements and make sure you correct each other if necessary. Apart from gaining in confidence yourself, practising movements like this helps leaders understand how children feel in a group situation. Some find some movements difficult, some feel self-conscious in a group, and some think they are stretching when they could stretch a little further.

The next step is to take any piece of hand apparatus that you have. Go through the check-list again and see how you can use your piece of apparatus to teach the skills. It is amazing how many ideas you can come up with. To help you get started use the foam cube ideas from the session plan.

And finally practise some theme ideas. I have given the example of going to the park (see page 160), but the list is endless. You can use everyday situations such as going into town, you can use fairy stories, special occasions such as Bonfire Night or you could link it to your topic work.

Theme work
Theme work needs imaginative planning. It is important that you do not confuse it with mime work, because you are looking for particular movement skills. Write out a story with the movements you require from the children, and practise it together as a staff. Be critical of each other and make sure it does contain a variety of movements.

You will notice that there is tremendous overlap in the movements being taught. To gain expertise children need to repeat skills. The listed skills will be repeated time and time again but because you are presenting them in a variety of ways the children will see it as something different each time.

The list of movement skills is long. Don't try and teach them all in one session! Use the list to help you plan several sessions so that after four or five sessions all the movements have been covered and many of them will have been repeated.

The session

What you do in your session depends on the availability of:
- ❑ Time - 30 minutes is a good length of time
- ❑ Space - if this is limited then movements have to be adapted.
- ❑ Apparatus (large and hand)
- ❑ Number of children - I am lucky and work with a ratio of one adult: six children
- ❑ Number of adults.
   The British Gymnastics Association recommends no more than 1:8. The more help you have the more you will be able to do for the children and the more they will get out of the session.

Divide your session into three parts

1) Warm-up
Children's bodies need very little warm-up time but an introductory activity helps to sharpen their concentration and focus on what is coming next. Make your warm-up interesting, varied and fun!
Ideas: An action song; response games eg Simon Says; a combination of running, skipping, jumping (on the spot if you are short of space).

2) Skills
You can choose one skill which is presented in a variety of different ways or a variety of skills. Varying the skills can be approached in terms of:
- ❑ Body shape eg balancing in various shapes - thin, wide, stretched, tucked.
- ❑ Direction eg walking forwards, backwards, sideways.
- ❑ Level eg clap hands above your head, out in front, down by your feet.

Skills may also be varied by performing them on or with apparatus eg jumping
- ❑ along the floor
- ❑ in and out of hoops
- ❑ along a low beam.

Teach the skills using
- ❑ Hand apparatus
- ❑ Music
- ❑ Theme work
- ❑ (Large apparatus)

3) Calming down
Use a song or action rhyme which allows the children to cool down. Remember that young children have limited concentration. Your session needs to consist of lots of short activities. Be flexible - if something isn't working move on to the next activity.

Safety check-list
As the leader you must be suitably dressed.

Wear trousers and trainers (there is a risk of injury if adults work in bare feet).

Remove all jewellery including watches and tie back long hair.

Ask the parents to dress children suitably.

Skirts and dresses get in the way so try and have a box of spare clothing for the ones who will inevitably come unsuitably dressed. Be aware that children from some cultural backgrounds are not allowed to undress in public. Discuss this with parents.

Providing the floor surface is suitable children should work in bare feet.

Make sure your space is safe!

Remove as much furniture as possible, and tie up anything which is leaning against the wall.

Inspect your floor for drawing pins, splinters and so on.

If possible, put mats down.

Avoid trailing electric wires.

Open the window for some fresh air.

Session check-list

Make your instructions simple and accurate.

Demonstrate where necessary (you can use a child!).

Stand where all the children can see you.

Space the children out. They will need positioning and re-positioning! Chalk marks or small carpet squares can help.

Physically assist the children if necessary eg support a child that cannot hop, or straighten up arms held out to aid balance.

Give lots of praise and encouragement.

Don't look for instant results - you are encouraging a steady improvement.

Movement skills check-list Skills can be divided into three categories. Within your session include actions from each category.

Locomotion

(These skills should stimulate respiration and cardio-vascular rate.)

1) **Running** - forwards, backwards, fast, slow, quietly, loudly. Head up, pick up knees, run into a space, keep on your toes.

2) **Walking** - forwards, backwards, sideways, on toes, on heels. Head up, swing arms, lift knees if marching.

3) **Skipping** - forwards and sideways (backwards is very hard!) Many will be learning this skill. Say 'step hop, step hop'. Slow it down. Head up, keep on toes, lift knees high, use arms to help lift.

4) **Jumping** - forwards, backwards, sideways, leaping, feet apart, feet together. Use arms to help lift, bend knees on landing, head up.

5) **Galloping** - on toes, head up, lift knees high.

6) **Hopping** - right leg and left leg. Many will be learning this skill. Support where you can. Keep on toes, keep free knee high.

7) **Crawling** - on hands and knees, on hands and feet.

   i) tummy down

   ii) tummy up (crab walk). Lift tummy high. Weight on hands and feet.

8) **Sliding** - on tummies, on backs.

9) **Rolling** - do not attempt to teach forward rolls. Log rolls - keep arms and legs straight, feet together, roll with trunk only on the floor.

Balance

Many balances will be helped by putting arms out to the side. Keep your eyes fixed on a stationary object ahead of you.

1) on right leg, on left leg

2) on bottom

3) on knees

4) on backs

5) on tummy

6) on tiptoes

7) in a crouch position

8) on two feet and one hand/two hands and one foot

9) on hands and feet
   - tummy up like a crab
   - tummy down

10) moving from one balance to another eg rocking on feet, seat, from seats to backs clutch knees with arms, chin on the chest

11) using hand apparatus
    a) balancing hand apparatus on various parts of the body
    b) using hand apparatus to help achieve a balance eg sit on your bottom, hold a bean bag between your feet, lift your feet up in the air
    c) balance on/in hand apparatus eg balance in a hoop, walk along a rope.

Co-ordination

Co-ordinating movements:

• jumping jacks • star jumps • tuck jumps

• half turn jumps • bunny hops • frog jumps

Using hand apparatus:

• kick/throw/roll at a target • throw and catch

• bounce and catch • jumping over

• tapping tap sticks together

• hitting (bat and ball)

There will no doubt be other movements that you and the children will discover.

Theme work: Going to the park

(Start in circle formation.)

Story	Actions

Let's get on our bikes.

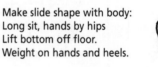

Lie on backs and pedal.
Vary speed, slow and fast.

Into the park, let's run.

Run round room.
(All run in same direction, run on toes.)

Big piles of leaves, let's jump over them.

Let's jump on them.

Leaping.

Go on the swings.

Feet together and jump. Use your arms to help.

Climb the climbing frame.

Stand feet apart, join hands to make a seat, bend over and swing hands between legs.

Down the fireman's pole!

Climbing action, stretch tall.

On the roundabout.

From stretch into tuck position.

On the slide.

Short sit, pivot round on bottom.

Make slide shape with body:
Long sit, hands by hips
Lift bottom off floor.
Weight on hands and heels.

On the see-saw.

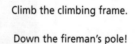

Lie on floor, balance on tummy
Straight arms off floor.
Straight legs off floor.

Let's walk down to the lake
and you can skip if you like.

Swing arms to and fro.
Lift knees high.

Let's look into the water.

Go on hands and knees.

See the fishes.

Make hands wiggle.

See the frogs.

Jump in squat position, hands and feet on floor.

Look at the ducks.

Flap arms up and down.

Let's take out a rowing boat.

Join hands with partner, sit on and sing 'Row the boat'.

Time to go home.

Back on to your bikes and pedal home

Calming down

Lie on backs and pedal legs.

Rhyme: 'Hands on hips'.

To become confident in their own abilities and able to understand the world children must be allowed to play creatively and to explore art and music in unstructured settings. Gay Wilkinson explains why and give some ideas how this can be achieved

Creative **Development**

Being creative is all about being able to use past experiences and rearrange or transform them to make and communicate new ideas. It means being able to respond to the world around us emotionally, using all the senses. It is about making believe, imagining the 'what if?', being willing to put oneself in other people's shoes and consider different ideas. It is about taking risks!

Future societies will need people who can develop novel solutions to all sorts of problems. Those who have been supported to develop as creative and divergent thinkers from early childhood will be better able to respond to those challenges.

Dramatic play

As young children play out different roles - being a mum or dad, a fireman, a dog - and recreate some event - looking after the children, putting out a fire - they transform themselves and objects through their imaginations. The beads become a bowl of food to be fed to the 'baby', the skipping rope becomes a hose gushing water. What they do not know about putting out a fire they make up from other experiences that, to them, seem similar! As they play with toy boats in the water they meet storms at sea and imagine dangers. As they play with the train set they feel the power and the responsibility of driving the train. As they drive the cars on the road built with blocks they deal with all the responsibilities of being a driver.

In their spontaneous play anything is possible; risks can be taken because they are in control and problems can be solved through the imagination.

Spontaneous play

All young children need help to be creative and imaginative. It is therefore important that they have substantial time each day when they can choose what they want to do and work through their ideas in their play. This spontaneous play is of the utmost importance since it gives them the freedom to explore their own ideas in their own way. In planning your curriculum you will need to be flexible whilst also maintaining a balance between spontaneous play and those focused or structured play activities which you have set up to introduce particular ideas. You will need to look at your environment both inside and outside.

❏ Does it help the children to develop their own play?
❏ Is there enough floor space for large constructions?
❏ Does the home corner have enough space for children to really explore roles?
❏ Do the experiences on offer outside complement those inside whilst reflecting the particular nature of either the outdoors or indoors - for example a sand tray indoors and a digging area outside, a home corner indoors and materials for making a den outdoors?
❏ Can children move around easily from one

space to another?
❏ Are there things for children to play with which are open-ended and so allow them to use their imagination?
❏ Do you have sets of different sized blocks, clay, dough, dressing-up clothes, dolls and so on?
❏ Do you allow them to use resources from one area in another - for example, can they use the counting cubes to represent food in the home corner (as long as they put things back in the right place when clearing up)?

It is sometimes useful to build up random collections of objects - shells, pebbles, fir cones, buttons, model people and animals, ribbons, bits left from withdrawn resources such as jigsaw pieces - which the children know they can use in any way, which will help to preserve more precious and expensive resources. The children might contribute to these collections by bringing in old toys from home.

You will also need to think about how you are going to support the children in their spontaneous play. You will need to observe the play activity first to intervene and support effectively.
❏ What ideas are they exploring and trying to make sense of?
❏ How can you help them sort out their ideas?

Without observation there is always the danger that you can misunderstand what the play is about and offer the wrong information or substitute your own ideas for theirs thus devaluing their creativity.
❏ When they share their ideas with you, how will you show them that you consider these to be really important?

The role of stories

If children are to play imaginatively they need a rich diet of experiences to feed their imagination. The richer the range of experiences from which the children can select the greater their opportunity to explore the things that interest them and develop new ideas.

Literature has a special contribution to make. Through story children can encounter people they may never meet, visit places they may never go, witness events they may never see, and worlds and times they may never live in. They can then choose from and transform this material as they create a story script for their own play - Superman meets Cinderella!

Some stories demonstrate how elements from one story can be transformed into a new story with surprising results. Alan Ahlberg's *The Jolly Postman* is one such example. Reading and talking about stories like this to children tells them that using your imagination to transform elements into something new and exciting is not only acceptable but fun!

Art and craft

Young children are continually reacting to, transforming and representing the world around them through play. Many of the experiences that you provide across the curriculum have the potential to contribute to children's aesthetic and creative development. However, there are particular experiences that make a special contribution to this aspect of the curriculum - art, craft, music, drama and dance - and it is these aspects that you will need to consider when planning your curriculum.

Art and craft includes painting, drawing, printing, collage, sewing, woodwork, sculpture and pottery. Some of these will result in two-dimensional work whilst others will lead to working in three dimensions.

Being creative means developing, representing and communicating your own ideas and experiences in your own way so it is important that children are allowed to do exactly that. Filling in someone else's

drawing with tissue paper, fabric or paint, drawing round templates, colouring in pre-drawn shapes, tracing and sticking pre-cut shapes to reproduce an adult's model pattern do not challenge children to think for themselves nor allow them to represent their ideas. As important is the damage that can be done to young children's self-esteem from the implicit message of such activities - that their ideas are of no value and their skills ineffectual. In other words, there is a right way and a wrong way - and they get it wrong!

To become skilful with different materials young children need time to explore them to find out what each can and can't do. It is only through such initial exploration that they will be able to make a considered choice about which material will best represent an idea or experience.

If children are to learn about and understand the properties of different materials then they need to have regular access to them and time to test out and consolidate their learning. Having access to clay on an occasional basis does not help children to develop an understanding of what clay might be most suitable for as a means of communication and how to work with it effectively.

This means that you will need to consider carefully the variety of materials that you can make available.

❑ Is there an area where children know there is a variety of mark making tools - pencils, crayons, coloured pencils, felt-tip pens, chalk, charcoal, and a range of paper (white is best) of different sizes - where they can draw?
❑ Are the pencils of differing quality not just HB? 2B and 3B pencils have quite different properties - they can be smudged and lines can be blended - and so offer different possibilities.
❑ Is the paper of good quality, capable of taking marks, and properly cut? It is hard for children to take care in their drawing and do their best when the quality of the materials say that this is not an important activity or where poor quality prevents them from realising their ideas.

❑ Is there a computer that they can use with an appropriate software package to explore computer imagery?
❑ Is there a printer so that they can print out their finished work?
❑ Is there an area where children can mix their own colours when painting so that they can better recreate experiences and are there ready mixed paints for those children who need to paint quickly in order to capture a personal event?
❑ Is there a range of brushes available - pointed, straight, bristle, sable - in different sizes, to suit the variety of painting tasks that the children might want to undertake?
❑ Are there opportunities to add other materials to paint - sand, glue, cornflour - to recreate texture?
❑ Is there an area where they can create three dimensionally, selecting from a range of materials - wood, soap bars, salt blocks, clay, dough, wet sand, reclaimed materials - and a range of tools and materials for joining and fastening that they can use to manipulate these materials?
❑ Is there an area where they can use fabrics and threads with sharp scissors that will cut?

What do you know about the materials you provide?
❑ How do they behave when they are handled?
❑ What are their constraints and their strengths?

Explore together each of the materials you provide one by one, then share your experiences.
❑ What skills did you need? Which tools were helpful and which weren't?
❑ What did you find frustrating? How did the material feel? What worked and why?
By doing this you will be better able to talk to the children about their experiences, teach appropriate skills as they are needed and help them to develop and refine their representations.

Children need to be presented with a range of experiences that will stimulate them to try out all these materials and arouse their imagination. Very young children can be introduced to the work of artists and craftsmen, both 2-d and 3-d, to enhance their knowledge about arts and crafts. Encourage them to talk about what they see, the use of colour, line, pattern and texture, how it makes them feel and what they think the person who created the painting or object was trying to say.

Looking at and talking about works of art from a range of cultural backgrounds provides them with a more extensive repertoire of what they might be able to do.

Can you involve a practising artist in your setting? (If there is an art group in your area this could be your first point of contact.) They could show the children a sketchbook diary in which they quickly record things that they have seen or explain how they select an image and compose a picture. Would they be prepared to come in sometimes as the children are working and talk to those painting, drawing or modelling about their work? If this is possible, bear in mind that they may need help when talking to young children.

The displays in your environment will also foster children's imaginative responses to the world about them.

If you can't mount displays on walls perhaps you can set up small 3-d displays of objects which have interesting shapes, textures or colours which can be put away at the end of sessions. If you do mount displays, make sure that they don't become like wallpaper - they are there to stimulate the children's aesthetic and creative sensibilities. It is far better to have less of high quality than so much that it is impossible to really see anything at all.

Music

Most young children have a substantial musical repertoire before they attend an early years setting. Music accompanies adverts on television, is used to create mood in television programmes, and is played in shops and stores as background music. Children may have family members who enjoy listening to music or who are musicians. Many will have tapes of songs and

rhymes that they listen to regularly. It is likely that many of them will have memories of being sung to. It is not unusual to hear children singing to themselves. They will often sing the jingles that accompany well-known adverts and make up their own words to known tunes. They delight in exploring sound! The early years setting needs to build on and extend these early experiences.

- ❑ Is there an area in your setting where children have regular access to a range of musical instruments and where they can explore sound patterns and make music spontaneously? Consider carefully where to position such an area since it can be noisy!
- ❑ Are there planned opportunities when they can come together to make music using untuned percussion instruments? Can the children make a collection of objects from your environment that make interesting sounds or even make their own instruments?
- ❑ Do you help them to understand and appreciate musical stories by providing opportunities for them to 'tell' a well-liked and familiar story using sounds instead of words? Encourage them to think how they might represent characters and events in the story with sounds. What sort of sounds would best describe the giant in 'Jack and the Beanstalk', for example, and how might these change when he's asleep? Or how might they represent the dragon at Chinese New Year?

- ❑ Can they write down their compositions so that they can be replayed? Instead of using conventional notation encourage them to listen carefully to each sound they make and then create a descriptive symbol to represent it. A crash on the cymbal might look like a spiral, a zigzag could be repetitive taps on a drum.
- ❑ Can you set up a quiet listening area where they can choose to listen to short pieces of carefully chosen music, representing a variety of styles and cultures, on tape? Provide planned opportunities when they can come together to listen to a piece of music; help them to listen carefully and talk about how the music made them feel and what it made them think of. Demonstrate the importance of the activity by sharing your own feelings and ideas created by the music at the end. Perhaps you could build up your own collection of musical pieces that seem to work well with children.

Most children love to sing and make sound. Help them to learn a range of simple songs and rhymes and provide them with opportunities to sing together. If you can't play the piano to accompany them don't worry, they will enjoy having you sing along with them.

Alternatively, see if you can get a pianist friend to tape record the piano accompaniment to a group of the most popular songs that you can use with the children during singing. If you do this, invite the pianist in to listen to the children singing before making the tape so that they are aware of what is needed. As well as singing, help the children to develop their awareness of rhythm, pace and pulse by teaching them rhythmic chants or by using repetitive refrains from familiar stories such as 'The Gingerbread Man'.

Bring in people from your community or professional musicians who can perform to the children or who might be willing to work with the children as they make and create music.

Gay Wilkinson

Music plays a part in everybody's life and its benefits go far beyond the structured learning of playing instruments and singing songs, says Anne Hunter

The **value** of **music**

Zoltan Kodaly, a Hungarian composer who revolutionised the teaching of music to young children, believed that music fosters self-discipline and a sense of community. Katalin Forrai, in her study of Kodaly's methods entitled *Music in Pre-school*, tells how Kodaly thought that:

'Music has such a strong influence on personal development that it affects the entire personality. Music of value makes the individual sensitive to beauty and forms (the child's) tastes and attitudes.'

Above all, Kodaly believed that it was the job of parents and early years professionals to instil a love of music in every child.

Try to recall some of the main events in your life, for instance a wedding, a funeral, birthdays, Christmas, Diwali. Now imagine these occasions without music! What is the climax of a child's birthday party? Of course - cake, candles and the performance of one of the most frequently sung songs in the world, 'Happy Birthday'! A life without music is unthinkable. When we come together and enjoy music, we are not only communicating our emotions and showing our sense of belonging, we are creating memories. Most of us have heard a piece of music and been immediately transported back to the time when it was important to us.

Musical confidence

There are many more ways in which music-making in a group can benefit young children. First and foremost, it is great fun! Children quite simply enjoy listening to music, singing, dancing and playing instruments. It is extremely important at this stage to praise their musical efforts, even when they don't sound very musical at all! You want to instil a musical confidence in your children, teaching them that music is for everyone, not just the elite few who have a 'special talent'. Incidentally,

don't worry that children will laugh at your singing - if you sing with joy and enthusiasm they will think you are wonderful! I have often heard people say that they are tone-deaf when they have perfectly adequate singing voices. This is usually due to some unfortunate remark remembered from schooldays; often made by peers, parents or even, sadly, their music teacher. Children look up to their carers and often imitate them. You cannot encourage children to be musically confident and then refuse to sing in front of them.

Music encourages social skills

Music-making is a social activity. In the early years it will almost always be enjoyed in a group, often involving the whole setting or class at once. So it is a way of encouraging a feeling of belonging; of being, as Kodaly said, part of a community. An organised music session will encourage teamwork and co-operation in two ways: firstly when there is

a common aim, like learning a song or getting ready for a 'show', and secondly when the children are asked to perform individual tasks within the group. The ability to take turns is an essential skill in music as in life - if all the members of an orchestra played what they liked, when they liked, the result would be chaos! By listening to each other, keeping in time with each other and copying each other, the children become more aware of the needs of their fellow group members and often prove to be supportive to those who may be struggling. Music really does seem to bring out the best in people, particularly at this early stage. This leads me on to the next point:

Music is for everybody

Kodaly believed that a musically cultured people is one in which 'music belongs to everyone'. Indeed, music can be one of the most accessible areas of the

Happy Birthday to you...

curriculum; particularly so in the early years, before children have to worry about the formalities of crotchets, quavers, sharps, flats and so on (and in providing music for pre-school children, you don't have to worry about them either!). Have you noticed how some quiet, passive children can light up at singing time? Children who might be considered 'non-academic' often shine in a musical environment. In my work with both children and adults with learning difficulties of varying degrees, I am constantly amazed by their capacity for rhythm, melody and sheer joy at being actively involved in music.

Music unites people

Just as music can bring together people of different strengths and abilities, so it is a wonderful means of uniting people of different cultures. You can increase your children's understanding and appreciation of other cultures by listening to examples of their traditional music. Try your local library for tapes or CDs, or ask parents if they have any to share with you. You may have some talented parents or grandparents from ethnic minority families who play instruments or who could teach the children a simple nursery song from their culture. Make time during your celebrations of Diwali, Chinese New Year, and so on, to listen to some appropriate music - the children love this - and ask them to comment. Do try to get hold of some taped traditional African drumming - even very young children can be inspired to join in with the infectious rhythms! *

Music is fabulous for improving listening skills, language development and for encouraging self-discipline. Listening to certain kinds of music is even thought by some to increase intelligence (there is currently a study taking place in the London Borough of Newham** to prove it)!

Anne Hunter

* I have a good CD Called *Africa* in the *World of Music* series from Hallmark (try your local library - you may be surprised at what they have to offer).

** see *Times Educational Supplement* 14 January 2000.

The main elements of music

While I cannot stress enough that you do not need to be a musician to run a successful pre-school music session, it is useful to be aware of the basic areas that make music what it is. I will briefly list them here:

Timbre

This is the quality and texture of the sound. At this level you should be thinking about the various ways in which sounds can be made and observing their differences. Think of the different ways we can use our voices (high/low, quiet/loud, gruff/squeaky) and our bodies (clapping, stamping, rubbing hands, tapping knees). Instrumentally, listen to the many different sounds you can make (triangles tinging, woodblocks tapping, maracas shaking). Listen to and imitate environmental sounds, like rain and traffic, in various ways.

Dynamics

This means loud, soft, getting gradually louder or gradually softer. Any familiar song can be experimented with in this way. It is useful for the children to learn that instruments can be played quietly as well as with gusto!

Tempo

This is the Latin word for time and it refers to the speed of the music. Again, sing familiar songs at different speeds or make up your own rhymes with an appropriate subject, for instance, 'Snails crawl slowly on the ground, mice run quickly round and round'!

Pitch

This is whether the notes are high or low. A melody will contain notes at several pitches, otherwise it would be a monotone or a chant. In choosing songs for young children, bear in mind that pitch is usually the last musical skill to develop. Keep it simple and sing at a level that is comfortable for both children and adults - not too low and certainly not too high! Do not be alarmed if most of the children sound out of tune - this is a developmental stage and will not last forever! Now is the time to build their confidence.

Rhythm/pulse

Rhythm is the pattern the sounds make. It is made up of long notes, short notes, silences and pauses. Pulse is the actual beat of the music and is usually regular throughout a song. If asked to clap along to a piece of music, an adult will invariably clap the pulse, whereas a child of three or four will often clap the rhythm. Imagine chanting the days of the week; the pulse would be the beginning of each word (MONday, TUESday, WEDnesday, and so on) while the rhythm would be the pattern made by each syllable. During their pre-school years, many children will learn to differentiate between rhythm and pulse, but it can be a tricky one!

Peter Morrell examines the part that performance can play in the life of the early years setting

The **value** of **performance**

Children are born actors and will be involved in performances daily - one minute they are a shopkeeper and customers in the theme corner, the next they are an architect with the Duplo or simply themselves in an impressive temper tantrum!

Children are spontaneous and love to tell you about all kinds of things. When they do, they are developing numerous social skills - speaking to an audience, using appropriate language and vocabulary, sharing experiences, keeping the audience's attention (who, in turn, are required to listen attentively), giving time to others, taking turns, formulating questions and developing memory.

By nurturing children's natural acting ability with their enthusiasm and spontaneity, you can lead them to a more structured performance that will help shape their character, develop confidence, heighten social and co-operative awareness and offer many opportunities for enjoyment and fulfilment. Memories of their performance often last a long time.

By taking part in performance, children can visit all six areas of learning.

Personal, Social and Emotional Development
❑ Establish effective relationships;

❑ Work as part of a group;

❑ Explore new learning situations;

❑ Respond to religious events.

Communication, Language and Literacy
❑ Listen and respond to stories, songs, nursery rhymes;

❑ Take part in role play with confidence.

Knowledge and Understanding of the World
❑ Talk about past events;

❑ Explore and recognise features of events in the made world;

❑ Talk about their observations and ask questions to gain information.

Mathematical Development

❑ Use mathematical language to describe position - 'in front of', 'semi-circle';

❑ Become familiar with number through rhymes and songs.

Physical Development
❑ Move confidently and imaginatively with increased control and co-ordination;

❑ Become aware of space and others;

❑ Handle appropriate objects with increased control.

Creative Development
❑ Through art, music, dance and stories, show increased ability to use imagination, listen and observe;

❑ Use a widening range of instruments and other resources to express ideas and communicate feelings.

One of the most important areas of competence for the young child is the development of social skills and self-awareness. How children feel about themselves and how they cope with the world around them (and come to terms with

decisions!) will often affect their social development. You will need to bear this in mind when you consider the criteria you will use to decide which child represents which character.

Cultural awareness

A Nativity performance may also form part of a more general objective or policy of developing cultural awareness through festivals. What clothes do the characters wear, what food would they eat, what kind of houses would they live in? Looking at and discussing cultural similarities and differences heightens cultural awareness and acknowledges the importance of showing respect for others whatever their race, colour or religion. If you can help children to understand that they are a valued member of their community they, in turn, will learn to respect and value people from other cultural backgrounds.

Learning opportunities

The Nativity offers good opportunities to discuss with the children aspects of family life such as the arrival of a sibling. Perhaps the children have photographs of themselves as babies. What gifts did they receive when they were born? How do they treat their younger brother/sister?

A child's ability to display kindness, care and affection contributes to their social skills development. Where a child is socially competent and respected by others, they are more likely to display kindness and support than children who regard themselves in a negative way and who feel they have little to give socially. Kindness and a caring approach are often absorbed through example. It is important, therefore, that the adults create (or maintain) an atmosphere of co-operation, help and support which children can sense.

You could look at different jobs in society. Joseph was a carpenter. There may be a parent /grandparent who works with wood and will talk to the children about this job.

Other possible areas of experience are the hustle and bustle of town life compared with village life, shepherds and sheep (visit a farm?), how to care for babies and animals, including the children's pets.

A Nativity performance will also be good preparation for the children as they in time come to National Curriculum music where performing/composing/listening are essential elements.

Peter Morrell

To *perform* or not to *perform?*

Chrys Blanchard joins the debate

There is pressure in many early years settings to stage a Christmas performance. I find myself asking the question 'Who is this for?' The Nativity is an important part of our culture and a wonderful story for the children. If the right language is chosen it is a story they will understand and remember and get much enjoyment from, as well as the educational spin-offs. It's ideal source material to base your Christmas activities around; but is a performance - with all the stress, extra work involved by staff, and time spent rehearsing - the best way for children of this age to experience the Nativity? Yes, you can teach them to say lines on cue, yes you can dress them up and stand them in the right places, but whilst parents love to see their offspring all dressed up and the centre of attention on stage, we need to consider what the child gets out of it. Do they understand their part in the whole?

We should consider all the options before we decide what to do at Christmas. Do the Nativity story, but don't spend hours rehearsing, use the time for many more Nativity and Christmas related activities. Tell the story many times in the weeks running up to Christmas. Let the children dress up in costumes and act out various bits as you tell the story time and again. Involve parents, encouraging them to make costumes for the Nativity dressing-up box. Let the children try out different costumes at different times, make stars, be angels together and all make angel music. Be animals - all try being donkeys and making 'clip-clop' music. Sing lullabies to baby Jesus. Have fun!

If you want to use this time of year to involve your parents why not invite them in for a Christmas coffee morning/evening with Christmas shaped biscuits and goodies, made by the children? Let the children dress up as they have been used to and tell the story in the style that people have used since time began, where everyone sits in a circle, and the storyteller (an adult) tells the story, giving the children opportunities to join in naturally and spontaneously. Play your 'clip-clop' music, sing like angels. Singing is a wonderful way to share and celebrate. Teach songs to the parents so they can join in. Maybe the parents would sing something especially for the children.

Whilst there are probably some nursery schools, with a high proportion of four-year-olds who are keen, confident and able, and who will enjoy a structured performance and the rehearsing involved, I feel that the majority of groups with a collection of two- to four-year-olds will get more out of the type of experience I have described above. Children may be natural performers so maybe natural is the best setting for this age group - they will have plenty of time to move on to more formal acting when they go to school.

Whatever you decide is right for you, enjoy yourselves and savour the magic that we are lucky enough to experience by sharing this time of year with our young children.

Take the opportunity this Christmas to try out customs and crafts from around the world. Judith Harries explains some of the traditions followed in different countries and suggests related activities

Christmas **around** the world

Christmas is a special festival for Christians all over the world when they celebrate the birth of Jesus in a stable more than 2,000 years ago. Christmas or 'Christ's mass' is usually celebrated on 25 December and lasts for 12 days from Christmas Eve until Epiphany, 6 January. There are many stories and traditions associated with Christmas and each country has its own customs.

Giving

Present giving is an essential part of Christmas in all countries, originating from the story of the three wise men who brought gifts for the baby Jesus.

St Nicholas was a rich bishop living in the third century in Asia Minor, famous for his generosity. He is usually depicted as an old white-bearded man with a red cloak and mitre. In Holland, 5 December is Sinterklaas Eve and presents from St Nicholas are hidden throughout the house, with clues and poems teasing the person who should find them. The presents are wrapped in ingeniously shaped parcels or hidden inside things.

It is easy to see how Sinterklaas (the Dutch name for St Nicholas) became Santa Claus, who brings gifts to children in America and Britain. Father Christmas, too, derived from an old British legend, wears a red fur-trimmed suit, black boots, and has a long

white beard. His mode of travel in different countries varies from a sleigh pulled by reindeer or goats or an eight-footed horse (Scandinavia) to a surf boat (Australia).

Activity idea:
❑ Collect together as many different pictures of Santa Claus, in his various guises, from greetings cards, magazines, wrapping paper and ask the children to cut them out and make a collage in the shape of a huge parcel or other Christmas shape. Talk about the different present giving traditions as you cut and stick.

Stories

In Russia there are many versions of the story of Baboushka who delivers presents to the children on Christmas Eve. She is usually depicted as an old woman who one cold night was visited by the three wise men. They invited her to join them on their journey, following the star, but when she saw how cold it was she chose to stay in her warm home. The next morning she changed her mind and tried to catch up with the travellers, carrying a basket of presents for the baby Jesus, but there was no star in the sky for her to follow. So she still wanders the world searching, visiting each house at Christmas and leaving presents.

Italian children receive gifts at Epiphany (6 January) from a kind old witch called La Befana. Her name originates from young children's efforts to pronounce Epiphania! She was too busy cleaning her house when the wise men called by on their way to Bethlehem and she is forever wandering from house to house, looking for the new baby and leaving gifts just in case. Today she

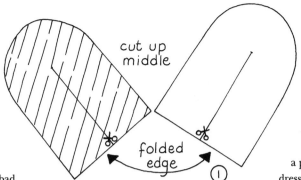

cut up middle

folded edge ①

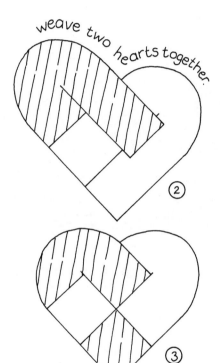

weave two hearts together.

②

③

fills good children's stockings or shoes with presents, and leaves only coal for bad children.

On 5 January in Spain, people fill the streets for the Magi Kings' Parade. Children hope to deliver letters listing their present requests to the three kings as they ride by on their camels. That night Spanish children fill their shoes with straw and leave them out for the three kings. The camels eat the straw and leave presents in exchange.

Activity ideas:
❑ If you have children in your pre-school from any Christian European countries you could invite them and their families to visit you and share their first-hand experiences of these Christmas traditions. There are many picture books of Christmas stories from around the world. You could create your own book of stories using the children's own words, pictures and paintings.

Nativity scenes
The Nativity story has inspired many traditional customs and crafts. The first Christmas manger scene or *precipio* was life-sized, with real people and animals. St Francis of Assisi set it up in his tiny chapel in Italy more than 700 years ago. Nowadays, many town squares in Europe and America have Nativity scenes with figures of Mary, Joseph, baby Jesus, the shepherds and the three wise men.

Often people have miniature crib scenes made from wood or card in their homes. In Brazil, hand-made cribs or *presebres* are an important part of the family Christmas. Each member of the family is included alongside the usual Nativity characters and as the family grows new figures are carved and added to the scene.

Activity ideas:

❑ Using a simple keyhole shaped template and lots of suitable collage materials, try making your own nursery Nativity scene together. When you have made all the Nativity characters get each child to make a figure of themselves and mount them all on the wall under a large outline of a stable.

Traditions
Many traditions have grown up around the original story of the Nativity. In Germany, the last Thursday before Christmas is Klopelnacht (Knocking Night). People dress up in scarey masks and go from house to house knocking on doors, rattling tin cans, ringing bells and making a noise! This originates from Mary and Joseph's search for

a place to stay; nowadays it is an excuse to dress up, visit people and have fun.

Mexicans believe that Mary and Joseph's journey to find shelter in Bethlehem took nine days. Every night for nine nights, the people of a neighbourhood join together to form a *posada*. Children stand at the front of the procession carrying figures of Mary and Joseph or dress up as characters from the story. The group goes from house to house, seeking a place to stay until one of the homes lets the groups inside. Each night of the *posada* ends with parties, music, fun and feasting.

The children often play *pinata* during this time. Clay pots, shaped like animals and decorated in paper, are hung from the roofs. They are filled with water, confetti or sweets. The children stand in a circle around them and take it in turns to be blindfolded and, using a stick, try to break the *pinatas* - hoping to be showered with sweets and not water!

Activity idea:
❑ Try making *pinatas* using balloons covered with several thin layers of papier maché. Cut the top off and remove the balloon. You could use paint or feathers to make them look more realistic. Fill them with confetti or perhaps raisins instead of sweets and replace the top. Suspend from the ceiling using ribbons at both ends and have fun trying to make them tip up. (There's no need to use a blindfold - some young children are nervous about this anyway.)

Decorations
Decorating homes and streets is a big part of most festivals and not least Christmas. The Christmas tree originates from Germany where it is decorated with gingerbread

shapes and lighted candles. The fairy or angel on the top is the *Christkindl* (Christchild) who brings gifts to the children on Christmas Eve.

In Finland, tiny candles shine in every window of the house. On Christmas Day, a straw framework is hung from the ceiling which the children decorate with coloured paper stars.

Danish homes pride themselves in decorating their trees with completely home-made decorations. One favourite traditional shape is the Danish heart.

Activity ideas:
❑ The children can try folding, cutting and weaving these hearts from red, green, gold and silver paper (see diagram on page 169). They can be hung on the tree with a sweet inside.

❑ Add some mixed spice or ground ginger to a simple biscuit dough and make Swedish spice stars to hang on the tree. Don't forget to make a hole at the top of each star before baking! You can decorate them with coloured icing and silver balls.

Feasting
Christmas is always a time for special food and each country has its own traditional seasonal fare. In Norway the children bake 'thaw' biscuits, so called because the heat from thousands of ovens is supposed to melt the winter snow. In Holland a special cake called *Letterbanket* is eaten on Christmas Eve. The pastry and marzipan mixture is shaped into the initials of every member of the family.

Activity idea:
❑ You could make a firm biscuit dough with the children and help them to shape it into their initial letters.

In Poland, supper is served when the first star appears in the sky on Christmas Eve. A thin layer of hay is spread over the floor and under the tablecloth to remind people of the

stable at Bethlehem. Before the meal a thin wafer of bread, an *oplatek*, with the Nativity scene imprinted on it, is passed around the table for each person to share. There are even places set for any absent friends or family members.

The traditional English Christmas pudding often contained money or charms to bring good luck to whoever found them.
In Denmark,
the traditional dessert is rice pudding. A single almond is hidden in the pudding and the person who finds it in their portion receives an extra present. At Epiphany in both France and Spain a special Kings' Cake is served. The *Roscon de Reyes* is a large doughnut-shaped sweet loaf decorated with red, green and yellow glace cherries. It is baked with a coin or ring hidden inside and whoever discovers this is crowned 'King for the day'.

Activity idea:
❑ Try making some bread dough with the children. You could either bake it as one large ring-shaped loaf or individual buns. Add a 10p coin to the dough before baking. Decorate the loaf with glace cherries and icing. On the last day of term you could share the Kings' Cake together. Help the children to look out for the coin when they are eating so nobody hurts their teeth! Whoever finds the coin is King for the day

and could have special privileges such as be first to have their snack, be first in the line or have their choice of activity, story or song.

Judith Harries

Books on a Christmas theme
The Star Tree by Gisella Colle (North-South Books) ISBN 1 558587411. An old man believes his simple paper stars will not be noticed. Then during a stormy Christmas night the lights in the city go out ...

Treasury of Christmas compiled by Robert Van de Weyer (Hunt & Thorpe) ISBN 1 856081273. A collection of simple Christmas stories from different countries.

Kaspar's Greatest Discovery by Campbell Paget (Frances Lincoln) ISBN 0 711211744. Kaspar, wisest of all the sultan's wise men, goes on a long journey following a star to make his greatest discovery yet.

This is the Star by Joyce Dunbar (Doubleday) ISBN 0 385406029. Simple but poetic retelling of the Nativity story accompanied by breathtaking oil paintings.

Celebration Song by James Berry (Hamish Hamilton) ISBN 0 241002095. A poignant picture book about Jesus on his first birthday told in a lyrical Carribean style.

The Greatest Gift - The Story of the Other Wise Man by Susan Summers (Barefoot Books) ISBN 1 898000581. A retelling of the Victorian story of the fourth wise man's search for truth.

Sewing is an activity which has the potential to develop a wide range of knowledge and skills and, through involving your children in sewing, you will cover all aspects of the Early Learning Goals. Katrina Foley explains

Sewing and needlework

Sewing is a rewarding experience to offer the children in your setting. If you provide sewing, you will be giving children a rich experience with varied opportunities to develop their learning in all areas identified by the Early Learning Goals. Not only does sewing develop children's creative and mathematical thinking, it is also a key experience for encouraging their problem-solving skills (How do I get this needle through that button? How do I sew these two pieces of material together?) and their ideas of pattern and sequence.

In our nursery, we always provide a sewing corner with a sewing table set up and ready for the children to use. The children can choose to use it when they wish and develop their learning over the course of several days or weeks, whichever they choose. Sometimes they take things home and bring them in the next day to finish. This helps to form important positive links between home and school.

At the sewing corner, children have the opportunity to create their own patterns with beads, materials and ribbons. Adults will show them how to use scissors and needles correctly and safely. Children are also shown adult reference books which encourage them to look at beads, jewellery and stitching ways and ideas from these may later be incorporated into their work. However, we don't suggest this as we feel that the most effective way of developing children's creative learning and thinking is by valuing and encouraging their own ideas and by helping them to develop and show these in practice.

Safety

Although we always provide a sewing corner where children can sew, needles are never threaded until the children ask for this to be done. It is important that staff always know

■ **Creative Development**
When they are sewing, children explore colour, texture and shape. They look at the size, shape and colour of beads and feel different textures of various materials, such as cork, when they are making necklaces.

■ **Physical Development**
Children will learn to handle tools (needles and scissors) with increasing control.

■ **Mathematical Development**
Children will be given opportunities to talk about, recognise and recreate simple patterns and use language to describe the shape and size of solid and flat shapes, for example when they use buttons and beads and material to make a necklace. They will use everyday words to describe position, for instance 'on top of', 'under', 'in', 'out'.

■ **Knowledge and Understanding of the World**
Children will look closely at similarities and differences between the beads and buttons and materials used in sewing. They will make and look closely at patterns, they will select the tools and techniques they need to shape, assemble and join the materials they are using when they are sewing.

■ **Communication, Language and Literacy**
Through discussion, children will use talk to organise, sequence and clarify their thinking particularly if they are trying to make something using binca or material (one of our children made a babygrow for example). Children will extend their vocabulary through discussion with the adult and with other children when sewing.

who is sewing so they can give advice or help when necessary. It also ensures that children use the area safely. The sewing corner is usually available to only two children at any one time. Two children to supervise, two pairs of scissors and two needles are enough for the busy adult in the nursery setting to look after.

At the sewing corner, the basic safety rules for children to remember are:

❏ Leave the needle in the pincushion and go and ask an adult to thread it for you.

❏ Sit down when you are at the sewing table.

❏ When you have finished, cut off the wool or thread and replace the needle in the pincushion before leaving the table. If you need help to do this, ask an adult.

We usually provide darning needles as they are real, not too small and not too sharp, but if children need a smaller needle we will provide this for them. As smaller needles tend to be sharper, staff usually supervise the children closely when they are using these. Remember, when you first set up this activity, you will need to supervise it very closely at all times. Gradually, as children learn to use the needles and scissors safely, and to select what they want to use to create their designs, they will need less and less supervision.

Progression

Children make necklaces, bracelets and sew onto pieces of binca, sometimes just starting with one large stitch! At all times, children are encouraged to experiment and often children, who have been sewing for some time, will start to stitch in an adult way without ever being told to do so. However, they will only do this independently if they are allowed to go through all of the earlier stages and if at these earlier stages their initial efforts are highly valued by staff and parents.

Children like to discuss what they are doing and we can use our discussions with children to extend individual learning. We also extend children's language through discussion, perhaps introducing new vocabulary such as next, the one before, lace and thread.

We want to let children have the chance to sew without worrying about what they produce. By sewing children develop their creative and mathematical thinking along with a wide range of other skills. The end product is not the most important part of the activity, it is the activity itself that develops thinking. If they are given numerous opportunities to sew, children's ability to use materials and tools will develop considerably over time. To do this, children need to be given time and space to explore the materials provided.

Role models

Sometimes adults will sit in the sewing corner mending the dressing-up clothes, sewing hooks onto towels or embroidering. While this makes the area real for the children, it also provides a model for them to copy and helps them to see the relevance of sewing to their everyday lives.

We always let children take all of their sewing home from the very beginning. It is really important that children enjoy sewing, then they are more likely to repeat it and therefore consolidate and extend their learning.

Katrina Foley

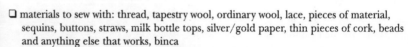

Set up a sewing corner

You will need:

❑ clothes horse with net curtain partition

❑ 1 small table

❑ 2 children's armchairs

❑ 1 chair for an adult

❑ 1 pincushion

❑ 2 pairs of scissors that cut - Rahmquist are good

❑ 2 darning needles provided in the pincushion and other needles that the adult keeps for particular occasions as outlined above

❑ materials to sew with: thread, tapestry wool, ordinary wool, lace, pieces of material, sequins, buttons, straws, milk bottle tops, silver/gold paper, thin pieces of cork, beads and anything else that works, binca

❑ a partitioned box or tray (you can make this) for buttons, beads, materials, laces, and so on, which can be sorted out by the children

❑ pictures of sewing and beads

❑ pictures of 'adult' embroidery and stitching, to give them ideas about this

❑ adult craft books, such as *The Complete Book of Beads* (ISBN 0863184375)

❑ pictures from magazines - good for using as display materials on or near a sewing table

Creative Development